The
Marketing Plan
Workbook

Commercial Finance
At Platinum Enterprise, we aim to search for sound but effective finance for your business.

Our business brokerage services include the following.

Commercial Finance
We will be happy to consider most propositions of finance for your business.

There are many products on the market ranging from:

*Invoice discounting	***Invoice factoring**
*Asset based finance	***Leasing finance**
*Business loans	***Property Finance**
*Trade Finance	***Stock Finance**

Commercial Mortgages
Commercial mortgages and remortgages are available for most sites including:

*Offices   *Warehouses   *Professional practices

*Shops   *Restaurants   *Hotels

*Post Offices

*Leisure facilities   *Care facilities

*Commercial and Residential Investment Properties

Adverse credit or non status applicants are acceptable.

Property Finance
There are many sources for property finance and so the market is competitive. We aim to find a suitable product for most cases.

The mail areas of property finance are:

*Land or Site finance   *Development finance

*Mezzanine finance

Buy to Let Mortgages
We can arrange Buy to Let mortgages with a large number of lenders and so are able to find a product which meets your requirements from a wide selection.

Insurance
Please remember to consider the benefits of insurance regarding property, mortgages or other loans.

Please contact us for further information.

We subscribe to the NACFB code of practice.
Insurance, security and a deposit may be required for secured Finance. Terms will be subject to circumstances. A Brokers fee of higher of £500 or up to 1% of loan value may apply.

PLATINUM
ENTERPRISE
L I M I T E D

THE SUNDAY TIMES

BUSINESS ENTERPRISE GUIDE

The Marketing Plan Workbook

JOHN WESTWOOD

RECOMMENDED BY
INSTITUTE OF DIRECTORS

KOGAN
PAGE

London and Sterling, VA

For Louise, Ben, Carolina and Lucinda for their help and advice.

First published in Great Britain and the United States in 2005 by Kogan Page Limited.

120 Pentonville Road
London N1 9JN
United Kingdom
www.kogan-page.co.uk

22883 Quicksilver Drive
Sterling, VA 20166–2012
USA

© John Westwood, 2005

ISBN 0 7494 4178 X

British Library Cataloguing-in-Publication Data

A CIP record for this book is available from the British Library.

Library of Congress Cataloging-in-Publication Data

Westwood, John, 1947–
The marketing plan workbook/John Westwood.
    p. cm.
  Includes index
  ISBN 0-7494-4178-X
  1. Marketing–Planning–Handbooks, manuals, etc. 2. Marketing–Planning–Problems. exercise. etc. I. Title.
HF5415.13.W482 2005
658.8'02–dc22

2004026585

Typeset by Datamatics Technologies Ltd, Mumbai, India
Printed and bound in Great Britain by Bell & Bain, Glasgow

totalfinance
SOLUTIONS

Business Finance Consultants

your first stop
for all business finance

- Commercial Mortgages
- Equipment Leasing
- Land Development
- Asset Based Finance
- Equity Finance
- Property Sale & Leaseback
- Factoring & Invoice Discounting

Tel 01509 816196
www.totalfinancesolutions.com

yourinsurancegroup (brokers) limited are specialist Insurance Brokers to the UK SME sector.

The team at yourinsurancegroup have researched the requirements and frustrations of the small business market place, so they understand what is important to their customers when dealing with their business insurance needs.

The yourinsurance product range for business includes features such as:

- Competitive premiums
- No form filling
- Instant, no-fuss cover
- Monthly premiums
- Plain English policies
- Cover for legal expenses

Policies are underwritten by a panel of reputable UK Insurers. yourinsurancegroup was founded in 1995 in Australia and established itself as the leading innovator in the SME Insurance Sector. Today, yourinsurancegroup of companies has operations in Australia and the United Kingdom and is establishing operations in South Africa and Canada.

The Group commenced operations in the United Kingdom in early 2000 and currently handles the insurance needs of over 20,000 SME customers.

yourinsurancegroup (brokers) limited are contactable on **0800 102 4810** or visit their web site **www.yourinsurance.co.uk**

yourinsurancegroup

Contents

If your bank
isn't prepared
to work your way,
give us a call

♻ NatWest

another way

Whatever kind of business you're in, you need a bank that will get to know your individual
requirements – and aims to offer services to suit you.

At NatWest, our Business Managers can meet you, to make sure we work the way you do.
You can choose how you bank with us (online, by phone, in branch or at a cashpoint).
And you can have exactly the amount of support you want.

To find out how easy it is to switch to **NatWest** call us on **0800 028 2677***
quoting ref yml. Monday to Friday 8am to 7pm. Textphone users please call
0800 917 0526.

BEST DIRECT
BUSINESS BANKING
PROVIDER

NATWEST

Starting your own
business?

Get your
FREE
guide

If you're considering going it alone, you don't have to do it on your own. NatWest's New Business Planner CD can help you with everything from writing a business plan to managing your accounts and invoices.

 **NatWest**   another way

For your FREE New Business Planner CD call us on

0800 028 2677

Quoting ref DW1

Lines open Monday to Friday 8am to 7pm. Textphone users, please call 0800 917 0526.

Introduction

When I first moved into marketing planning more than 20 years ago, I found books on the subject to be highly academic, full of theory and short on examples. Also, most were written from the viewpoint of large multinational companies in the consumer goods field with multi-million pound marketing budgets. I found it impossible to use these books to teach my salespeople how to prepare and implement their own marketing plans and so I decided to write my own book and try to make marketing planning accessible to salesmen, accountants, production and shipping people – in fact to anyone who has lots of other things to do as well as preparing marketing plans.

That was 15 years ago and over that time I have continued to work in sales and to prepare and implement my own marketing plans. So I know just how important it is to get the best results, while spending a minimum of time working on the preparation of the plans themselves. Standard formats and practice make this possible.

Small businesses do not have surplus people to do their marketing planning. This book will enable busy people to prepare marketing plans in a time-effective manner.

1

What is marketing planning and how can it help a small business?

Planning is one of the most important roles of management. A company's corporate or business plan runs the business. A company's marketing plan is a key input to the business plan. It should identify the most promising business opportunities for the company and outline how to penetrate, capture and maintain positions in identified markets. It is a communication tool combining all the elements of the marketing mix in a coordinated action plan. It spells out who will do what, when, where and how, to achieve its ends.

A marketing plan is a tool to help you identify the most promising business opportunities and to outline how to penetrate, capture and maintain your position in identified markets. It is a dynamic tool, not a weighty document. It can be as short or as long as it needs to be.

A marketing plan is a map to help you develop your business. The important thing about a map is that when you look at it you can find where you are and where you want to get to. You can then decide the best way from one place to the other. The shortest route may be over a hill and if you have a four-wheel drive vehicle this may be the best way. But if you have no car at all, you may have to take the bus or the train. It is the same with a marketing plan. Before you can decide where you want to get to you need to know where you are now.

An overall company marketing plan can be made up of a number of smaller marketing plans for individual products or areas. These smaller plans can be prepared as and when the occasion requires.

When should you prepare a marketing plan? I would say: when it will help you to understand your business and how to develop it. It is important to carry out a marketing audit or 'situation analysis', as explained in Chapters 2 to 4 of this book. That will tell you what your business really is and where you are with your products, applications and customer base. If you have already done this to prepare your business plan, then use the concepts in this book to update your information.

Most books on marketing planning concentrate on theory. This approach is fine for business academics but makes the whole process too complicated for the average manager. The approach in this book is a practical one, including only as much theory as is necessary to understand the planning process. Working your way through this book will broaden your understanding of the principles of marketing planning so that you will be able to carry out the background work necessary to put together any type of marketing plan.

Large companies have sales departments, marketing departments and sometimes even strategic planning departments. Smaller companies have salespeople and in some cases the salespeople (or person!) have many other tasks as well. In small companies it is these people who will be putting together marketing plans. They will often need to put together individual plans for a product or an area very quickly. They will want to be able to prepare simple and short plans. This book is designed as much to provide guidance in the preparation of individual marketing plans as it is to assist managers in putting together an overall marketing plan for their business.

Preparing a marketing plan is not just an academic exercise, so you should only put in the work to prepare one when it will help you to develop your business. You should not do it just because you think it will impress your bank manager! Use the frameworks shown later in this book, but only use the parts that you feel are relevant to *your* business.

Throughout the book we will follow the fortunes of a number of small businesses in a wide range of industries. They will be used in examples and as the basis of a marketing plan. To get the best out of this book, you should follow these examples and prepare your equivalents for a product for your own company as we progress through the planning steps one by one.

Adopting and following the formal structure of a marketing plan, shown later in this book, will make it easier for you to order your thoughts and the facts logically. It will be easier for people reading the plan to follow your arguments and to see how you reached your conclusions, and for you to present a professional-looking and complete document from even a relatively small amount of information.

To help us with our planning, I have chosen six small companies. Three are small 'local' companies – Jane's Beauty & Health, AH Building and Prestige Cars; one is a 'regional' company – Global Fuels; and two are companies that operate nationally and internationally – The Pure Fruit Jam Company and Precision Valves Ltd.

THE COMPANIES

- Jane's Beauty & Health. A beauty parlour employing eight people. Turnover £410,000.
- AH Building. A building and roofing company employing 10 people. Turnover £700,000.
- Prestige Cars. A taxi and chauffeur drive company employing 10 people. Turnover £800,000.
- Global Fuels. A distributor of fuel oils and heating oils, employing 15 people. Turnover £1.8 million.
- The Pure Fruit Jam Company. A company employing 20 people, which manufactures and sells a specialist range of jams and conserves. Turnover is £2.5 million, of which £500,000 exported.

■ Precision Valves Ltd. Employs 18 people and manufactures and imports valves used in the water treatment industry. Turnover £2.5 million, of which £500,000 exported.

If we look in a bit more detail at these companies, we can list the key data.

Company name	Jane's Beauty & Health
Annual turnover	£0.41 million
Export sales (if applicable)	none
Operating profit	£0.05 million
Number of employees	8
Main products	facials, massage, manicure

Company name	AH Building
Annual turnover	£0.7 million
Export sales (if applicable)	none
Operating profit	£0.05 million
Number of employees	10
Main products	building modifications and roof repairs

Company name	Prestige Cars
Annual turnover	£0.8 million
Export sales (if applicable)	none
Operating profit	£0.05 million
Number of employees	10
Main products	taxi hire and chauffeur drive hire

Company name	Global Fuels
Annual turnover	£1.8 million
Export sales (if applicable)	none
Operating profit	£0.15 million
Number of employees	15
Main products	fuel and heating oils

Company name	The Pure Fruit Jam Company
Annual turnover	£2.5 million
Export sales (if applicable)	£0.5 million
Operating profit	£0.6 million
Number of employees	20
Main products	specialist jams and conserves

Company name	Precision Valves Ltd
Annual turnover	£2.5 million
Export sales (if applicable)	£0.5 million
Operating profit	£0.5 million
Number of employees	18
Main products	ball valves

EXERCISE

List the same information below for your own company or business unit.

Company name ....
Annual turnover ....
Export sales (if applicable) ....
Operating profit ....
Number of employees ....
Main products ....

Before we proceed, we need to cover some basic definitions. So first of all answer the following questions:

What is selling?
....
....
....

What is marketing?
....
....
....

What is marketing planning?
....
....
....

Check your answers with the definitions given below.

WHAT IS SELLING?

Selling is a straightforward concept that involves persuading a customer to buy a product. It brings in 'today's orders'. It is, however, only one aspect of the marketing process.

WHAT IS MARKETING?

The dictionary definition of marketing is: 'the provision of goods or services to meet consumers' needs'. In other words, marketing involves finding out what the customer wants and matching a company's products to meet those requirements, and in the process making a profit for the company. Successful marketing involves having the right product available in the right place at the right time and making sure that the customer is aware of the product. It therefore brings in 'tomorrow's orders'.

It is the process that brings together the abilities of the company and the requirements of its customers. Companies have to be flexible in order to achieve this balance in the marketplace. They must be prepared to change products, introduce new products and/or enter new markets. They must be able to read their customers and the marketplace.

A company manufacturing radio sets in the 1960s and 1970s would have had to change to radio/cassette players in the 1980s and to Walkmans or portable CD players in the 1990s. A television manufacturer that made black-and-white television sets in the 1950s would have been making colour TV sets in the 1970s and widescreen surround-sound and digital TV sets by 2000. Even a modern invention like the video player/recorder is now being replaced by the next generation DVD players and recorders. Each of these products satisfied the same basic customer desire, but at a different moment in time. If the companies had not changed products, they would have gone out of business. This balancing process takes place in the 'marketing environment', which is not controlled by individuals or by companies, is constantly changing and must be monitored continuously.

Marketing therefore involves:

▨ the abilities of the company;
▨ the requirements of the customer; and
▨ the marketing environment.

The abilities of the company can be managed by the marketing function. It can control four main elements of a company's operation, which are often referred to as 'the marketing mix', also known as the 'four Ps'. They are four controllable variables that allow a company to come up with a policy that is profitable and satisfies its customers:

1. the product sold (product);
2. the pricing policy (price);
3. how the product is promoted (promotion);
4. methods of distribution (place).

'Promotion' and 'place' are concerned with reaching your potential customers in the first place and 'product' and 'price' will allow you to satisfy the customer's requirements.

The marketing mix for a product of each of our companies is given below:

Jane's Beauty & Health has chosen the product 'manicure':

Pricing   This is a luxury product – we offer two levels: basic and full
                       service.
Promotion   For this product, we have adopted the following approach:

                       – we advertise in the local press;
                       – we use Yellow Pages;
                       – we use our website.

Distribution   We take orders by phone, by post and in person.

For AH Building the product is 'conservatories', which is part of its 'home
extension' product:

Pricing   This is a 'quality' product and as such is relatively expensive.
                       We aim the pricing to be 20 per cent below the cost of a
                       brick-built extension. Since we buy the product from
                       'Monarch', we are limited by the discounts we get on the
                       basic wood/window part of the product.
Promotion   For this product we use the following:

                       – adverting in the local paper, free papers;
                       – Yellow Pages and Thomson directory;
                       – Monarch's website.

Distribution   We take orders by post and e-mail and also through
                       Monarch's website.

The marketing mix for Prestige Cars for its product 'stretched limo hire':

Pricing   This is a 'prestige product'; we offer at the same price as our
                       Rolls Royce, and we offer a list of extras such as bar, TV, hi-fi.
Promotion   For this product, we have adopted the following approach:

                       – we advertise in the local press;
                       – we use Yellow Pages;
                       – photos are on our website.

Distribution   We take orders by phone, e-mail and in person.

Global Fuels chose 'red diesel':

Pricing   Red diesel is a cheap product aimed not only at farmers, but also at gardeners and leisure (boat) users. Since we compete with other suppliers in the area, we cannot overprice the product. But because of our ability to distribute by tanker, we can charge 2p to 3p more than they can.

Promotion   For this product:

                 – we advertise in the local press;
                 – we advertise in gardening centres, boat clubs, etc;
                 – we use Yellow Pages.

Distribution   We take orders by phone and e-mail and intend to expand our website to take orders online.

The Pure Fruit Jam Company highlights 'mini-pots':

Pricing   We sell mini-pots in packs of 30. The pricing is actually triple the price of the equivalent amount of jam sold in large jars. This reflects the packaging costs and is in line with our competitors' pricing. We pitch the pricing 15 per cent above the price of competitors selling jam in mini-foil containers.

Promotion   For this product:

                 – we advertise in magazines aimed at catering for hotels and airlines;
                 – we have a single page advert that we use as a flyer for targeted mailshots.

Distribution   We normally sign supply contracts for a set amount of product per month.

Precision Valves Ltd's cast iron type 'B' ball valves:

Pricing   For this product we have adopted a 'discount policy'. We are offering quantity discounts to encourage larger unit purchases; we are offering a quantity retrospective discount based on the level of purchases for the whole year; we are offering a discount level for next year based on the level of purchases this year.

| | Product 1 | Product 2 | Product 3 |

Promotion | For this product, we have adopted the following approach:

– we advertise this product in the technical press;
– we have a range of product brochures;
– we carry out regular mailshots.

Distribution | This product is sold in the UK through our own sales force and independent distributors. Overseas it is sold through independent distributors.

EXERCISE

Consider the marketing mix for your company's products. For each of your main products write some notes on the pricing policy, how the product is promoted and how the product is distributed:

	Product 1	Product 2	Product 3
Pricing	....	....	....
	....	....	....
	....	....	....
Promotion	....	....	....
	....	....	....
	....	....	....
Distribution	....	....	....
	....	....	....
	....	....	....

WHAT IS MARKETING PLANNING?

The term 'marketing planning' is used to describe the methods of applying marketing resources to achieve marketing objectives. This may sound simple, but it is in fact a very complex process. The resources and the objectives will vary from company to company and will also change with time. Marketing planning is used to segment markets, identify market position, forecast market size, and to plan viable market share within each market segment.

The process involves:

- carrying out marketing research within and outside the company;
- looking at the company's strengths and weaknesses;
- making assumptions;
- forecasting;
- setting marketing objectives;
- generating marketing strategies;

- defining programmes;
- setting budgets;
- reviewing the results and revising the objectives, strategies or programmes.

Each of these will be discussed individually in later chapters.
   The planning process will:

- make better use of company resources to identify marketing opportunities;
- encourage team spirit and company identity;
- help the company to move towards achieving its corporate goals.

In addition, the marketing research carried out as part of the planning process will provide a solid base of information for present and future projects.
   Marketing planning is an iterative process and the plan will be reviewed and updated as it is implemented.
   Don't be concerned that the process will be too difficult – it will not be. A complete company marketing plan can be broken down into individual plans for products and areas. If you only have one product, you only have one plan. You may think you only have one product, but when you look at it more closely there will probably be differences that allow you to split the product and segment the individual market niches that you have.

WHAT IS A MARKETING PLAN?

A marketing plan is a document that formulates a plan for marketing products or services. Although 'products' are referred to in this chapter, the product would nearly always include some 'service' component such as after-sales service, advice by technically trained salespeople or in-store merchandising. A marketing plan has a formal structure, but can be used as a formal or informal document that has great flexibility. It can be used to:

- prepare an argument for introducing a new product;
- revamp the marketing approach for existing products;
- put together a complete company marketing plan to be included in the business plan.

It can refer to a local, national or even to a worldwide market. The types of plan you would consider would depend on the type of company you are. The Pure Fruit Jam Company and Precision Valves Ltd are thinking locally, nationally and internationally; Global Fuels is thinking regionally as well as locally; but Prestige Cars, AH Building and Jane's Beauty & Health are only thinking locally.
   In a company operating out of one base, the split of products and areas can be represented as in Table 1.1. It is therefore possible for such a company to prepare not only an overall marketing plan for all products in all areas, but also individual plans for individual products or individual sales areas. These are represented in Tables 1.2 and 1.3 respectively.

Table 1.1 Company sales by area

OVERALL COMPANY SALES	Area 1 Product A Product B Product C	Area 2 Product A Product B Product C	Area 3 Product A Product B Product C

Table 1.2 Marketing plans prepared by area

OVERALL COMPANY MARKETING PLAN	Plan for Area 1 All Products	Plan for Area 2 All Products	Plan for Area 3 All Products

Table 1.3 Marketing plans prepared by product

OVERALL COMPANY MARKETING PLAN	Plan for Product A All Areas	Plan for Product B All Areas	Plan for Product C All Areas

Table 1.4 Marketing plans prepared by product for a company operating only in one area

OVERALL COMPANY MARKETING PLAN	Plan for Product A	Plan for Product B	Plan for Product C

A company operating in only one area, region or town would normally prepare individual product plans, as shown in Table 1.4.

So how might some of our small companies decide to structure their marketing plans?

The smaller companies operating only in one town or city would probably only prepare one overall company marketing plan, but it could be split into separate product sections as shown in Table 1.4. This allows different methods of marketing different products in the portfolio to be clearly shown.

The company marketing plan for Jane's Beauty & Health could be made up of separate plans for the different main products or main groups of products.

Table 1.5   Marketing plans prepared by product for a company operating only in one area, Jane's Beauty & Health

JANE'S BEAUTY & HEALTH MARKETING	Plan for facials	Plan for manicure and pedicure	Plan for massage

In practice, because the plan will be relatively short, it is unlikely that a company as small as Jane's Beauty & Health would produce individual plans unless it was a matter of preparing an individual plan for an individual product to support a business plan for expanding the business on the basis of that product alone.

Similarly, if AH Building was making individual plans it would probably be split as shown below.

Table 1.6   Company with a number of subsidiary marketing plans, AH Building

AH BUILDING COMPANY MARKETING PLAN	Plan for building extensions and conservatories	Plan for roof repairs and guttering
	Plan for modifications	Plan for specialist work – damp, insulation, etc

Prestige Cars might go for a similar breakdown of subsidiary plans

Table 1.7 Company with a number of subsidiary marketing plans, Prestige Cars

PRESTIGE CARS MARKETING PLAN	Plan for taxi business	Plan for chauffeur-driven cars
	Plan for chauffeur-driven people carriers	Plan for chauffeur-driven luxury cars

In practice it would probably just prepare one plan for people carriers and luxury cars on the basis that although they have different markets, they are both up-market products.

Global Fuels operates in the counties of Devon, Cornwall, Somerset and Wiltshire. It has separated the customer base in Bristol and Avonmouth into a an area it has called 'Bristol and Avon'. It has decided to prepare plans as shown below.

Table 1.8 Marketing plans prepared by area, Global Fuels

GLOBAL FUELS COMPANY MARKETING PLAN	Plan for Bristol & Avon All Products	Plan for Wiltshire & Somerset All Products	Plan for Devon & Cornwall All Products

There would be different ways for Global Fuels to proceed. It could either prepare individual marketing plans for its three areas or it could make these subsidiary parts of one main plan.

The Pure Fruit Jam Company wants to prepare a number of marketing plans

Table 1.9 Company with a number of subsidiary marketing plans, The Pure Fruit Jam Company

| PURE FRUIT JAM COMPANY MARKETING PLAN | Plan for UK market for standard jams (340 gm jars) | Plan for UK market for special products |
| | Plan for UK market for marmalades | Plan for overseas markets for all products |

Precision Valves Ltd has decided to produce one plan for the UK market and one plan for its export markets.

Table 1.10 Company with marketing plans prepared by area, Precision Valves Ltd

| PRECISION VALVES MARKETING PLAN | Plan for UK market | Plan for export market |

In practice, after much deliberation, our companies have decided to prepare the following marketing plans:

Jane's Beauty & Health	Overall company marketing plan
AH Building	Overall company marketing plan
Prestige Cars	Overall company marketing plan
Global Fuels	Overall company marketing plan
The Pure Fruit Jam Company	Separate UK and export plans
Precision Valves Ltd	Marketing plan for the UK market

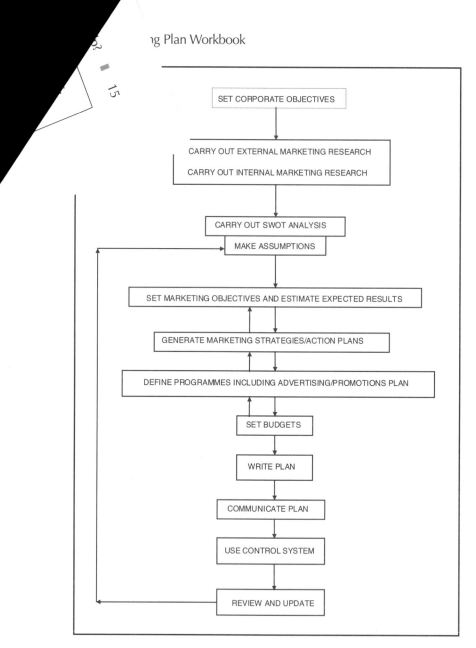

Figure 1.1 The marketing planning process

STAGES IN THE PREPARATION OF A MARKETING PLAN

The stages in the preparation of a marketing plan are shown in Figure 1.1.

Set corporate objectives

Corporate objectives are set by top management and this may not be in your brief. Even so, you must be aware of your company's corporate objectives and the ultimate plan should be in line with them.

Carry out external marketing research

Since companies exist and operate in the marketing environment, the first step in a marketing plan is research into that environment. Research is carried out into the markets themselves and then the information collected is analysed in the context of the marketing of the products.

Carry out internal market research

Perhaps even more important than general market information is historical information available 'in house'. This will be sales/order and margin/profit data relating to the products and areas for the plan. This information needs to be put into context in the form of market shares by geographical area and industry type for individual products and in total.

Carry out a SWOT analysis

When all the information and opinions have been collected by market research, the materials need to be analysed and presented in a way that will help to make the best decisions. This can be done by selecting the key information and carrying out a SWOT analysis. The method of carrying out a SWOT analysis is explained in detail in Chapter 4.

Make assumptions

The plan itself is based on a clearly understood set of assumptions. These relate to external economic factors as well as technological and competitive factors.

Set marketing objectives and estimate expected results

The next step is the key to the whole marketing process: the setting of marketing objectives. This is what you want to achieve – the fundamental aims of the plan. How to set objectives is covered in Chapter 5.

Generate marketing strategies and action plans

Marketing strategies are the methods that will enable you to achieve your marketing objectives. They relate to the elements of the marketing mix – product, price, promotion and place. For each objective, strategies need to be developed relating to these individual elements. First the marketing strategy needs to be set out and then action plans are prepared. This is covered in Chapter 6.

Define programmes

Defining programmes means defining who does what, when, where and how.

Set budgets

Objectives can be set and strategies and action plans devised, but they need to be cost-effective. The setting of budgets defines the resources required to carry out the plan and quantifies the cost and also the financial risks involved; it is explained in Chapter 9.

Write the plan

Once all the above steps have been carried out you will be in a position to prepare the written plan. The written plan should only contain the key information that needs to be communicated.

Communicate the plan

If a plan is not properly communicated to those who will be implementing it, it will fail.

Use a control system

This system will be used to measure the performance of the plan in achieving its objectives and to recommend any necessary corrective action.

Review and update

Conditions and situations will change and the plan should be regularly reviewed in the light of changing circumstances.

SUMMARY

Planning is one of the most important roles of management. The company's business plan runs the business. The marketing plan is only one part of the business plan and the marketing planning process therefore needs to be carried out as a part of the overall company planning and budgeting process.

Because of major changes in the business environment in the past few decades, the focus has shifted away from long-term planning to the implementation of action plans that will produce visible short-term results and against which the results of longer-term strategic plans can be further refined. This new 'strategic' planning is designed to react to and exploit new information as it is acquired. This is the approach adopted by marketing planners.

Selling involves persuading the customer to buy your product, but it is only one aspect of the marketing process. Marketing involves finding out what the customer wants and matching your company's products and services to meet these requirements and in the process making a profit for your company. This involves understanding:

- the abilities of your company;
- the requirements of your customers;
- the marketing environment in which you operate.

The abilities of the company can be managed by controlling four main elements of a company's operation, often referred to as the marketing mix. These elements are:

1. the product sold (product);
2. the pricing policy (price);
3. how the product is promoted (promotion);
4. methods of distribution (place).

Marketing planning involves the application of marketing resources to achieve marketing objectives. It is used to segment markets, identify market position, forecast market size and plan viable market share within each market segment. A marketing plan is a document that formulates a plan for marketing products and/or services. A company marketing plan sets out the company's marketing objectives and suggests strategies to achieve them.

There is a fixed procedure for carrying out the marketing planning process to enable you to prepare a marketing plan. Whether you are preparing a marketing plan for a single product in a single market or a full company marketing plan, the planning procedure is the same; it is the scope of each part of the planning process that will differ. The planning process is an iterative procedure.

2

The marketing audit – internal

The marketing audit is a detailed examination of the company's internal marketing activities, its marketing system and its marketing environment. We will begin with an internal audit looking at a company's marketing activities. In later chapters we will carry out an audit of the marketing environment and the company's marketing system.

INTERNAL MARKET RESEARCH

In addition to the external market research, your company has a wealth of data that is invaluable in the preparation of a marketing plan. In fact the problem is more likely to be that there is too much data, so you cannot easily see which information is the most important. It is likely that much data will not be available in the right form. You may have overall sales data, but not data itemised for individual product lines or market segments.

The historical data relevant to the preparation of your marketing plan is basically sales/order data separated and analysed in such a way that it reflects the key market segments into which you sell your products.

WHAT IS MARKET SEGMENTATION?

Different customers have different needs. They do not all require the same product and they do not all require the same product benefits. Even with an individual product, not all customers will buy it for the same reasons. Market segmentation allows you to consider the markets you are actually in and the markets that your company *should* be in.

You need to be able to split up your customer base into groups of customers who all have similar needs. Each of these groups constitutes a market segment.

For consumer goods and services, it is usual to classify the end-users by socio-economic group, age, sex, occupation or region.

The marketing of industrial goods and services is different, because the customer is usually another company or a government department. The number of customers is more likely to be 10,000 than 10,000,000 and could be only a few hundred in the case of suppliers to power stations, coal mines, etc. The main ways of defining segments here are:

- by geographical area;
- by industry or industry sub-sector;
- by product;
- by application;
- by size of end-user;
- by distribution channel – distributor, equipment manufacturer, end-user.

Segmentation can also be based on:

- order size;
- order frequency;
- type of decision-maker.

The key to market segmentation is to let the marketplace segment itself, because the individual segments exist independently of the company and its products.

For the products and markets covered by your plan, you should collect and present information going back two or three full years together with this year's historical sales. You should show margin information relating to those sales, where it is available. You should also adjust figures for inflation and have them available in their actual and adjusted forms.

INFORMATION CHECKLIST

It is useful to prepare an information checklist for a marketing plan, before you start to collect data. The exact content will vary, depending on the scope of your plan, but it should include the segmentation that you want for sales, the split of your customer base, and competitor activity/market shares. The detail of the information will vary, depending on the type of company and this will mean that detail listed in the checklist will also vary and should be customised to your company.

The checklists for our six companies are shown below.

Jane's Beauty & Health

1. Sales history

The last three years' sales by value (including margins where available) for:

- sales areas – city centre, suburbs, out of town, home;
- product groups, ie facials, manicure, pedicure, massage, aromatherapy;
- young singles, mature business, young mothers, 'preferring home visits'.

Also unit sales:

- number of appointments by length and type;
- number of appointments by day of week, time of day.

2. Customers

Total number of customers by:

- sales area – city centre, suburbs, out of town, home;
- products bought, ie facials, manicure, pedicure, massage, aromatherapy;
- sector, ie young singles, mature business, young mothers, 'preferring home visits';
- key customers, ie top 40 by sales turnover.

3. Competition?

- Who are the competitors for each product group?
- What are the market shares for each product–for each competitor?

AH Building:

1. Sales history

The last three years' sales by value (including margins where available) for:

- product groups, ie extensions, modifications, damp treatment, roofing;
- sales areas – town centre, Old Town, seaside, suburbs;
- customer type, ie one-off, repeat, multiple.

Also unit sales:

- number of extensions by type;
- number of bird deterrent devices.

2. Customers

Total number of customers by:

- products bought, ie extensions, modifications, damp treatment, roofing;
- customer type, ie renovators, expanding families, affluent retired, do up/resell;

- sales area – town centre, Old Town, seaside, suburbs;
- key customers, ie top 40 by sales turnover.

3. Competition?

- Who are the competitors for each product group?
- What are the market shares for each product–for each competitor?

Prestige Cars

1. Sales history

The last three years' sales by value (including margins where available) for:

- sales areas, ie town centre, suburbs, out of town;
- product groups, ie taxi hire, cars, people carriers, luxury cars;
- markets, ie business, leisure, travel.

Also unit sales:

- numbers of car hires by car size/type;
- number of chauffeur drives by car size/type.

2. Customers

Total number of customers by:

- sales area, ie town centre, suburbs, out of town;
- products bought, ie taxi hire, cars, people carriers, luxury cars;
- industry sector, ie business, leisure, travel, etc;
- key customers, ie top 40 by sales turnover.

3. Competition?

- Who are the competitors for each product group?
- What are the market shares for each product–for each competitor?

Global Fuels

1. Sales history

The last three years' sales by value (including margins where available) for:

- sales areas – Devon/Cornwall, Somerset/Wiltshire, Bristol/Avon;
- product groups, ie fuel oils, heavy fuel oils, diesel, red diesel, lubricating oils;
- markets – home heating, industrial, farming, leisure.

Also unit sales:

- number of litres by product;
- sales split for lubricating oils.

2. Customers

Total number of customers by:

- sales area – 1, 2 or 3;
- products, ie fuel oils, heavy fuel oils, diesel, red diesel, lubricating oils;
- markets – home heating, industrial, farming, leisure;
- key customers, ie top 40 by sales turnover.

3. Competition?

- Who are the competitors for each product group?
- What are the market shares for each product–for each competitor?

The Pure Fruit Jam Company

1. Sales history

The last three years' sales by value (including margins where available) for:

- sales areas, UK – South, North, Wales, Scotland/NI;
- sales areas, export – USA, Europe, Japan, Australia;
- product groups, ie standard jams, marmalades, mini-pots, gift packs;
- markets – supermarkets, quality shops, hotels, airlines.

Also unit sales:

- number of standard jars – by product;
- number of mini-pots – by product;
- number of gift packs.

2. Customers

Total number of customers by:

- sales areas, UK – South, North, Wales, Scotland/NI;
- sales areas, export – USA and Canada, Europe, Japan, Australia;

■ product groups, ie standard jams, marmalades, mini-pots, gift packs;
■ markets – supermarkets, quality shops, hotels, airlines;
■ key customers, ie top 40 by sales turnover.

3. Competition?

■ Who are the competitors for each product group?
■ What are the market shares for each product–for each competitor?

Precision Valves Ltd

1. Sales history

The last three years' sales by value (including margins where available) for:

■ sales areas – South, Midlands, North, Wales, Scotland/NI;
■ product groups, ie type 'A', type 'B', type 'S', packages;
■ markets – water treatment, waste water, chemicals, other.

Also unit sales:

■ unit sales by valve type, size and material;
■ package sales by type and size.

2. Customers

Total number of customers by:

■ sales areas – South, Midlands, North, Wales, Scotland/NI;
■ product groups, ie type 'A', type 'B', type 'S', packages;
■ markets – water treatment, waste water, chemicals, other;
■ key customers, ie top 40 by sales turnover,

3. Competition?

■ Who are the competitors for each product group?
■ What are the market shares for each product–for each competitor?

EXERCISE

Now prepare an information checklist for your own company for the products and areas to be covered by your plan.

1. Sales history

Prepare last three years' sales by:

....
....
....

2. Customers

Segment customers by:

....
....
....

3. Competition?

How do we want to present competitor information?

....
....
....

HOW TO PRESENT THE FIGURES

Depending on the scope of the plan, the sales data may be split up into separate tables geographically, by product, by industry or under all of these categories.

The figures can be easily prepared on computer spreadsheets such as Excel or Lotus 1-2-3. These programs have the facility for the data entered into the spreadsheet tables to be displayed graphically as well. It is usual when producing tables of historical data on a spreadsheet to extend the form layout to include columns for the years that the marketing plan will cover. The columns for future years will remain blank at this time as the current task is to record historical and current sales data, but it makes it easier later on to project sales figures so that comparisons can be made and trends can be seen.

Table 2.1 shows how the figures could be presented by Jane's Beauty & Health for use in its marketing plan.

Inflation over the last three years has been 3 per cent per year. The sales figures therefore need to be adjusted downwards to take inflation into account; see Table 2.2.

Another way to look at volume growth is to analyse unit sales rather than sales value; see Table 2.3.

Table 2.1 Sales figures for all products, Jane's Beauty & Health

JANE'S BEAUTY & HEALTH
SALES FIGURES (Historical and Forecast)

SALES AREA: ALL

					forecast	
YEAR	20X3	20X4	20X5	20X6	20X7	20X8
(all values in £k)						
FACIALS	90	100	100			
MANICURE	70	80	90			
PEDICURE	40	50	60			
MASSAGE	20	40	80			
AROMATHERAPY	60	70	80			
TOTAL	280	340	410			

Table 2.2 Sales turnover adjusted for inflation, Jane's Beauty & Health

JANE'S BEAUTY & HEALTH
SALES FIGURES (Historical and Forecast)

SALES AREA: ALL

					forecast	
YEAR	20X3	20X4	20X5	20X6	20X7	20X8
(all values in £k)						
FACIALS	85	97	100			
MANICURE	66	78	90			
PEDICURE	38	49	60			
MASSAGE	19	39	80			
AROMATHERAPY	57	68	80			
TOTAL	265	331	410			

Table 2.3 Unit sales of different products, Jane's Beauty & Health

JANE'S BEAUTY & HEALTH
SALES FIGURES (Historical and Forecast)

SALES AREA: ALL

					forecast	
YEAR	20X3	20X4	20X5	20X6	20X7	20X8
number of sessions						
FACIALS	4150	4220	4200			
MANICURE	2520	3067	3800			
PEDICURE	1620	1955	2420			
MASSAGE	825	1750	3220			
AROMATHERAPY	2010	2555	3000			
TOTAL	11125	13547	16640			

AH Building presents its sales figures in a similar way; see Table 2.4.

However, instead of unit sales, AH Building examines customer growth by looking at the number of customers it has each year purchasing each product; see Table 2.5.

Table 2.4 Sales figures for all products, AH Building

AH BUILDING
SALES FIGURES (Historical and Forecast)

SALES AREA: ALL

YEAR	20X3	20X4	20X5	20X6	forecast 20X7	20X8
(all values in £k)						
EXTENSIONS	120	180	220			
MODIFICATIONS	250	220	230			
DAMP TREATMENT	90	80	100			
ROOFING	20	50	100			
OTHER	40	60	50			
TOTAL	520	590	700			

Table 2.5 Number of customers for each product, AH Building

AH BUILDING
NUMBER OF CUSTOMERS

SALES AREA: ALL

YEAR	20X3	20X4	20X5	20X6	forecast 20X7	20X8
EXTENSIONS	23	35	44			
MODIFICATIONS	118	107	115			
DAMP TREATMENT	11	10	13			
ROOFING	38	88	144			
OTHER	76	72	63			
TOTAL	266	312	379			

> As well as presenting its sales figures by product, Prestige Cars looks at the number of taxi call-outs or chauffeur car hires; see Tables 2.6 and 2.7.
>
> For Prestige Cars, the number of call-outs/hires is important, because it knows the average duration of each call-out and can therefore estimate how many drivers it needs if it wants to expand the business further.

Table 2.6 Sales figures for all products, Prestige Cars

PRESTIGE CARS
SALES FIGURES (Historical and Forecast)

SALES AREA: ALL

					forecast	
YEAR (all values in £k)	20X3	20X4	20X5	20X6	20X7	20X8
TAXI SERVICE	200	180	200			
CARS (WITH DRIVER)	250	220	250			
PEOPLE CARRIERS (WITH DRIVER)	100	150	200			
LUXURY CARS (WITH DRIVER)	50	100	150			
TOTAL	600	650	800			

Table 2.7 Call-outs by product per year, Prestige Cars

PRESTIGE CARS
SALES FIGURES (Historical and Forecast)

SALES AREA: ALL

					forecast	
YEAR No of hires/call-outs	20X3	20X4	20X5	20X6	20X7	20X8
TAXI SERVICE	18500	17220	18570			
CARS (WITH DRIVER)	3125	2750	3080			
PEOPLE CARRIERS (WITH DRIVER)	1020	1528	1890			
LUXURY CARS (WITH DRIVER)	310	580	972			
TOTAL	22955	22078	24512			

Global Fuels has to operate in an area of activity where its raw material costs fluctuate with the price of oil and where a significant amount of its selling price is made up of fuel taxes. It therefore shows figures net of taxes and duties; see Table 2.8.

Global Fuels is interested in the volume of product it sells, so it also shows its sales in thousands of litres of product sold; see Table 2.9.

Table 2.8 Sales figures for all products, Global Fuels

GLOBAL FUELS
SALES FIGURES (Historical and Forecast)

SALES AREA: ALL

Net sales after deducting tax & duty

YEAR	20X3	20X4	20X5	20X6	forecast 20X7	20X8
(all values in £k)						
FUEL OILS	850	920	900			
HEAVY FUEL OILS	300	280	300			
DIESEL	270	310	300			
RED DIESEL	50	100	200			
LUBRICATING OILS	60	80	100			
TOTAL	1530	1690	1800			

Table 2.9 Sales by volume of product sold, Global Fuels

GLOBAL FUELS
SALES FIGURES (Historical and Forecast)

SALES AREA: ALL

YEAR	20X3	20X4	20X5	20X6	forecast 20X7	20X8
thousands of litres of sales						
FUEL OILS	1400	1500	1490			
HEAVY FUEL OILS	430	400	430			
DIESEL	600	690	670			
RED DIESEL	125	250	500			
LUBRICATING OILS	30	40	50			
TOTAL	2585	2880	3140			

A larger company with more diverse sales will need to segment the figures even more. The Pure Fruit Jam Company sells its products throughout the UK and also exports about 20 per cent of its turnover. In the past it has produced regional plans for various parts of the UK, where it was developing sales, but it has not prepared an overall plan for several years. It has decided to prepare separate plans for its UK market and for its export markets.

The Pure Fruit Jam Company is using the figures shown in Tables 2.10 and 2.11 in its UK marketing plan.

It has also prepared the figures shown in Tables 2.12 and 2.13 for its export plan.

Table 2.10 Sales figures for the UK, all products, The Pure Fruit Jam Company

THE PURE FRUIT JAM COMPANY
SALES FIGURES (Historical and Forecast)

SALES AREA: UK

YEAR (all values in £k)	20X3	20X4	20X5	20X6	forecast 20X7	20X8
STANDARD JAMS (340 gm)	1000	1000	1000			
MARMALADES (340 gm)	350	350	420			
MINI-POTS	100	180	250			
GIFT PACKS	90	70	50			
SPECIAL PRODUCTS	150	200	280			
TOTAL	1690	1800	2000			

Table 2.11 Unit sales of jam products for the UK, The Pure Fruit Jam Company

THE PURE FRUIT JAM COMPANY
SALES FIGURES (Historical and Forecast)

SALES AREA: UK

YEAR 000s of jars/packs	20X3	20X4	20X5	20X6	forecast 20X7	20X8
STANDARD JAMS (340 gm)	1100	1130	1160			
MARMALADES (340 gm)	290	265	325			
MINI-POTS	400	700	950			
GIFT PACKS	47	33	25			
SPECIAL PRODUCTS	80	105	140			
TOTAL	1917	2233	2600			

Table 2.12   Sales figures for export, all products, The Pure Fruit Jam Company

THE PURE FRUIT JAM COMPANY
SALES FIGURES (Historical and Forecast)

SALES AREA: EXPORT

| | | | | | forecast | |
| YEAR | 20X3 | 20X4 | 20X5 | 20X6 | 20X7 | 20X8 |
(all values in £k)						
STANDARD JAMS (340 gm)	100	200	300			
MARMALADES (340 gm)	50	80	100			
MINI-POTS	0	20	50			
GIFT PACKS	0	30	50			
SPECIAL PRODUCTS						
TOTAL	150	330	500			

Table 2.13   Unit sales of jam products for export, The Pure Fruit Jam Company

THE PURE FRUIT JAM COMPANY
SALES FIGURES (Historical and Forecast)

SALES AREA: EXPORT

| | | | | | forecast | |
| YEAR | 20X3 | 20X4 | 20X5 | 20X6 | 20X7 | 20X8 |
000s of jars/packs						
STANDARD JAMS (340 gm)	80	160	240			
MARMALADES (340 gm)	70	115	145			
MINI-POTS		100	250			
GIFT PACKS		15	25			
SPECIAL PRODUCTS						
TOTAL	150	390	660			

Precision Valves Ltd also operates throughout the UK and in certain export markets, but for now it has decided just to concentrate on the UK market and to produce its marketing plan for that. The UK sales figures are shown in Table 2.14.

Again, inflation slightly changes the picture; see Table 2.15.

Precision Valves Ltd is particularly interested in how many of each type of valve it is selling; see Table 2.16.

Table 2.14 Sales figures for the UK, all products, Precision Valves Ltd

PRECISION VALVES LTD
SALES FIGURES (Historical and Forecast)

SALES AREA: UK

| | | | | ←——— forecast ———→ | | |
| YEAR | 20X3 | 20X4 | 20X5 | 20X6 | 20X7 | 20X8 |
(all values in £k)						
TYPE 'A' VALVES	450	450	400			
TYPE 'B' VALVES	1000	900	800			
TYPE 'S' VALVES	100	200	400			
PACKAGES	50	100	200			
SPARE PARTS	180	180	200			
TOTAL	1780	1830	2000			

Table 2.15 Sales figures adjusted for inflation, Precision Valves Ltd

PRECISION VALVES LTD
SALES FIGURES (Historical and Forecast)

SALES AREA: UK

| | | | | ←——— forecast ———→ | | |
| YEAR | 20X3 | 20X4 | 20X5 | 20X6 | 20X7 | 20X8 |
(all values in £k)						
TYPE 'A' VALVES	424	437	400			
TYPE 'B' VALVES	943	874	800			
TYPE 'S' VALVES	94	194	400			
PACKAGES	47	97	200			
SPARE PARTS	170	175	200			
TOTAL	1678	1777	2000			

Table 2.16 Unit sales, Precision Valves Ltd

PRECISION VALVES LTD
SALES FIGURES (Historical and Forecast)

SALES AREA: UK

| | | | | ←——— forecast ———→ | | |
| YEAR | 20X3 | 20X4 | 20X5 | 20X6 | 20X7 | 20X8 |
unit sales of valves						
TYPE 'A' VALVES	4200	4400	4000			
TYPE 'B' VALVES	4800	4300	4000			
TYPE 'S' VALVES	220	480	1000			
PACKAGES	40	80	220			
TOTAL	9260	9260	9220			

The *profitability* of sales is very important. It is therefore necessary also to show the margins being made on the sale of different products.

> The margins for Jane's Beauty & Health are shown in Table 2.17.
>   The low margins on 'massage' in 20X3 and 20X4 reflect the fact that this was contracted out and in-house staff were only recruited in 20X5.

Table 2.17   Sales figures including margin information, Jane's Beauty & Health

JANE'S BEAUTY & HEALTH SALES FIGURES + MARGINS						
SALES AREA: ALL						
YEAR	20X3		20X4		20X5	
	SALES	GROSS PROFIT	SALES	GROSS PROFIT	SALES	GROSS PROFIT
	£k	%	£k	%	£k	%
FACIALS	85	45	97	50	100	52
MANICURE	66	38	78	47	90	51
PEDICURE	38	40	49	48	60	51
MASSAGE	19	15	39	15	80	40
AROMATHERAPY	57	48	68	50	80	60
TOTAL	265	41	331	45	410	51

> AH Building is slowly improving its overall margins, as shown in Table 2.18.

Table 2.18   Sales figures including margin information, AH Building

AH BUILDING SALES FIGURES + MARGINS						
SALES AREA: ALL						
YEAR	20X3		20X4		20X5	
	SALES	GROSS PROFIT	SALES	GROSS PROFIT	SALES	GROSS PROFIT
	£k	%	£k	%	£k	%
EXTENSIONS	120	45	180	48	220	50
MODIFICATIONS	250	40	220	44	230	45
DAMP TREATMENT	90	35	80	33	100	34
ROOFING	20	30	50	35	100	36
OTHER	40	35	60	35	50	35
TOTAL	520	39	590	42	700	43

Prestige Cars is trying to maintain a steady margin as taxi sales stagnate and other product lines grow; see Table 2.19.

Table 2.19 Sales figures including margin information, Prestige Cars

PRESTIGE CARS
SALES FIGURES

SALES AREA: ALL

YEAR	20X3		20X4		20X5	
	SALES	GROSS PROFIT	SALES	GROSS PROFIT	SALES	GROSS PROFIT
	£k	%	£k	%	£k	
TAXI SERVICE	200	30	180	27	200	25
CARS (WITH DRIVER)	250	37	220	36	250	35
PEOPLE CARRIERS (WITH DRIVER)	100	42	150	41	200	40
LUXURY CARS (WITH DRIVER)	50	65	100	58	150	55
TOTAL	600	38	650	38	800	38

Table 2.20 shows Global Fuels' sales figures including margin information.

Table 2.20 Sales figures including margin information, Global Fuels

GLOBAL FUELS
SALES FIGURES

SALES AREA: ALL

YEAR	20X3		20X4		20X5	
	SALES	GROSS PROFIT	SALES	GROSS PROFIT	SALES	GROSS PROFIT
	£k	%	£k	%	£k	
FUEL OILS	850	32	920	31	900	33
HEAVY FUEL OILS	300	28	280	26	300	27
DIESEL	270	30	310	32	300	33
RED DIESEL	50	31	100	32	200	35
OTHER	80	50	90	50	100	50
TOTAL	1550	32	1700	31	1800	33

Precision Valves Ltd can see from its margin information (Table 2.21) that the more type 'S' valves and packages it sells, the better margins it makes.

Table 2.21 Sales figures including margin information, Precision Valves Ltd

PRECISION VALVES
SALES FIGURES + MARGINS

SALES AREA: UK						
YEAR	20X3		20X4		20X5	
	SALES	GROSS PROFIT	SALES	GROSS PROFIT	SALES	GROSS PROFIT
	£k	%	£k	%	£k	
TYPE 'A' VALVES	450	34	450	35	400	34
TYPE 'B' VALVES	1000	30	900	32	800	33
TYPE 'S' VALVES	100	40	200	40	400	40
PACKAGES	50	40	100	40	200	40
SPARE PARTS	180	60	180	58	200	58
TOTAL	1780	35	1830	37	2000	38

The Pure Fruit Jam Company is able to compare margins on its UK and export business; see Tables 2.22 and 2.23.

It can be seen that the margins for the export business are much lower than those it makes in the UK.

Table 2.22 Sales and margins for UK business, The Pure Fruit Jam Company

THE PURE FRUIT JAM COMPANY
SALES FIGURES + MARGINS

SALES AREA: UK						
YEAR	20X3		20X4		20X5	
	SALES	GROSS PROFIT	SALES	GROSS PROFIT	SALES	GROSS PROFIT
	£k	%	£k	%	£k	
STANDARD JAMS (340 gm)	1000	50	1000	51	1000	51
MARMALADES (340 gm)	350	48	350	50	420	54
MINI-POTS	100	60	180	65	250	65
GIFT PACKS	90	60	70	60	50	65
SPECIAL PRODUCTS	150	60	200	58	280	60
TOTAL	1690	52	1800	53	2000	55

Table 2.23 Sales and margins for export business, The Pure Fruit Jam Company

THE PURE FRUIT JAM COMPANY
SALES FIGURES + MARGINS

SALES AREA: EXPORT

YEAR	20X3		20X4		20X5	
	SALES	GROSS PROFIT	SALES	GROSS PROFIT	SALES	GROSS PROFIT
	£k	%	£k	%	£k	%
STANDARD JAMS (340 gm)	100	25	200	30	300	30
MARMALADES (340 gm)	50	31	80	32	100	33
MINI-POTS			20	32	50	32
GIFT PACKS			30	40	50	40
SPECIAL PRODUCTS						
TOTAL	150	35	330	37	500	38

For small local companies like Jane's Beauty & Health, AH Building and Prestige Cars, the split of sales by product or application and unit sales is adequate. In Chapter 3 we will look at how they could start to look at their types of customer or application, but they will not have this information available in the breakdown of their historical sales.

On the other hand, the distribution and manufacturing companies like Global Fuels, The Pure Fruit Jam Company and Precision Valves Ltd will also be able to look at sales by customer or industry type and by geographical area.

> Global Fuels has split its sales by industry sectors; see Table 2.24.

Table 2.24 Sales by industry sector, Global Fuels

GLOBAL FUELS
SALES FIGURES (Historical and Forecast)

SALES AREA: ALL

Net sales by application after deducting tax & duty   ←——— forecast ———→

YEAR (all values in £k)	20X3	20X4	20X5	20X6	20X7	20X8
HOME HEATING	850	920	900			
INDUSTRIAL	600	640	660			
FARMING	50	70	120			
LEISURE	0	20	70			
OTHER	30	40	50			
TOTAL	1530	1690	1800			

> The Pure Fruit Jam Company has a similar split of sales by market sector; see Table 2.25.

Table 2.25   Sales by market sector, The Pure Fruit Jam Company

THE PURE FRUIT JAM COMPANY						
SALES FIGURES (Historical and Forecast)						

SALES AREA: UK

					forecast	
YEAR (all values in £k)	20X3	20X4	20X5	20X6	20X7	20X8
SUPERMARKETS	490	470	490			
QUALITY SHOPS	830	850	850			
HOTELS	80	140	220			
AIRLINES	40	80	140			
OTHER	250	260	300			
TOTAL	1690	1800	2000			

> Precision Valves Ltd sells into a small number of main markets; see Table 2.26.

Table 2.26   Sales by application, Precision Valves Ltd

PRECISION VALVES LTD						
SALES FIGURES (Historical and Forecast)						

SALES AREA: UK

					forecast	
YEAR (all values in £k)	20X3	20X4	20X5	20X6	20X7	20X8
WATER TREATMENT	650	680	760			
WASTE WATER	750	780	830			
CHEMICALS	200	210	210			
OTHER	180	160	200			
TOTAL	1780	1830	2000			

These three companies operate regionally for the main geographical areas of the plan. Global Fuels has split sales in its main sales areas; see Table 2.27.

Table 2.27 Sales by geographical area, Global Fuels

GLOBAL FUELS
SALES FIGURES (Historical and Forecast)

SALES AREA: ALL

Net sales by area after deducting tax & duty

YEAR (all values in £k)	20X3	20X4	20X5	20X6	forecast 20X7	20X8
DEVON/CORNWALL	280	360	430			
SOMERSET/WILTSHIRE	330	370	380			
BRISTOL/AVON	920	960	990			
TOTAL	1530	1690	1800			

The Pure Fruit Jam Company sells more product in the south of England than in any other area; see Table 2.28.

Table 2.28 Sales by geographical area, The Pure Fruit Jam Company

THE PURE FRUIT JAM COMPANY
SALES FIGURES (Historical and Forecast)

SALES AREA: UK

YEAR (all values in £k)	20X3	20X4	20X5	20X6	forecast 20X7	20X8
SOUTH	1010	1080	1190			
NORTH	550	590	650			
WALES	50	40	60			
SCOTLAND/NI	80	90	100			
TOTAL	1690	1800	2000			

Precision Valves Ltd includes sales for its type 'B' valves by geographical area; see Table 2.29.

Table 2.29 Sales figures for type 'B' valves in the UK, Precision Valves Ltd

PRECISION VALVES LTD						
SALES FIGURES (Historical and Forecast)						
SALES AREA: UK						
PRODUCT 'B' VALVES					forecast	
YEAR (all values in £k)	20X3	20X4	20X5	20X6	20X7	20X8
SOUTH	320	330	305			
MIDLANDS	300	245	215			
NORTH	305	250	210			
WALES	30	32	30			
SCOTLAND/NI	45	43	40			
TOTAL	1000	900	800			

Sometimes, showing information graphically makes more of an impact. This could be used in your plan or in a presentation.

Jane's Beauty & Health uses a pie chart to show its relative sales values; see Figure 2.1.

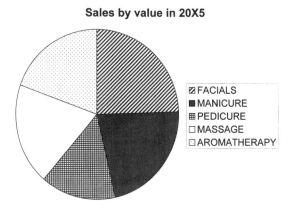

Sales by value in 20X5

- FACIALS
- MANICURE
- PEDICURE
- MASSAGE
- AROMATHERAPY

Figure 2.1 Sales for all products, Jane's Beauty & Health

Also, use of a bar chart shows the relative importance of the different products in terms of numbers of customer sessions; see Figure 2.2.

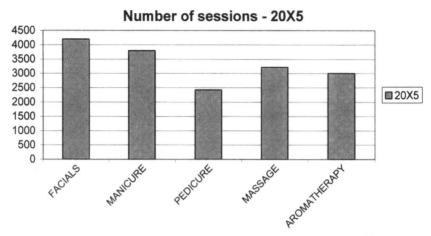

Figure 2.2   Number of sessions for each product, Jane's Beauty & Health

This shows the relative importance of the different products much better than a table.

Similar types of graphics could be used for all of the companies preparing their marketing plans.

AH Building analyses its customer base, as shown in Figure 2.3.

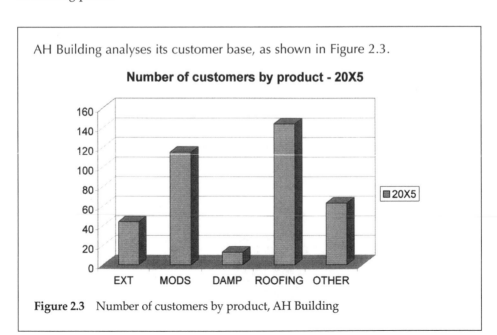

Figure 2.3   Number of customers by product, AH Building

Prestige Cars shows its sales growth, in Figure 2.4.

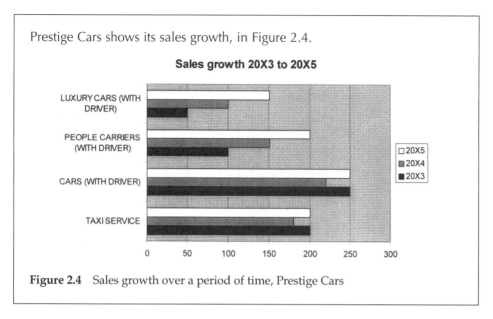

Figure 2.4 Sales growth over a period of time, Prestige Cars

Global Fuels shows its sales by market segment, in Figure 2.5.

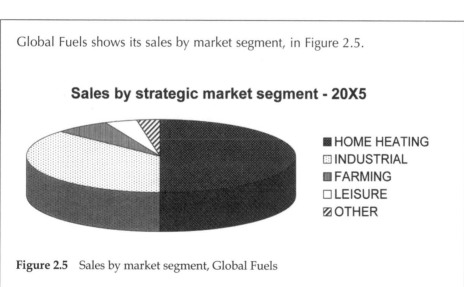

Figure 2.5 Sales by market segment, Global Fuels

The Pure Fruit Jam Company looks at its product split, in Figure 2.6.

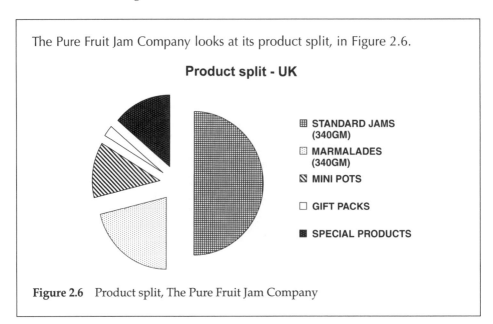

Figure 2.6 Product split, The Pure Fruit Jam Company

Finally, Precision Valves Ltd looks at its sales growth by region, in Figure 2.7.

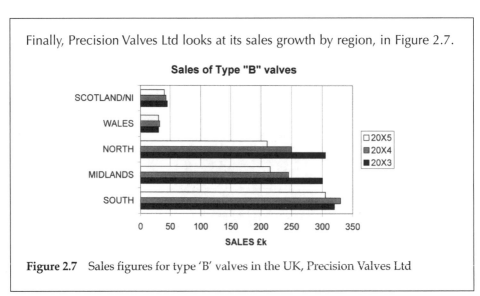

Figure 2.7 Sales figures for type 'B' valves in the UK, Precision Valves Ltd

EXERCISE

Now prepare a similar set of data for your product for your own example plan. It is important that you carry out the exercise even if you do not have all the data available to complete all of the tables.

THE USE OF DATABASES

The widespread use of computer technology has revolutionised the ability of even small companies to have comprehensive databases. Software has also become much more 'user friendly' than it was even 10 years ago. There are now standard packages that can be customised for individual company use. Many manufacturing companies have installed MRP (materials resource planning) systems which, in effect, act on a database of the company's current and expected order intake and sales. These systems normally include a sales and finance package with the facility to extract information from the database for the purpose of sales analysis.

Further useful analysis can be carried out if it is possible to segregate customers by SIC (Standard Industry Classification) codes and to split order intake related to these specific industries. Every single order has to be allocated the SIC code relevant to the industry that it is being sold into and the analysis work is carried out on the codes. Information can be obtained based on values and numbers of units of different products sold into different industries.

Even if your company does not have such a system or if the system you have does not include the parameters that you want to measure, it is still possible for you to use a PC with database programs to analyse data. It may mean that someone has to go back through order data for the past three years and extract the relevant information to put it manually into a database.

There is no excuse for companies – however small – not to keep some information on databases for use in marketing planning. Such databases can be on a PC, linked by means of a network, so that the information can be shared. Or they can be held as a main file on a file-server in such a way that they can be updated by any authorised user, so that they are always current.

A computer database can be a powerful tool and it is not necessary to have a detailed knowledge of computers to use one. In its simplest form you can use the database functions of spreadsheet programs such as Microsoft Excel or Lotus 1-2-3. These allow you to sort data alphabetically or by date or number. The next stage is to use the associated database – Access (with Excel), Approach (with Lotus 1-2-3) or FileMaker Pro.

The difference between a database and a spreadsheet is that a spreadsheet is essentially two-dimensional and a database is three-dimensional. The possibilities of sorting and analysing data are therefore greater with a true database.

Before setting up your database you need to decide *all* of the parameters that you want to record – not just for now, but for the future. At the moment you may only be interested to know how many units were sold over the last three years and not their size or colour, but it is wise to construct a list of data for the database to include other parameters that may be needed for future analysis work. A database is effectively a set of individual entries of data that can be sorted by the computer in a variety of ways. It can sort just as easily on 'colour' as on 'size of unit' or 'customer industry code'.

With the transparency of modern software, it is quite possible to enter data in an Excel spreadsheet and then regularly download it into an Access database to process it further. It is also possible to maintain a dynamic link between the two programs so that when data in one is changed, the other is automatically modified.

Before you import spreadsheet data into a database you should ensure that the format of the data is appropriate for a database table. For example, be sure that the data has the same fields in every row and that the information in each column is of the same data type.

Once a database has been installed, it should be continuously kept up to date so that it can be analysed as and when required for planning purposes.

Most databases will present the final data as lists or as a spreadsheet. The advantage of integrated office software packages is that they usually include a high-quality presentation program. Graphs can be prepared in Excel, but Microsoft Office includes the PowerPoint presentation package and data and images can be transferred between the two.

SUMMARY

Your company is a valuable source of data for use in your marketing plan. This historical 'in-house' data will be added to the more general market information that will be collected using the techniques outlined in Chapter 3.

Before collecting data you should prepare an 'information checklist' for your plan. The exact detail will vary, depending on the scope of your plan, but it should include details of the segmentation that you want for sales, the split of your customer base and competitor activity/market shares.

You should present data to show:

■ invoiced sales;
■ number of units sold;
■ gross margins/profits.

The information should be collected and presented in such a way as to reflect the key market segments into which you sell your products. For the products and markets covered by your plan you should collect and present information going back two or three full years, together with this year's forecast sales.

The historical information should be entered in a format that includes space for forecast data as well, even though this would be left blank at this stage. If seasonal sales are a significant part of total sales, the information should also be presented to show monthly sales throughout the year. You should indicate the affect of inflation/price increases and exchange rate fluctuations on the figures you present. You should also present figures for the number of units sold, because this is a measure that removes inflation.

You should not include individual figures that are too small to be relevant. More detail and smaller individual figures may be more relevant in a plan for an area or product than in an overall plan.

The information collected will also need to be put into context in relation to market information that will be collected in Chapter 3, and the information year on year needs to be compared and contrasted.

Company databases can provide useful information for this internal market research, and once set up, they will continue to provide such information for future marketing planning.

3

The marketing audit – external

The external marketing audit is a detailed examination of the company's marketing environment.

The audit of the marketing environment

This is an examination of the company's markets, customers, competitors and the overall economic and political environment. It involves marketing research and the collecting of historical data about your company and its products. It is an iterative process. It is only when you start to analyse your own in-house data that you realise which market sectors you need to look at outside, and once you look at the external data you may notice applications that are small for your company, but larger in a market context and therefore require further investigation.

The audit of marketing activity

This is a study of the company's marketing mix – products, price, promotion and place.

The audit of the marketing system

This involves looking at the current structure of the marketing organisation together with its systems.

THE MARKETING ENVIRONMENT – MARKET RESEARCH

At the same time that you consider historical sales data for your company, you need to collect information that will allow it to be put into perspective. This involves market research – collecting information about your markets and then analysing it in the context of the marketing of the products.

Why is marketing research necessary?

In today's highly competitive business environment there is no substitute for keeping in touch with the marketplace. Markets are constantly changing and so are the requirements of customers. It is easy for a company to get so involved in one market or one sector of a market that it is not able to consider the whole market for its products and may be missing potential opportunities in other markets or market sectors.

Equally, product offerings are constantly changing and evolving in the marketplace. Competitors may have new ideas and if you do not find out about them quickly enough, you could find parts of your market starting to disappear.

Small businesses do not have huge resources to commit to market research, but much information is easy to get hold of if you know where to look for it. In fact, for small local businesses, much can be obtained by looking at competitors, both in your own town and in larger cities.

Your in-house acquired knowledge is important, as is feedback and market intelligence from your sales force, but they need to be supplemented by marketing research obtained from outside sources. If you are in the consumer goods field, your contacts with the trade are unlikely to say enough about customers' attitudes and what you find out will be limited by your contacts with retailers and will not represent all views. Even if you are one of your sales force (or *the* sales force), your selection and interpretation of what is important will be affected by the fact that information gathering is secondary to your selling function. Although information from salespeople and other sources will be of considerable qualitative value, you need to be sure that the information on which decisions will be based is as complete as possible and is representative and objective. So additional information is required, and this would be key information relating to the companies or customers that you sell to and the industries and areas in which your product or service is being sold.

As well as information on customers, you also need information on competitors and their products. You should also obtain information about how the market and your customers perceive *your company and its products*. This could include company and product image, before- and after-sales service, price and quality. You should research advertising and sales promotion methods to find out which methods are the most effective for your type of product or service. In its simplest form this process is shown in Figure 3.1.

Market research is used to:

▪ give a description of the market;
▪ monitor how the market changes;
▪ decide on actions to be taken by a company and evaluate the results of these actions.

Description of the market

This is the primary purpose for which research is needed. It is of particular use to a company entering a market or launching a new product or service. In order

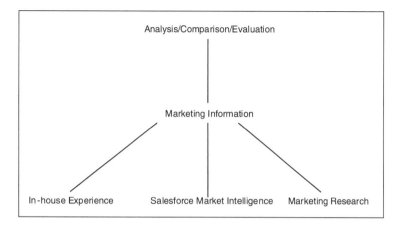

Figure 3.1 The collection and evaluation process

to work out overall strategy, formulate the product or service correctly, and decide how to market it, it is important to learn all relevant information that is known about the products or services that are already in the market (if there are any), their market share, how they are distributed, who the users are, how frequently they use them, whether they only use one brand or several, and why they make their choices. A company entering a market would have to learn these things, but it is equally important for companies with established products to keep up to date with how and why their product is purchased.

Monitor how the market changes

This means periodic checking for changes in a product's or brand's share or distribution, usage or image. It is dangerous to put together plans based on out-of-date information if significant changes have occurred since the original information was collected.

Decide on or evaluate potential courses of action

'Description' and 'monitoring' refer to obtaining information about the 'marketing environment'. 'Deciding on actions' relates to ways in which market research information can help a company to decide how to operate in the marketing environment. It can include:

- test marketing;
- new product launches (and developments);
- acceptance testing of modified products;
- promoting company image;
- developing and evaluating advertising and promotion campaigns, mailshots and e-mail marketing.

Market research data consists of primary data and secondary data. Primary data is data obtained from primary sources, ie directly in the marketplace. This is

Table 3.1 Expenditure on market research in the UK in 1999

INDUSTRY	%
1. Food, drink and tobacco	16
2. Pharmaceuticals and cosmetics	14
3. Media and advertising	12
4. Government and public services	9
5. Motoring	7
6. Financial services	7
7. Telecom and IT	6
8. Retailers	5
9. Household products	4
10. Travel and tourism	4
11. Industrial products	2
Other	14

gathered either by carrying out field research directly yourself or by commissioning a consultant or market research company to carry out the fieldwork for you. Secondary data is not obtained directly from fieldwork, and market research based on secondary data sources is referred to as 'desk research'.

Small businesses will usually carry out limited market research themselves. Some large companies in the consumer goods field employ some of their own people for market research, but even so, most work is carried out by specialist market research companies. The sector has grown rapidly in recent years. Worldwide spending on market research is now in excess of £10 billion, with the UK accounting for about 10 per cent of this. Companies belonging to the British Market Research Association (BMRA) account for 80 to 90 per cent of all interviewing in the UK. The UK market research industry is now some four times larger in real terms than it was 20 years ago. Market research employs over 10,000 people in the UK, more than 8,000 of whom belong to the Market Research Society.

The major users of market research are the food and drinks companies and other consumer goods companies. The distribution of market research expenditure in 1999 estimated by BMRA is shown in Table 3.1.

It can be seen that the proportion of expenditure by companies marketing industrial products is very small.

FIELD RESEARCH

In field research the information is collected by obtaining the answers to a set of questions from a number of respondents. The sample used needs to be representative and objective.

Methods of carrying out field research

Field research can be carried out in person, by telephone, by post or by e-mail. Large companies often use outside companies to do the work, but small businesses usually do the work themselves and limit it to just what is really necessary. Because it is an expensive process, it is best used to obtain specific information or to answer particular questions about your market. There are other methods of obtaining information in the consumer field that are partway between carrying out your own field research and desk research. These are methods such as retail audits and consumer audits.

Retail audits

The retail audit was pioneered by Nielsen in the USA. It can provide very accurate information on broad market shares, market sizes and sales trends. The principle is very simple. A representative sample of retailers is selected in a particular field (typically grocers, supermarkets, off-licences, chemists, etc). An auditor visits the retailers at regular intervals (usually twice a month). On his or her first visit, the auditor notes the stock of the audited items on display and in the storeroom. On the next visit he or she notes the quantity of stock delivered since the last visit. The product sold between the visits is then calculated from the formula:

$$\text{sales} = \text{initial stock} + \text{deliveries} - \text{final stock}$$

The audit is maintained over a period of time and builds up a picture of the sales of the products and of competitive products over that period. Setting up a retail audit is expensive and they are normally arranged so as to be syndicable (ie, the information from the audit is sold to a number of clients, most with different products). Syndication is economically possible because once the investment has been made in selecting and carrying out initial visits to the retailers, it is relatively inexpensive to collect data for a large number of products. Clients pay agreed subscriptions for packages of selected brands within a defined product field. The information is reported and presented in the way that the client requests it.

Consumer audits

Consumer audits use a panel of consumers to measure changes in attitudes or behaviour. This has the same effect as interviewing the same sample over and over again. It is either a sample that agreed on recruitment to be available to be contacted on all sorts of subjects or, more commonly, a panel is recruited to provide information continuously over a period. The information would need to be recorded daily otherwise it would not be remembered, so a diary is used to record purchases and consumption of particular goods. In some cases special containers are provided for used cans or cartons of the product being measured (the so-called 'dust-bin check'). Consumer audits can be used to evaluate the effect of various advertising campaigns on usage of products. They are often syndicated because of their cost.

Reactive marketing research with questionnaires

This is what most people associate with market research – the interviewer with the clipboard in the street. It is still the backbone of the market research industry and will probably remain so for some time, although computer techniques and e-mail can be expected to become increasingly used over the next decade or so. There are in fact many ways of getting questionnaires completed. As well as personal interviews, questionnaires can also be completed by telephone interviews, as postal questionnaires or increasingly as e-mail questionnaires. Nowadays it is quite common to find questionnaires in magazines, left in hotel rooms or given out in fast-food restaurants. It is a widespread method of gathering data because it is a flexible technique, which is not necessarily that expensive, and it can be designed for statistical analysis of the questionnaires by computer. It becomes a very expensive technique if the questionnaire is badly designed so that ambiguous or inadequate data are obtained.

Questionnaires need to be specific to the area to be researched and the list of questions should be designed to give as much information as possible without ambiguity. The results can be influenced by loading questions, and even the order of questions can have an effect on the answers. A questionnaire needs to be designed and set out with skill by someone with knowledge of the techniques. Even then, before it is used on the full samples, it should be pilot tested on a small section of the sample. This will highlight any problems such as ambiguous questions or omissions, and the questionnaire can then be modified before being used on the full sample. More detailed guidance on questionnaire design is given later in this chapter.

The methods of getting the respondent to answer the questionnaire are compared below.

Personal interviews

This can be the most comprehensive method of carrying out field research. It allows the respondent time to ponder and to answer the questions, and it allows the interviewer the opportunity of asking additional questions or for clarification of a particular answer. It is, however, very costly in terms of both time and money. It involves travelling time and expenses as well as the actual time of the interview. There is also time required to set up the interviews.

In the consumer field the cost is increased by the need for interviewers to work unsocial hours, because with more women working and with the requirement to contact men and women in employment rather than just the unemployed, interviewing needs to be carried out in the evenings and at weekends as well as in normal daytime hours.

Nevertheless, for many purposes personal face-to-face interviewing is considered an absolute necessity. A good interviewer can form a rapport with the respondents so that they focus on the subject under discussion in a relaxed and concentrated way. He or she can lead the respondent through the questions and can also show stimuli, such as pictures, photographs or the actual product itself – this is not possible with the other methods such as telephone and postal interviewing, although it can be possible using e-mail techniques with web links.

Telephone interviews

Telephone interviewing is less expensive than personal interviewing because it does not incur the costs of sending interviewers out to people's homes to make the contact. People tend to be more receptive since it involves a much smaller amount of a respondent's time. This can be important in the service and industrial sector where interviews are with businessmen or engineers at work. Such people may be reluctant to agree to a personal interview because of the time involved but would rarely refuse a telephone questionnaire *so long as it was not too long*. Since instant answers are demanded, it is often easier to get a full set of answers from a telephone interview than from other techniques. This must be offset by the fact that instant answers are not always the answers that would be given after due reflection. In telephone interviewing the interviewer's voice is all-important, but other aspects of his or her personality are less important than in personal interviewing. Much greater productivity can be achieved in telephone interviewing, because there is no lost travelling time and many more interviews can be conducted in a day. There is also the facility for instant supervision and the correction of interviewer error. An additional advantage of this type of interview is that the answers can be entered directly into a computer for immediate processing.

Many companies now carry out telephone interviews when customers phone up with complaints or problems. (To encourage phone calls many companies include freephone numbers on their product packaging.) In addition to or as a means of solving the problem, a standard list of questions are asked and the answers noted. This provides the company with valuable feedback, which can be analysed for reoccurring problems or trends.

Postal and e-mail questionnaires

This is a relatively low-cost method, where the questionnaire is sent by post, fax or e-mail and the respondent is left to complete it in his or her own time. Increasingly, questionnaires are sent out with bills, supplied with new equipment, or given to the customer as he or she leaves after using the service. It has the advantage, as with telephone interviewing, that it does not incur the high costs involved in sending interviewers to people's homes.

It also has a number of disadvantages. There is no personal contact. Because of this, it is likely that a considerable number of questionnaires will end up in waste-paper bins. There is no way of checking whether the person it was addressed to was really the right person to ask. The respondent can scan the whole questionnaire before answering it and cannot be led through the questionnaire one stage at a time. He or she can take as long as he or she wishes in formulating replies to the questions, so that postal surveys are only suitable for considered opinions and not for instant reactions. Response rates are often low and replies may come in over a long period of time, making it difficult to collate and analyse the results. Most questionnaires are sent out with a reply-paid envelope, and a reminder and a further questionnaire are usually sent about two weeks later.

Because of the low response rates it is important to know whether the bias of those that did not reply would affect the results of the survey. For this reason it is common to check the non-response bias by telephone calls to a sub-sample. It is also important to note that recent legislation has made it more difficult to use faxes for this purpose.

E-mailing is by far the cheapest method of sending out questionnaires. If e-mails are sent to individual people, they can only now be sent by using an 'opt-in' list. An 'opt-in' list contains customers that have chosen to receive e-mail shots. This is now a legal requirement following a European Directive governing Privacy and Electronic Communications. The Directive favours the 'opt-in' system and prohibits the sending of unsolicited electronic mail (spam). Specialist companies like Email Factory UK (www.emailfactory.co.uk) and Emailvision UK Ltd (www.emailvision.com) can provide a cheap and effective e-mail service and can obtain 'opt-in' lists from third-party e-mail list brokers. But to grow your list, you need to initiate or optimise an e-mail address collection operation at all your customer points of contact (website, point-of-sale, invoices, etc).

Typical questionnaires

You will have to put together your own questionnaires based on your particular requirements, but the information given here will give you some guidelines on the type of questions that you may use and the layout of the questionnaire.

Although the requirements in the consumer, service and industrial sectors are different, there are many factors in questionnaire design that are universal. The content, order and layout of questionnaires will also vary, depending on whether they are designed for personal or telephone interviews or for postal or e-mail questionnaires.

The following points are important:

▦ The questionnaire needs to be specific to the area being researched and without irrelevant questions.
▦ The list of questions should be designed to give as much information as possible without ambiguity.
▦ Each question should be simple and relatively short.
▦ Most questions should require a simple yes/no answer or a choice from a number of answers.
▦ Do not use loaded questions as these will tend to give a biased result.
▦ Consider the order of questions carefully, since questions earlier in the questionnaire could influence later answers.
▦ Lay out the questionnaire in such a way that the answers can easily be analysed statistically.
▦ Avoid 'omnibus' questionnaires with a hundred questions or more – most people will not be prepared to answer more than about 20 questions.

In service industries, the emphasis of questionnaires is usually on the quality of the service as perceived by the customer.

Figure 3.2 shows a questionnaire prepared by Jane's Beauty & Health. This questionnaire is on a single page, which can be folded, sealed and the resulting 'envelope' is then either left at reception or posted back to the company.

Date of visit: _____

Sex   male ☐   female ☐

How was our reception service on arrival?

very good ☐ good ☐ adequate ☐ bad ☐ very bad ☐

What services did you use?

facial ☐   manicure ☐   pedicure ☐   massage ☐   aromatherapy ☐

Was the service you received

above expectations ☐   as expected ☐   below expectations ☐

Did you find staff generally

very helpful ☐ helpful ☐ adequate ☐ unhelpful ☐

Would you use our services again ?

yes ☐   perhaps ☐   no ☐

Figure 3.2 Questionnaire for Jane's Beauty & Health

Figure 3.3 is a questionnaire for AH Building.

Date work carried out:

Which of our services did you use?

Home Extension ☐   Roofing ☐   Damp Treatment ☐   Other ☐

How would you rate the quality of our work?

excellent ☐   very good ☐   good ☐   adequate ☐   unacceptable ☐

How would you rate our time to complete the job?

excellent ☐   very good ☐   good ☐   adequate ☐   unacceptable ☐

Was the service you received from us:

above expectations ☐   as expected ☐   below expectations ☐

Would you use our services again?

yes ☐   perhaps ☐   no ☐

Figure 3.3 Questionnaire for AH Building

Figure 3.4 is an extract from a similar questionnaire for Prestige Cars.

Date of hire: _____

Sex   male ☐   female ☐

How was our reception service on arrival?

very good ☐   good ☐   adequate ☐   bad ☐   very bad ☐

Was the cleanliness of the vehicle

very good ☐   good ☐   adequate ☐   bad ☐   very bad ☐

Was the size and quality of the car:

above expectations ☐   as expected ☐   below expectations ☐

Did you find staff generally

very helpful ☐   helpful ☐   adequate ☐   unhelpful ☐

Would you use our services again?

yes ☐   perhaps ☐   no ☐

Figure 3.4   Questionnaire for Prestige Cars

Industrial companies also prepare questionnaires based on the quality of their service, but in addition they use questionnaires to extend their customer base for existing products and to sound out the interest in new products.

Global Fuels wants to find out what the demand would be for red diesel among its existing customers for home heating oil for houses or farms. It has prepared the questionnaire shown in Figure 3.5. This will be sent out to all prospective customers with their next bill.

Area code: _____   Date: _____   Customer number: _____

Please complete the following information:

What products do you currently purchase from us?

heating oil ☐   diesel ☐   red diesel ☐   other ☐

Did you know that we supply red diesel?   yes ☐   no ☐

Do you already use red diesel   yes ☐   no ☐

If you do use red diesel, please advise quantity you use per month _____ litres

Is your use for:

farm vehicles ☐   gardening equipment ☐   leisure equipment ☐

If you use ordinary diesel, you should be made aware that red diesel is less than half the price of ordinary diesel. If you do not know when and where you can use it, please request our free fact sheet.

Please send me your free fact sheet on red diesel   yes ☐   no ☐

Figure 3.5   Questionnaire for Global Fuels

It is also thinking of preparing a questionnaire to sound out its industrial customers on its range of lubricating oils.

The Pure Fruit Jam Company is considering launching a range of specialist flavoured marmalades. It has prepared the questionnaire shown in Figure 3.6. It needs to establish a number of things relating to the market. It has already obtained information on the sales levels for jams and marmalades in the UK from published data in reports prepared and sold by the Leatherhead Food Research Association. It wants to find out details about the typical consumer of marmalade. Are they male or female, young or old, how often do they purchase and where do they purchase from? This will influence the type of advertising and promotion campaign that the company will use.

Area code: _____ Date: _____ Interview no: _____

Please complete the following information:

Sex   Male ☐   Female ☐

Age   10–15 yrs   16–20 yrs   21–25 yrs

         26–30 yrs   31–35 yrs   36–40 yrs

         41–50 yrs   51–64 yrs   over 65 yrs

Do you buy marmalade?

Do you buy mainly traditional Seville orange marmalade?   Yes ☐   No ☐

Do you buy specialist marmalades with other fruits or flavours?   Yes ☐   No ☐

How often do you buy marmalade?

once a week ☐   once a month ☐   less often ☐

Do you buy from   supermarket ☐   delicatessen ☐   by mail order ☐   other ☐

If a specialist range of marmalades was available, which of these flavours would you be interested in?

whisky ☐   brandy ☐   Cointreau ☐   sherry ☐   vodka ☐   gin ☐

Would you consider buying specialist marmalades?

for normal use ☐   at Christmas ☐   as a present for others ☐

Figure 3.6   Questionnaire for The Pure Fruit Jam Company

The questionnaire starts with the more general questions relating to age and sex and then moves on to the types of marmalade and allows the company to sound out the flavours it is thinking of introducing (whisky, brandy, Cointreau, as well as flavours such a vodka and gin that it thinks will have less appeal).

Most questionnaires are one or two pages in length. Some questions are put on the second page of the questionnaire so that the answer does not affect preceding questions.

Sometimes in the industrial goods sector there is a requirement for more specific information that cannot be obtained by a simple yes/no answer. Also, many companies involved in industrial goods marketing are active in markets where there are only a small number of suppliers and often only a small number of customers. A supplier of consumer goods may potentially have many millions of end- customers. Many industrial goods companies have less than a thousand active customers on their files. For this reason it is common for such companies to structure questionnaires in a more general way, mixing qualitative and quantitative types of questions. Some of the major areas that these companies often want to have their customers or potential customers views on are:

- buying factors that influence them;
- how they view the company and its competitors;
- how they find out about new products;
- their approach to new products.

Precision Valves Ltd has prepared a number of questionnaires on more general subjects, which are shown in Figures 3.7 to 3.11.

Buying factors that influence customers

> When you buy product A, there are a number of factors that you will take into account in making your decision. Please list the factors given below, numerically, in order of priority (1 to 5).
>
>
> PRICE
>
> DELIVERY
>
> QUALITY
>
> TECHNICAL SPECIFICATION
>
> AFTERSALES SERVICE

Figure 3.7 Questionnaire – buying factors

How customers view your company and its competitors

A similar questionnaire could also be used to establish customer's feelings about your company. The same list of factors would be shown, but with a different question (Figure 3.8).

Based on the buying factors listed below, how would you rate our company?

PRICE

DELIVERY

QUALITY

TECHNICAL SPECIFICATION

AFTERSALES SERVICE

Please rank as follows:

1 – Best on the market

2 – Better than average

3 – Average

4 – Worse than average

5 – Worst on the market

Figure 3.8   Questionnaire – image in marketplace

Precision Valves Ltd will use this questionnaire. The same questionnaire could be used by a wider range of companies, including all of our example companies, if it was modified as shown in Figure 3.9.

Based on the buying factors listed below, how would you rate our company?

PRICE

AVAILABILITY

QUALITY

Please rank as follows:

1 – Best on the market

2 – Better than average

3 – Average

4 – Worse than average

5 – Worst on the market

Figure 3.9   Questionnaire – image in marketplace

How customers find out about new products

> From what sources do you learn about new products in your industry?
> (please tick)
>
> ☐ TRADE ASSOCIATION
>
> ☐ MANUFACTURERS' SALES VISITS
>
> ☐ EXHIBITIONS (PLEASE STATE WHICH ONES)
> -
> -
> ☐ JOURNALS/MAGAZINES (PLEASE STATE WHICH ONES)
> -
> -

Figure 3.10   Questionnaire — awareness of new products

Customers approach to new products

> When purchasing a new product do you:
>
> A) Contact existing users   Y/N
>
> B) Carry out your own tests   Y/N
>
> C) Seek other advice   Y/N (If 'yes', please specify)
> -
> -
> In view of past experience, how long does it take for new products to be accepted into the industry:
>
> A) For purchase by existing plants _____
>
> B) For inclusion in specifications _____
>
> Who would specify XYZ products in your company? _____
>
> What approvals (if any) would be required? _____

Figure 3.11   Questionnaire — approach to new products

DESK RESEARCH

Desk research involves the collection of data from existing sources. These sources can be:

- government statistics;
- company information;
- trade directories;
- trade associations;
- ready-made reports;
- the internet.

Desk research is often referred to as being cheap, since the main costs involved are the researcher's time, expenses, telephone charges, and buying directories and reports. It is, however, only 'relatively' cheap in relation to the costs involved in carrying out field research. It could be a complete waste of money if the researcher chosen to do the work did not have the knowledge to work in a way that would get the required results. For this reason care needs to be taken in the selection of personnel for this task and a reasonably senior qualified person needs to be chosen to supervise the desk research. In fact, you may need to do this yourself.

There are a number of companies that specialise in carrying out research and publishing reports. The most prominent are Euromonitor, Mintel, Keynote and Frost and Sullivan. These organisations publish lists of reports that they have available on their websites. Euromonitor has about 25 business reference handbooks and hundreds of reports covering 26 different industry sectors. Reports have titles as diverse as 'Healthfoods in France' and 'The Market for Disposable Paper Products in Asia-Pacific'. The reports include information on the market, its segmentation, the products, competition, distribution systems, and the consumer. Most reports are now available both as a hard copy and as a CD ROM.

Most companies use a mixture of field and desk research and it is clearly a waste of money to carry out your own research to obtain information that is already available and can be purchased in the form of a ready-made report. Many reports can be purchased for between £50 and £150.

The internet is a valuable source of information for desk research. There are many specific websites for individual industries, eg, www.sugarinfo.co.uk; patent information, eg, uspto.gov; and of course all of your competitors will have websites, which are by far the easiest way of getting up-to-date information on their companies and their products. Even small companies like Jane's Beauty & Health have their own website and can gain much information on local competitors by looking at their websites.

Government support

UK Trade & Investment, the government organisation for assisting UK exporters, has a huge amount of information and reports available on export markets. On its website (www.trade.uktradeinvest.gov.uk) you can access market information on over 200 locations across the world. It also produces sector and market reports such as 'The Software & Computer Services Market in India' and 'The Food & Drink Market in Japan'. There are currently over 600 sector and market reports live on the website, all of which can be accessed free of charge.

UK Trade & Investment has an Information Centre, based in Kingsgate House, London, which is a free information resource for exporters. It contains market information as well as statistical, marketing and contact information. From April 2005 this information will be available in a purely electronic format. From April 2006 this will be available as an electronic service via the UK Trade & Investment website.

There is also an Export Marketing Research Scheme, which is administered by the British Chambers of Commerce on behalf of UK Trade & Investment. Companies with fewer than 250 employees may be eligible for a grant of up to 50 per cent of the agreed cost of an approved marketing research project. Details of the scheme can be obtained by contacting the Export Marketing Research Team at the British Chambers of Commerce (e-mail: emr@britishchambers.org.uk) or via the website (www.chamberonline.co.uk/exportzone/emrs).

Types of data

The marketing research information that we need for our plan is market information and product information.

Market information needs to tell us:

- The market's size
    - How big is it?
    - How is it segmented/structured?

- Its characteristics
    - Who are the main customers?
    - Who are the main suppliers?
    - What are the main products sold?

- The state of the market
    - Is it a new market?
    - A mature market?
    - A saturated market?

- How well are companies doing
    - Related to the market as a whole?
    - In relation to each other?

- Channels of distribution
    - What are they?

▦ Methods of communication

- What methods are used? Press, TV, internet, direct mail?
- What types of sales promotion?

▦ Financial. Are there problems caused by:

- Taxes/duties?
- Import restrictions?

▦ Legal

- Patent situation
- Product standards
- Legislation relating to agents
- Trademarks/copyright
- Protection of intellectual property (designs/software, etc).

▦ Developments

- What new areas of the market are developing?
- What new products are developing?
- Is new legislation or new regulations likely?

Product information relates to your own company, your competitors and the customers:

▦ Potential customers

- Who are they?
- Where are they located?
- Who are the market leaders?
- Do they own competitors?

▦ Your own company

- Do existing products meet customers' needs?
- Is product development necessary?
- Are completely new products required?
- What would be the potential of a new product?
- How is your company perceived in the market?

▦ Your competitors

- Who are they?
- How do they compare with your company in size?
- Where are they located?
- Do they operate in the same market sectors as you?
- What products do they manufacture/sell?
- How does their pricing compare with your own?
- What sales/distribution channels do they use?
- Have they recently introduced new products?

There are four main areas of published data that can be used in marketing research to provide the market and product information required. These are:

- market reports;
- company information;
- product and statistical information;
- consumer information.

In addition to these there is the internet. The internet is probably the easiest and cheapest means for small companies to start to research their markets and their competitors. We will show you later in the chapter how to use the internet to best advantage for the purposes of market research.

Market reports

Market information and market reports are the most comprehensive types of market research information. They look at all aspects of the market including companies, products, customers and trends. They present an overview of the whole market and allow a company to assess where it is positioned in the market.

The key areas covered by market reports are:

- a history of the market;
- the structure of the market;
- the size of the market;
- data on major companies in the market;
- market trends;
- distribution channels;
- recent market developments;
- future market developments.

Reports may be on a single market, a single market sector or on a number of related markets. Reports may be obtained from the organisations mentioned above or from specialist research or consulting organisations such as the Leatherhead Food International (www.lfra.co.uk) for food industry reports, or Jaakko Pöyri Group (www.poyry.com) for pulp and paper industry reports.

Many of our sample companies are only operating at a local level, so a report on health and beauty practices in Asia is not going to be of much interest to Jane's Beauty & Health. But Jane belongs to a trade association, the Guild of Professional Beauty Therapists. By contacting her trade association she may well be able to find more localised reports and information that will be of greater use to her than more general reports.

Company information

We need information on other companies in order to investigate potential customers and distributors and also to monitor our competitors and potential competitors. Company information is of two types: directory information and financial information.

Directory information gives key data on companies. This includes names, addresses, telephone numbers, trademarks, details of directors, and who owns whom. They usually list companies operating in particular markets.

The main trade directories such as Kompass Directories and Kelly's Directories cover all of the larger companies and include a great deal of information with a detailed analysis of activities and products. Kompass has a wide range of directories covering many foreign countries as well as its UK directories. It also has a business-to-business search engine on its website (www.kompass.com). There is also a wide range of more specialised directories covering single industries or industry sectors (such as the chemical industry, offshore oil and gas and the textile industry). These directories are often not as detailed as the main trade directories and often they only show the name, address and telephone numbers of companies, with a brief list of products, but they do have the advantage of being specific to their industry.

Many small businesses will find they can obtain the sort of information that they need from their trade association. In the case of a company operating locally, much useful information can be obtained from the local Yellow Pages, Thomson Directories or via the internet.

Financial information relates to the trading performance of a company and is normally an analysis of a company's financial accounts for one or more years. By law all UK companies have to file copies of their financial accounts with Companies House. The information must include:

- the directors' report and accounts;
- the annual return;
- the mortgage register;
- the memorandum and articles of association;
- changes in registered office or name;
- details of any bankruptcy proceedings.

The amount of information required from small companies is not the same as that required for large companies and it is quite common for small companies to give no details of turnover. This can be a problem in analysing information where small companies are involved.

Copies of companies' financial accounts can be obtained by requesting a copy from Companies House. More detailed information on individual companies can be obtained from companies such as Dun and Bradstreet.

A sensible way of obtaining this kind of information for an industry is to obtain a Business Ratio Report for that industry from a company such as The Prospect Shop, which specialises in producing such reports. These reports analyse industries by examining the results of the leading companies in the industry. The sample usually covers from 50 to 150 companies. In the reports, firms are often grouped into sub-sectors in order to give a thoroughly comparative analysis. The reports include up to 26 tables of ratios, such as return on capital, return on assets, profit margin, and stock turnover. The companies are ranked according to ratio performance. In addition, averages are calculated for the whole industry and where applicable each sub-sector. Information for these reports is derived from the annual audited accounts of companies filed at Companies House. In each report the tables of ratios are preceded by an informative commentary and followed by individual financial and directory profiles on all companies included in the report.

There are currently over 140 business ratio reports available. These reports can also be useful in relating your company's performance to others in your own industry. Using the ratio approach, you can compare the performance of your company with the performance of major competitors.

Product and statistical information

Government statistics are a useful source of information. These relate to business activity, as well as to details of imports and exports of products and commodities. Another useful source of international trade and production statistics is information produced by United Nations organisations such as the Food and Agriculture Organization (FAO). This type of information may well be irrelevant to many small businesses, but if you are involved in exporting or in the sale of industrial goods, you can find useful information to assist you. If this is not for you, please move on to the next section of this chapter.

To find your way around such statistics, it is necessary to have a basic understanding of the main coding and classification systems used for economic activity and products. There have been major changes to these systems in the last few years and a good guide to the development of and relationship between the systems is given in *Standard Industrial Classification of Economic Activities 1992. UK SIC (92)*. The latest updated version of this book was published in 1997 by The Stationery Office.

The system that is most commonly used by directories or financial reports classifies companies into industries by relating their main activities to the official standard industrial classification (SIC) codes. The codes in use in the UK are the SIC codes (revised 1992). (Care should be taken to differentiate from the US SIC codes, which are not the same. They are still in use, although they in turn are now being replaced by the NAICS system.)

The UK SIC codes are based on NACE Rev 1, which is an EU regulation requiring the use of common codes throughout the EU, but where it was thought necessary a fifth digit has been added to form subclasses of the NACE Rev 1 four-digit classes. Thus SIC(92) is a hierarchical five digit system. At the highest level of aggregation, SIC(92) is divided into 17 sections each denoted by a single letter from A to Q. These sections are given in Table 3.2.

Some sections are, in turn, divided into subsections (each denoted by the addition of a second letter). The letters of the sections and subsections do not need to be part of the SIC/NACE codes because they can be uniquely defined by the next breakdown, the divisions (denoted by two digits). The divisions are then broken down into groups (three digits), then into classes (four digits) and in some cases again into subclasses (five digits). Here is an example:

Section D	Manufacturing (divisions 15–37)
Subsection DB	Manufacture of textiles and textile products (divisions 17 and 18)

Division 17   Manufacture of textiles
Group 17.4   Manufacture of made-up textile articles, except apparel
Class 17.40   Manufacture of made-up textile articles, except apparel
Subclass 17.40/1   Manufacture of soft furnishings

Table 3.2 SIC codings

Section	Industrial Classification
A	Agriculture, hunting and forestry
B	Fishing
C	Mining and quarrying
D	Manufacturing
E	Electricity, gas and water supply
F	Construction
G	Wholesale and retail trade; Repair of motor vehicles, motorcycles and personal and household goods
H	Hotels and restaurants
I	Transport, storage and communication
J	Financial intermediation
K	Real estate, renting and business activities
L	Public administration and defence; Compulsory social security
M	Education
N	Health and social work
O	Other community, social and personal service activities
P	Private households with employed persons
Q	Extra-territorial organisations and bodies

In 1989 the UN Statistical Commission agreed a Central Product Classification (CPC), which provides direct links to the Harmonised Commodity Description and Coding System (HS). The HS, known generally as 'tariff numbers', replaced the Custom Cooperation Council Nomenclature (CCCN) in 1988 and is the coding system used for trade worldwide.

Only the first eight digits of the HS code are of major importance. The first two digits denote the chapter, the next two digits denote the part of the chapter, the third set of two digits denotes the section and the fourth set of two digits denotes the subsection. If further digits are used, the ninth digit is a special subdivision for use in a particular country and the tenth and eleventh digits are for non-EU countries. Thus the coding HS 841360 41 0 is broken down as follows:

Chapter	84	Machinery, mech/elec appliances and parts
Part	13	Pumps for liquids
Section	60	Other rotary PD pumps
Subsection	41	Gear pumps
National	0	National breakdown (used for statistics)

The EU preferred a product classification that was more akin to the industrial activity classification and devised the Classification of Products by Activity (CPA). One of the uses of the CPA is to code the PRODCOM lists. PRODCOM is a system that was agreed in 1992 to harmonise the collection of statistics throughout the EU. PRODCOM stands for Products of the European Community. All EU countries are now using this system. The UK was the first country to start publishing statistics, in May 1995. Other EU countries have followed, but not all have yet achieved the same level of coverage as the UK. The information is in the form of reports that are published annually – quarterly for some of the most popular products. The reports provide Total Market Data (UK production, or more precisely, UK manufacturer sales, exports, imports and net supply to the UK market in both value and volume terms as well as average price) on a wide range of products. The PRODCOM reports are published online by National Statistics, the official UK statistics site (www.statistics.gov.uk). The reports can be found in the 'Bookshelf' of online products under 'commerce and industry'. Not only can you read the summaries of the reports, but you can also view or download the entire documents free of charge.

Consumer information

A considerable amount of data is available relating to consumers and consumer goods. In fact no major consumer goods company could survive for long without carrying out very specific marketing research and analysis. Such information is of value not only to companies operating in consumer markets, but also to those operating in the industrial market supplying goods to the manufacturers of consumer goods.

Consumer goods markets differ from industrial markets by having a large number of customers who are all different. Since advertising and selling on a national scale is expensive, consumer goods suppliers target sections of the consumer market for their product.

Consumer markets are usually segmented by the characteristics of their consumers and this involves the analysis of a group of factors. Generally, consumers are classified by:

- socio-economic group;
- age;
- sex;
- occupation;
- region.

The classification system developed by Research Services Ltd is the most commonly used system for determining socio-economic groups in the UK. It divides consumers into six broad groups, shown in Table 3.3.

Other classifications can be used to classify family types, housing types and area groups. These include the classification system for area of residence called ACORN (A Classification of Residential Neighbourhoods) developed by CACI market analysis group (see Table 3.4) and the alternative residential based classification of consumers called PIN (Pinpoint Identified Neighbourhoods) developed

Table 3.3 Consumer classification by socio-economic groups

Group	Social Status
A	Upper middle class
B	Middle class
C1	Lower middle class
C2	Skilled working class
D	Working class
E	Lower class

Table 3.4 Consumer classification by ACORN groups

	Category
A	Agricultural areas
B	Modern family housing, higher incomes
C	Older housing of intermediate status
D	Older terraced housing
E	Council estates – category I
F	Council estates – category II
G	Council estates – category III
H	Mixed inner metropolitan areas
I	High status non-family areas
J	Affluent suburban housing
K	Better-off retirement areas
L	Unclassified

by Pinpoint Analysis Ltd. Each ACORN and PIN group can be further divided into subgroups.

In the consumer goods industry, advertising research is also important. It is essential to know how much your competitors are spending and what they are spending it on. Advertising research can also assess which media channel is most used by customers of a given product.

HOW TO PLAN YOUR MARKETING RESEARCH

We have now covered all of the main methods and data available for marketing research, but it is important to plan how you will carry out the research in your particular case to obtain the right information for your plan. You will not need to use all of the methods and all of the types of data in every case. Obviously the scope of the work will be much more comprehensive if you are preparing an overall marketing plan for all of your company's products in all markets than if you are preparing a plan for one product in one market only. Figure 3.12 shows the principle of planning marketing research.

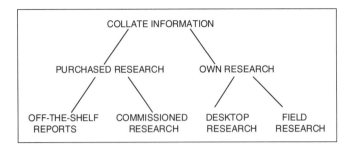

Figure 3.12   Planning marketing research

Much time, effort and cost is wasted by starting marketing research projects without defining the objectives.

The key steps to carrying out the marketing research are as follows:

- define the objectives;
- decide what information needs to be obtained;
- decide the best way of obtaining it;
- collect the data;
- analyse the data.

The objectives

The objectives must be clearly defined. This should include the timescale that is necessary for completion of the work to fit in with the timescale of preparation of the overall marketing plan. If the plan concerns equipment to be sold into the jam manufacturing industry, then the objective of the research would be to gather information about this industry, including its size, major companies involved, growth patterns, etc. Time should not, however, be wasted gathering wider-ranging information about the food industry in general.

The information required

A list should be prepared, detailing all of the information required. This needs to be a complete list of everything needed, because it is extremely costly to have to go back later to collect additional information that was not considered in the first place.

How to obtain the information

This is one of the most crucial decisions to be taken. It involves deciding who will obtain the required information and how it will be obtained. The options are:

- use own staff;
- use an outside market research company;
- carry out field research;
- carry out desk research.

Only the very largest companies have market research professionals on their staff. A project involving more than a minimal amount of fieldwork is best carried out by a professional. In marketing research you get what you pay for. It should be noted that in the UK, government grants are often available for marketing research projects.

In practical terms large amounts of fieldwork are rarely necessary in the capital goods or service fields, but are quite usual in the consumer goods field.

If the requirement is for a small amount of fieldwork and a large amount of deskwork, then it is usually carried out in-house. The staff chosen to do this work must be capable of understanding what they are doing. It should not be seen as just a clerical job and should only be entrusted to someone who will be able to understand the methods of marketing research and the full objectives of the project. In most small companies this task will fall to the managing director/owner or sales manager/director.

In the capital goods industries, the small amounts of fieldwork required are often carried out by the field sales staff in the course of their normal duties. The person carrying out the project will prepare a form to be completed by field sales staff based on their individual knowledge of their territory and their customers.

Collecting the data

Collecting the data involves using the methods and the data sources detailed earlier in the chapter. The names and websites for some key sources of information are listed at the end of the book in Useful Websites.

Analysing the data

The data on its own is of no use to anyone. It needs to be verified and analysed. Verification really means being sure that the information has been collected in a logical and unbiased way. It should be representative and needs to be as complete as possible. The assumptions used in interpreting the data need to be stated.

The analysis of the data needs to be carried out by your marketing professional (this may be you). It will only be as good as the understanding of the person carrying out the analysis.

In some areas, in-house knowledge is crucial. How many people do you know in sales and marketing who have a rule of thumb to calculate potential sales of their product? Many people have worked out such rules and they can be crucial in working out the total potential market for a product.

PRACTICAL EXAMPLES

Jane's Beauty & Health only operates locally and it is based near the city centre in Greentown. It is looking for information on competitors to use in its marketing plan for expanding its business into new applications. It is a member of The Guild of Professional Beauty Therapists. It contacts the Guild, which gives it a list of useful websites, including its own. Jane has a broadband connection, so research on the internet will only cost her time.

Jane goes onto the internet and uses the Google search engine (www.google.com). She first does a search by entering 'beauty salon'. She gets a list of hundreds of matches. But she can see immediately that many of these are in the USA and in other countries around the world. One website which is near the top of the list is thebeautysalonyellowpages.com, which is described as the site of the National Association of Beauty Salon Owners. She knows that she really wants only information on the UK, so she now types in 'beauty salon + UK'. This will give her a search of sites relating to beauty salons in the UK. Again, she get lists of hundreds of sites, but this time there is much more of interest. She finds www.beauty-guild.co.uk, which is the website of the Guild of Professional Beauty Therapists. It gives her details of the UK Beauty Salon Directory, which she can get hold of through www.uk-beauty-directory.co.uk. She searches further and finds details of The Indian Head Massage Directory and the UK Beauty Salon Equipment directory. Then she finds the site www.beauty-salon.searchmole.co.uk operated by yell.com, which says 'yell.com can help you find beauty salons and mobile therapists near your home, near your work or anywhere in the UK.' Jane uses this search engine to locate eight beauty salons and 20 mobile therapists in the region of Greentown.

She also checks in her local Yellow Pages and Thomson Directory and finds seven of the same companies listed. Eight are within a 20-mile radius of the town and one is in the city centre.

Jane now takes a city map and segments it into areas – city centre, outer areas, north, south, east and west and suburbs. She then places the locations of all of the competitors on the map.

The next stage of her research is to check the websites of those competitors that have one. She then visits all of the competitors' sites to list the actual products offered and the size and quality of the establishment. The information is summarised in Table 3.5.

Table 3.5 Beauty salons in Greentown, Jane's Beauty & Health

Company	Size (people)	Distance from us (miles)		Facials	Manicure	Pedicure	massage Aromatherapy
Jimbo's	4	5	Y	Y	Y	N	N
Nail Bar	2	10	N	Y	Y	N	N
Beauty Room	6	5	Y	Y	Y	Y	Y
Monique's	2	1	Y	Y	Y	Y	Y
Arturo	2	1	N	N	N	Y	Y
Massage R us	4	2	N	N	N	Y	Y
Healthstyle	8	1	Y	Y	Y	Y	Y
Arcadia	2	5	Y	Y	Y	N	N

AH Building wants to find out more information on the building industry. It sends someone to the local library for them to look through the publications *Current British Directories* and the *Directory of British Associations*. Here he finds directories relating to roofing and building and several trade associations that look interesting, including the Federation of Master Builders. Much of the information is general or lists companies covering the whole country. He wants to narrow the search down to the local area.

So next he looks through the local Yellow Pages and lists all other local companies advertising for general building and roofing work. Then he decides to phone the local Chamber of Commerce. The contact at the Chamber of Commerce suggests that he looks on the Chamber's website, where there is a directory of members. He finds that the members directory has a search engine and he first types in 'builders'. He gets 15 companies with the company name and address, a category of their trade and a short description of the company. Under 'category', some companies are just listed as 'Builders, Contractors & Allied Trades', but others are specifically listed as 'Roofing Contractors' or 'Plastering Contractors'. He narrows his search to specific categories and also searches under 'Conservatories', where he finds five companies. Some of the company details also give websites, so he is able to piece together a lot of information about the local companies.

Having used the internet once, he does so again and goes onto the website of the Federation of Master Builders, which is the trade association for the UK building industry. Here he finds that there is a directory of the 13,000 member companies, with a search engine that allows him to type in AH Building's postcode and select a category of builder. He then gets details of all the members of the Federation in AH Building's postcode area that offer the particular service.

So with the information gathered from all of these sources, AH Building is able to piece together a fairly accurate picture of the competition in its area for the different products it is selling.

Prestige Cars also only operates locally, so its first approach to finding information about local companies is to use the Yellow Pages and its local Chamber of Commerce. Again on the local Chamber of Commerce website, it is able to find details of three local companies doing chauffeur-driven cars and five companies offering a taxi service. By going onto the companies' websites it is able to put together a detailed picture of the local competition. It is able to supplement this information by going onto a number of other websites: the National Taxi Association at www.national-taxi-association.co.uk, where there is a link to TaxinetUK at www.sable.co.uk/taxi/associationlinks.asp. From here Prestige also finds details of the National Federation of Taxicab Associations and the National Private Hire Association.

Global Fuels also uses its local Chamber of Commerce and Yellow Pages to get information on locally based competitors offering the same oil products that it does. But because oil products are traded nationally and internationally, it also goes onto the Google site. From here it goes to the Google Business Directory (directory.google.com) and eventually finds the page http://directory.google.com/Top/Business/Energy)_andEnvironment/Oil_andGas/Petroleum. Here there are details of lots of companies supplying oil products nationwide. Global can immediately see some companies it competes with locally. It also finds websites for speciality lubricating oils with pricing information, which enables it to check how competitive it is for its really special products.

It uses Companies House to obtain financial information on its major local competitors. For some companies, annual turnover is given, so it can compare its company in size and turnover with some companies it thought were of similar size. Obviously it cannot get local turnover information for national oil companies operating in its local area, and getting an annual report on BP or Shell would serve no useful purpose.

The Pure Fruit Jam Company wants to find out more about the UK market for jams and marmalades to use in its marketing plan for the UK market. It knows its own sales of different types of product by region of the UK, but has no idea what market share it has and how it compares with larger manufacturers.

It contacts the Leatherhead Food Research Association and finds that there is a report called 'The UK market for jams, conserves and preserves 2003'. As non-members it can buy a copy of the report for £350. From this report it can see that the UK market is estimated to be about £250 million, so its share of the market is only 1 per cent. It is very small compared with the market leaders, which each sell more than £60 million. In fact in size, it is nearer to some of the specialist imported brands from France (La Belle Confiture) and Germany (Rein Konfitüre). So it becomes clear that it is a niche market player.

It can also see from the regional spread of jam sales, that its major markets are the South and South West. It has weak sales in the Midlands, the North, Scotland and Northern Ireland.

It goes onto the Google website and types in 'jam manufacturers + UK + association'. This search brings up the website www.catalogue.marketing-file.com with a connection to www.catalogue.marketingfile.com/jam_manu-facturers. From this site it is offered a list of the 22 jam manufacturers in the UK with details by region and county. When it purchases the list it is able to get a significant amount of information on all of these manufacturers, including turnover and main products. It also gets a list of the websites of all of these companies, so that it can carry out further research on the most interesting companies.

Precision Valves Ltd sets about carrying out external market research. It is looking for information on valves and companies that manufacture them. For this particular marketing plan it is concentrating on the UK market.

With regard to information on valves, it already has a lot of information. The company belongs to the British Valve Manufacturers Association (BVMA). The BVMA produces a publication called *Valves from Britain,* which gives company profiles of all the valve manufacturers in the UK that belong to the Association, together with details of the types of valves that they produce.

'Our company manufactures ball valves and we can see that there are six other manufacturers of ball valves in the BVMA. Other companies manufacture other types of valves – diaphragm, gate, butterfly, etc.

'The next source is the Central Statistical Office, which produces Prodcom statistics. These are details of the value of production, imports and exports of products for the UK. They use the Prodcom headings set by Eurostat. They are normally produced in the form of annual data publications, but some products, including valves, have quarterly reports. The reports are on "Manufacture of Taps and Valves", so we have to separate out the information relating to ball valves. By subtracting imports from exports and taking this figure from UK production we are able to establish that the UK market for ball valves is £20 million. We sell £2 million in the UK market. Prodcom statistics also tell us that imports are £8 million, of which £4 million come from other EU countries.

'We then go to Companies House and get annual reports for our UK competitors. The information given varies – small companies do not have to give turnover and divisions of larger companies may have individual reports. Nevertheless a considerable number of companies still show annual sales split between UK sales and export sales.

'Finally, the BVMA advises us that there are a number of published reports by companies like Frost & Sullivan and small market research companies. We are able to obtain a number of reports, including "Pumps and Valves in the Water Industry" and "A Survey of Equipment Suppliers to the Food Industry".

'We have now been able to establish that the UK market for our product is £20 million, we have sales of £2 million; imports are £8 million, of which £4 million come from the EU. From this data we can produce a table showing UK market shares.' (See Table 3.6.)

Table 3.6 Market share information, Precision Valves Ltd

| Company | UK MARKET SHARE – BALL VALVES | |
	£000	%
PRECISION VALVES LTD	2000	10
ACE VALVE COMPANY	4400	22
SPARCO VALVES	1600	8
DVK (GERMAN)	3200	16
TEXAS VALVES (USA)	1600	8
OTHERS	7200	36
TOTAL	20000	100

EXERCISE

Now consider the product(s) and area(s) that you will use for your marketing plan. Follow through the same exercise that we have just carried out for our sample companies. Do you have a trade association? If so, start by contacting them, and your local Chamber of Commerce. Use the internet to track down other information relating to your market and your competitors. Put together as much information as you can on the products, the markets, competition, market shares, etc.

SUMMARY

In today's highly competitive environment, there is no substitute for keeping in touch with the marketplace. Markets are constantly changing and so are the requirements of customers.

In-house knowledge needs to be supplemented by marketing research acquired from outside sources.

Market research data consists of primary and secondary data. Primary data is obtained directly in the marketplace by carrying out field research, whereas secondary data is obtained by desk research.

Field research can be obtained by personal interviews, telephone interviews, postal questionnaires or e-mail questionnaires. Desk research involves the collection of data from existing sources such as government statistics, company information, trade directories, trade associations or ready-made reports.

The marketing research information required for marketing planning is market information and product information.

There are a number of systems for classifying companies, products and consumer types. Companies can be classified by activity using Standard Industrial Classification (SIC) codes. Socio-economic groupings for consumers can be classified by the Research Services Ltd system or by the ACORN or PIN grouping systems.

Marketing research must be planned and it is important to set objectives, list the information required and decide how to obtain this information before proceeding with the project.

The data obtained from market research must be sensibly analysed and presented so that the best use will be made of it in the marketing planning process.

4

The marketing audit – situation analysis

Completing the market research and collecting the historical data about your company and its products is only the first step. You need to analyse this information and present it in a way that can be used for planning. Before you can decide on your marketing objectives and future strategies, you need to understand clearly the present position of your company and its products in the marketplace. Situation analysis is a process that helps you do this:

■ it reviews the economic and business climate;
■ it considers where the company stands in its strategic markets and key sales areas;
■ it looks at the strengths and weaknesses of the company – its organisation, its performance and its key products;
■ it compares the company with its competitors;
■ it identifies opportunities and threats.

The results of this analysis are included in the marketing plan under the headings:

■ assumptions;
■ sales;
■ strategic or key markets;
■ key products;
■ key sales areas.

It is only when the process of situation analysis is complete that marketing objectives can be set. The results of the analysis will also be used in deciding strategies and tactics. Situation analysis is therefore the key to the preparation of any marketing plan.

ASSUMPTIONS

The first part of the situation analysis involves reviewing the economic and business climate. This is because all marketing plans must be based on a set of assumptions. It is these assumptions that will decide what can and cannot be achieved. They should be few in number and should relate only to key issues.

If it is possible for the plan to be implemented regardless of an assumption, then it is not necessary and should be removed from the plan. The only assumptions included in the plan should be the key planning assumptions that would significantly affect the likelihood of the marketing objectives being achieved. They would normally relate to external factors over which the company has no control. They could include such things as:

- The market growth rate – are markets expanding? Is recession likely?
- Interest rates – are they likely to rise or fall? How will this affect business?
- Government plans or legislation – is there any planned government legislation that will impact on the plan?
- Employment/recruitment – how easy/difficult is it to recruit and retain personnel?
- The exchange rate – if you export, or compete with imports – what effect would a declining or appreciating pound/euro/dollar have on the plan?

The exchange rate is more likely to affect companies that operate internationally or who sell products that are imported, or compete with imported products.

Jane's Beauty & Health has made the following list of assumptions for its plan:

- Inflation will remain at 3 per cent in 20X6, rising to 4 per cent in 20X7 and 20X8.
- Interest rates will remain in the range 5 to 6 per cent over the period of the plan.
- Company wage increases will not exceed inflation over the next three years.

For this company, wage inflation and cost inflation are the most important outside influences.

The same set of assumptions are valid for AH Building and Prestige Cars. None of these companies is significantly affected by exchange rates.

It is different for Global Fuels. Exchange rates, oil prices and government legislation can significantly impact on its business. Its assumptions for its plan are:

- Tax increases on our products will be in line with inflation at 3 per cent in 20X6, rising to 4 per cent in 20X7 and 20X8.
- The oil price will remain in the range $25 to $40 per barrel over the next three years.
- The £:$ exchange rate will remain in the range £1:$1.65 to £1:$1.85 over the next three years.
- There will be no governmental changes relating to the sale of red diesel.

The Pure Fruit Jam Company is concerned about wage and cost inflation, but it is also concerned that exchange rates will impact on its ability to compete in export markets and European competition selling in to the UK. Its assumptions are:

- Inflation will remain at 3 per cent in 20X6, rising to 4 per cent in 20X7 and 20X8.
- Interest rates will remain in the range 5 to 6 per cent over the period of the plan.
- Company wage increases will not exceed inflation over the next three years.
- UK GDP will grow at 2 to 3 per cent per year over the next three years.
- The £:$ exchange rate will remain in the range £1:$1.65 to £1:$1.85 over the next three years.
- The £:€ exchange rate will remain in the range of £1:€1.4 to £1:€1.6 over the next three years.

Precision Valves Ltd has the most extensive set of assumptions. It is concerned about both the dollar and euro exchange rates and also the impact of government legislation:

- Inflation will remain at 3 per cent in 20X6, rising to 4 per cent in 20X7 and 20X8.
- Company wage increases will not exceed inflation over the next three years.
- UK GDP will grow at 2 to 3 per cent per year over the next three years.
- Interest rates will remain in the range 5 to 6 per cent over the period of the plan.
- The £:$ exchange rate will remain in the range £1:$1.65 to £1:$1.85 over the next three years.

> ▨ The £:€ exchange rate will remain in the range of £1:€1.4 to £1:€1.6 over the next three years.
> ▨ There will be no delay in the timescale for the UK water industry to implement the EU directives on drinking water and effluent.

EXERCISE

Now prepare a set of assumptions to include in your own marketing plan.

Assumptions

▨   ....
▨   ....
▨   ....

These assumptions will be carried forward to your written plan, but you should constantly review them, both at the planning stage and during the course of implementation of your plan, in the light of changing circumstances.

SALES

The company performance in terms of sales and profit for key products in key areas will be known from the historical sales data collected in Chapter 2 and separated into the categories shown above. You now need to look at this data and analyse it. It will be presented under the section 'sales' in the marketing plan. In addition you will need to consider trends in sales:

▪ What are the trends in the sales of your product/service?
▪ How do sales/profits compare with targets year on year for the last three years?
▪ How good is your forecasting?
▪ What amount of your business is new business?
▪ How does this compare with the growth in repeat business?
▪ How does your company compare with your competitors?
▪ How does your company's sales growth compare with the growth of key competitors?
▪ What is your estimated market share for key products in key markets? How has this changed over the last three years?
▪ Why do customers buy from you?
▪ Why do customers not buy from you?
▪ Do you record lost sales and find out why they were lost?
▪ How do your prices compare with those of your main competitors?

You now need to consider your key market segments by industry or industry segment. These are your 'strategic markets'.

STRATEGIC MARKETS

Strategic markets are 'market sectors' or 'industries' rather than geographical markets. If the marketing plan is for a complete range of products in all industries, your strategic markets will be the main industries into which the product is sold. If the marketing plan is for that one product in only one industry, strategic markets will be key application areas in that one industry.

Strategic markets for a dairy equipment manufacturer would be:

- dairies;
- cheese-making plants;
- butter-making plants;
- yoghurt production plants;
- milk tankers;
- milking parlours.

For a package holiday company, the strategic markets could be:

- UK holidays;
- Mediterranean holidays;
- USA and Canada holidays;
- exotic holidays.

Strategic markets for Jane's Beauty & Health are denoted by customer types and are:

- young singles;
- mature business;
- young mothers;
- 'preferring home visits'.

This is the list for AH Building:

- renovators;
- expanding families;
- affluent retired;
- do up/resell.

Prestige Cars has three strategic markets:

- business;
- leisure;
- travel.

Global Fuels has selected the following:

- home heating;
- industrial;
- farming;
- leisure.

The Pure Fruit Jam Company has the same strategic markets for its UK market and its export markets:

- supermarkets;
- quality shops;
- hotels;
- airlines.

Although Precision Valves Ltd has its main activity in water and waste treatment, this is not its only strategic market:

- water treatment;
- waste water;
- chemicals.

EXERCISE

List your strategic markets for your plan:

- ....
- ....
- ....
- ....

For your strategic markets, you need to detail information on the size of each market, growth rates and your own position in each market now and in the future. Also draft out a short description of the markets for your plan.

KEY PRODUCTS

In Chapter 5 we will look in more detail at the product portfolio and how to analyse it and decide where to make changes.

Sales values for the different products a company has need to be collected. This will show the relative importance of each product and whether sales of some products are increasing or declining.

Jane's Beauty & Health has separated its sales into the following key product categories:

- facials;
- manicure;
- pedicure;
- massage;
- aromatherapy.

For AH Building the key products are:

- extensions;
- modifications;
- damp treatment;
- roofing.

Prestige Cars has:

- taxi hire;
- chauffeur-driven cars;
- chauffeur-driven people carriers;
- chauffeur-driven luxury cars.

With Global Fuels it is:

- fuel oils;
- heavy fuel oils;
- diesel;
- red diesel;
- lubricating oils.

The Pure Fruit Jam Company has:

- standard jams;
- marmalades;
- mini-pots;
- gift packs;
- special products.

Precision Valves Ltd has:

- type 'A' valves;
- type 'B' valves;
- type 'S' valves;
- packages.

EXERCISE

Now prepare a list of your own company's key products to use in your plan.

- ....
- ....
- ....
- ....

KEY SALES AREAS

'Sales areas' in the context of a marketing plan means geographical areas. The way that you split your sales areas will depend on how you define your markets within your company. A company operating locally may assume it has only one sales area, but even small areas can be further subdivided if there is reason to do so.

Jane's Beauty & Health operates only in its home town, but it has found that it can split its sales into the following areas:

- city centre;
- suburbs;
- out of town;
- home.

AH Building also has key sales areas:

- town centre;
- Old Town;
- seaside;
- suburbs.

Prestige Cars operates in three key sales areas:

- town centre;
- suburbs;
- out of town.

Global Fuels is producing a complete marketing plan and has segmented into key sales areas as follows:

- Devon/Cornwall;
- Somerset/Wiltshire;
- Bristol/Avon.

If it had been doing a smaller plan – just for the region of Bristol and Avon – the key sales areas would have been:

- Bristol (city);
- Avonmouth;
- Bath.

The Pure Fruit Jam Company operates both nationally and internationally. For its UK plan it has the following key sales areas:

- South;
- North;
- Wales;
- Scotland/NI.

Precision Valves Ltd also operates nationally and internationally. For its UK plan it selects the following sales areas:

- South;
- Midlands;
- North;
- Wales;
- Scotland/NI.

Overseas markets could be classified in a number of ways, as:

- Europe/Americas/Asia/Africa/Australia; or
- Western Europe/USA/Rest of World; or
- Western Europe/USA/Japan/Rest of World.

There may be reasons other than geographical for markets to be classified together. A company may have subsidiary or associated companies in some countries and may wish to record details of these companies separately. For a company with subsidiary companies in Germany, the USA and Australia, the markets could be classified as: intercompany/other Europe/other USA/Asia/Africa.

The Pure Fruit Jam Company has significant exports to the USA and Canada, certain European countries, Japan and Australia. So for its export plan it is looking at the following key markets:

- the USA and Canada;
- Europe;
- Japan;
- Australia.

> If Precision Valves Ltd were producing an export plan, its key sales areas would be:
>
> ▩ Europe;
> ▩ USA;
> ▩ Africa.

In selecting key sales areas, only areas with a significant level of sales should be chosen, unless the purpose of the plan is to propose expansion into certain areas where sales at present are small but there is good potential for growth.

EXERCISE

Now list your own key sales areas for the plan:

▩   ....
▩   ....
▩   ....
▩   ....

SWOT ANALYSIS

The key process used in situation analysis is SWOT analysis. SWOT stands for: 'Strengths and Weaknesses as they relate to our Opportunities and Threats in the marketplace'.

The strengths and weaknesses refer to the company and its products, whereas the opportunities and threats are usually taken to be external factors over which your company has no control. SWOT analysis involves understanding and analysing your strengths and weaknesses and identifying threats to your business as well as opportunities in the marketplace. You can then attempt to exploit your strengths, overcome your weaknesses, grasp your opportunities and defend yourself against threats. This is one of the most important parts of the planning process. SWOT analysis asks the questions that will enable you to decide whether your company and the product will really be able to fulfil your plan and what the constraints will be.

In carrying out SWOT analysis it is usual to list the strengths, weaknesses, opportunities and threats on the same page. This is done by segmenting the page into four squares and entering strengths and weaknesses in the top squares and opportunities and threats in the bottom squares, as shown in Figure 4.1.

The number of individual SWOTs will depend on the scope of your plan.

STRENGTHS	WEAKNESSES
OPPORTUNITIES	THREATS

Figure 4.1 Presentation of SWOT analysis

First you should carry out a SWOT on your company and its organisation (for a very small company, this may be just one combined SWOT). You should also do the same for your main competitors and for your products and the geographical areas and market segments covered by the plan.

Company organisation

Before you consider your product and markets, you need to understand how your company and its organisation will affect your business. You must list its strengths and weaknesses and consider any threats and opportunities.

The strengths of a company and its organisation could be such things as:

- *For a large company* – it is well known in the marketplace; it has good resources.
- *For a small company* – it could be more flexible; all customers are personally known.
- It has a good internal sales organisation.
- It has a good external sales organisation.
- It has a good distribution network.
- It has a captive sales network covering the UK.
- The company manufactures in the UK.
- The company has various industry standard approvals.
- It has a 'quality' image.

Weaknesses could be such things as:

- Competitors are larger and well known in the marketplace.

- It has an inadequate internal sales organisation.
- It has an incomplete or inadequate external sales organisation.
- The sales manager needs to be replaced.
- There is an inability to recruit satisfactory staff.
- It has a bad image for 'quality'.
- The company lacks a distributor network or has an inadequate distributor network.
- It has an inadequate or non-existent service network.
- It has only one manufacturing centre and this is in a high-labour-cost area.
- It has long or unreliable deliveries.
- Its competitors have a better or more complete distributor network.
- The company's competitors have industry standard approvals that your company does not.

Opportunities could be such things as:

- The company has been taken over by a company that is a large potential customer for its products.
- The company has recently been merged with another company, giving it the advantage of economies of scale in manufacturing.
- Recent investment has given the company an edge over its competitors.

Threats could be such things as:

- Its largest customer has recently taken over one of its major competitors.
- The pound sterling has risen, making the company's products more attractive in overseas markets and overseas competitors more expensive in the UK.
- Foreign competitors are building a new factory in the UK.

An example of a company SWOT analysis is given in Figure 4.2.

STRENGTHS	WEAKNESSES
– part of UK group – good image – quality company – good resources – financial – technical – established export sales	– sales in UK are not growing – thought of as 'old fashioned' – few marketing staff
OPPORTUNITIES	**THREATS**
– owners are prepared to invest to develop new products – source components from Asia	– low-priced products from the Far East – niche products from other EU countries

Figure 4.2 Company SWOT analysis for medium sized company

The company SWOT analysis will vary considerably, depending on the type of company and where its marketplace is. The above SWOT would certainly not be relevant to the smallest companies in our group.

Jane's Beauty & Health has prepared the following SWOT analysis for the company.

STRENGTHS	WEAKNESSES
– well known locally – good image – known for quality at a competitive price – well-qualified staff	– high-cost city centre location – only one qualified in-house masseuse
OPPORTUNITIES	**THREATS**

– could open second shop outside town
– to expand using contract staff for
   massage
	– move to home massage favouring
	   contract staff who could leave

Figure 4.3   Company SWOT for Jane's Beauty & Health

AH Building prepared the following company SWOT.

STRENGTHS	WEAKNESSES
– good image – Monarch home extension range	– not known for roofing – only two bricklayers
OPPORTUNITIES	**THREATS**
– expand Monarch sales – grow roofing sales	– if we lose Monarch range to AF Jones & Son – Jim Smith retires next year

Figure 4.4   Company SWOT for AH Building

Here is the SWOT analysis for Prestige Cars.

STRENGTHS	WEAKNESSES
– well known locally – strong with business customers – we are only local luxury chauffeur hire company	– taxi business still a large part of our turnover – need new computer system to handle bookings
OPPORTUNITIES	**THREATS**
– we can expand luxury hire – people carriers on school runs and playgroup feed	– if other local companies move into luxury chauffeur hire – much of our taxi business is on contract; they could set up in competition

Figure 4.5   Company SWOT for Prestige Cars

Global Fuels prepared this SWOT analysis.

STRENGTHS	WEAKNESSES
– we are well known in the South West – we have our own fleet of tankers – we will deliver any quantity	– we only operate in a small regional area – many national competitors – difficult to recruit qualified drivers in the area
OPPORTUNITIES	**THREATS**
– to develop red diesel sales in the leisure industries – to expand lubricating oil sales in mechanical industries	– further tax increases from the chancellor – further increases in world oil prices

Figure 4.6   Company SWOT for Global Fuels

The Pure Fruit Jam Company has also prepared a company SWOT.

STRENGTHS	WEAKNESSES
– we have a quality image – good resources – financial and technical – we are known for our use of fresh fruit and natural ingredients	– small advertising spend compared to major players – still not well known in major European markets – our export distribution is weak outside the area
OPPORTUNITIES	**THREATS**
– to grow sales in export markets – to develop new products – to further reduce costs	– well-known European brands benefit from high pound sterling – a weakening US dollar would affect sales growth in USA

Figure 4.7   Company SWOT for The Pure Fruit Jam Company

Precision Vales Ltd made the following assessment of itself.

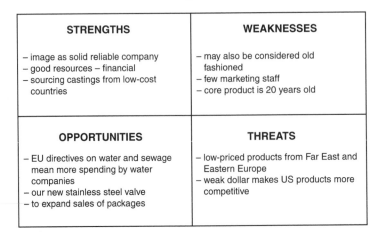

STRENGTHS	WEAKNESSES
– image as solid reliable company – good resources – financial – sourcing castings from low-cost countries	– may also be considered old fashioned – few marketing staff – core product is 20 years old
OPPORTUNITIES	**THREATS**
– EU directives on water and sewage mean more spending by water companies – our new stainless steel valve – to expand sales of packages	– low-priced products from Far East and Eastern Europe – weak dollar makes US products more competitive

Figure 4.8   Company SWOT for Precision Valves Ltd

STRENGTHS	WEAKNESSES
OPPORTUNITIES	THREATS

Figure 4.9 SWOT analysis exercise

EXERCISE

Now prepare a company SWOT analysis (Figure 4.9) for your own company.

The SWOT analysis will be used in the development of the marketing plan. All four sections are of use to us. The strengths can be further exploited by the company in its advertising and sales promotion, the weaknesses give a list of issues that need to be addressed for improvement. The opportunities need to be exploited in the plan, and contingency plans can be prepared to counter the threats.

Sales organisation

In addition to carrying out a SWOT analysis on the company, you can use the technique on the sales organisation itself and also to appraise your staff and sales personnel. This will allow you to understand where you have strengths and weaknesses in these areas. Typical questions that you might ask are given below.

Structure

- Do you have a clear organisation chart for your company? Is everyone in the company aware of this?
- Has the company structure changed to meet changing markets or is it fixed and likely to remain so?
- Do you have too few or too many staff in key areas?

Staff

- What are the strengths and weaknesses of each member of your staff?
- How often do you hold progress meetings, planning meetings, sales meetings?

- Do you and your staff need training? If so, in what areas?
- Do your staff have job descriptions? Are these regularly updated?
- What is your rate of staff turnover? Is it high or low?
- Is the relationship between members of staff good?
- Do your staff know the objectives of the company?

Sales personnel

- Do your sales personnel have sufficient knowledge of the operation of other departments?
- Do you have a proper training programme for your key sales personnel?
- Are their commissions/bonuses sufficiently performance related?
- Do your staff work to sales targets on a weekly/monthly/yearly basis?
- Do you carry out regular individual staff appraisals?
- If you died/left, who would take your place? Is there a proper succession plan for key people in the company?
- When did you last attend a training course?
- When did you last test the product knowledge of your sales personnel for your products? Your competitors' products?
- How do you measure/appraise individual performance?
- How do your salesmen spend their working day? Have you analysed this?
- Are your salesmen deployed by geographical area or by product?

You should now carry out a complete appraisal of the strengths and weaknesses of all of your staff. It would be appropriate for individual managers to carry out the appraisals for their own staff.

Figure 4.10 shows an example of a form to be used for this staff appraisal. The results of the individual appraisals would remain confidential, but the key information would be used in the SWOT analysis of the sales organisation.

```
┌─────────────────────────────────────────────────────────┐
│                    STAFF APPRAISAL                        │
│                                                           │
│                                                           │
│   Name/Position        Strengths        Weaknesses        │
│                                                           │
│   ...................................................     │
│   ...................................................     │
│   ...................................................     │
│   ...................................................     │
│   ...................................................     │
│   ...................................................     │
│   ...................................................     │
│   ...................................................     │
│                                                           │
└─────────────────────────────────────────────────────────┘
```

Figure 4.10 Staff appraisal form

STRENGTHS	WEAKNESSES
– good sales team – large field sales force in UK – high calibre of sales personnel – good distributor network in UK – have industry specialists	– some new staff – staff training required – sales manager needs replacing – limited coverage of export
OPPORTUNITIES	**THREATS**
– to expand share in existing markets	– competitors expanding field sales force – overseas distributors have better distribution in overseas markets

Figure 4.11 SWOT analysis for a sales organisation

A typical SWOT analysis for a sales organisation is given in Figure 4.11.

Again, the list of weaknesses needs to be addressed. The strengths and opportunities can be exploited.

Jane's Beauty & Health only employs eight people. Of these, Jane does most of the selling and marketing, assisted by Jenny. The other staff take orders for repeat business either in person, or when they are looking after the phone. But for a small unit like Jane's, a SWOT on the whole organisation is more meaningful than just on the sales organisation, which doesn't really exist as a separate entity.

STRENGTHS	WEAKNESSES

– I know the business
– Jenny is reliable
	– if Jenny or I were on holiday or sick,
	  there is no backup
	– if Jenny left to start her own business,
	  there is no successor

OPPORTUNITIES	**THREATS**

– develop our website
– use home visits to tout for more
  business
	– a national beauty parlour chain has
	  applied for planning permission in town

Figure 4.12 Organisation SWOT for Jane's Beauty & Health

AH Building carried out the same check.

STRENGTHS	WEAKNESSES
– Jim and I are well known locally – all our people are qualified craftsmen	– we only have two bricklayers – Jim Smith is due to retire
OPPORTUNITIES	**THREATS**
– if we can hire more bricklayers we can expand the business – we have enough roofers to grow that business	– how safe is our contract with Monarch?

Figure 4.13   Organisation SWOT for AH Building

Prestige Cars on its organisation.

STRENGTHS	WEAKNESSES
– our staff drivers are professional and smartly dressed	– we rely on contract drivers for our taxi service
OPPORTUNITIES	**THREATS**
– develop our website – use our senior drivers to sell their products	– contract workers have little company loyalty

Figure 4.14   Organisation SWOT for Prestige Cars

Global Fuels' organisation.

STRENGTHS	WEAKNESSES
– John is our main salesman – we employ only fully qualified drivers	– three staff nearing retirement
OPPORTUNITIES	**THREATS**
– John knows the leisure market and will visit potential clients	– national chains are getting more aggressive

Figure 4.15 Organisation SWOT for Global Fuels

The Pure Fruit Jam Company has a sales director, a sales manager and a marketing assistant.

STRENGTHS	WEAKNESSES
– sales director knows the industry well – we have a quality product	– only one person for all marketing and sales promotion
OPPORTUNITIES	**THREATS**
– new sales manager has export experience	– sales director is nearing retirement age

Figure 4.16 Sales Organisation SWOT for The Pure Fruit Jam Company

Prestige Valves Ltd has a sales director and a sales manager.

STRENGTHS	WEAKNESSES
– sales director and sales manager know water industry	– sales director does all marketing and does not have much time – staff training required
OPPORTUNITIES	**THREATS**
– to recruit salesman for water industry – carry out advanced sales training	– no in-house successor to sales director – competitors expanding field sales

Figure 4.17   Sales organisation SWOT for Prestige Valves Ltd

EXERCISE

Now prepare a SWOT (Figure 4.18) for your own company for your sales organisation or total organisation.

In addition to SWOTs on the company and its sales organisation you should prepare SWOTs for a product, a market segment, a sales area and a competitor.

To help you we have prepared a set of SWOTs for our chosen companies; see Figures 4.19 to 4.42.

STRENGTHS	WEAKNESSES
OPPORTUNITIES	**THREATS**

Figure 4.18   SWOT analysis exercise

STRENGTHS	WEAKNESSES
– we do a wide range of treatments – skin care is a particular skill we have	– we cannot offer the laser treatment – we only have three qualified specialists
OPPORTUNITIES	**THREATS**
– extend product to include electrolysis – extend product to include waxing – combine with neck massage	– low-cost visiting therapists – laser treatment – Healthcare Health Salon already offers it

Figure 4.19 Jane's Beauty & Health SWOT for a product — facials

STRENGTHS	WEAKNESSES
– captive market – we are the only beauty parlour in town exploiting home visits	– customers may not be working and therefore may have lower disposable income – travelling time adds to working time on-site for our employees
OPPORTUNITIES	**THREATS**
– this market is largely untapped – 'grey market'	– our competitors may move in and force price down

Figure 4.20 Jane's Beauty & Health SWOT for a market segment — 'preferring home visits'

STRENGTHS	WEAKNESSES
– more affluent customer base – easy transport links	– travelling time from centre of town
OPPORTUNITIES	**THREATS**
– home visits – satellite salon in Kingsland	– if competitors set up in suburbs, we could lose much of the business

Figure 4.21 Jane's Beauty & Health SWOT for a key sales area — suburbs

THEIR STRENGTHS	THEIR WEAKNESSES
– larger company – part of national chain – financial muscle	– old-fashioned treatments – all their staff are new and some are inexperienced
OPPORTUNITIES FOR US	**THREATS TO US**
– we have a wider range of products – they have high prices	– they are considering setting up satellite salons in the suburbs

Figure 4.22   Jane's Beauty & Health SWOT for a competitor – Healthstyle Health Salon

STRENGTHS	WEAKNESSES
– good range of sizes – quality product – solidly built	– limited range of woods available
OPPORTUNITIES	**THREATS**

– new products available from Monarch
  from next year
– can combine with brickwork
	– cheaper imports from Europe and USA
	– how secure is our contract with
	  Monarch?

Figure 4.23   AH Building SWOT for a product – extensions

STRENGTHS	WEAKNESSES

– finance usually not a problem
– getting property 'how they have always
  wanted it'
	– limit to available projects, so need to
	  continually find new customers

OPPORTUNITIES	**THREATS**

– home extensions
– modifications
	– pension crisis and stock market falls
	  could reduce this segment in future
	– potential to increase inheritance tax
	  liability

Figure 4.24   AH Building SWOT for a market segment – affluent retired

STRENGTHS	WEAKNESSES
– affluent clientele – large old houses	– some older people will not want to spend money on their houses
OPPORTUNITIES	**THREATS**
– much roofing work available – council grants may be available on older properties	– Bloggs Building Systems are based there – change in government policy on grants

Figure 4.25   AH Building SWOT for a key sales area – Old Town

THEIR STRENGTHS	THEIR WEAKNESSES
– wide product range – good name	– they do not have a product like Monarch for extensions
OPPORTUNITIES FOR US	**THREATS TO US**
– they are high priced (even if the product is good) – we can do extensions and include brickwork	– they are talking to Dorfilger (Monarch's German competitor)

Figure 4.26   AH Building SWOT for a competitor – Bloggs Building Services

STRENGTHS	WEAKNESSES
– good range of products: Rolls Royce, Bentley, stretched limos – product enthuses luxury	– each car costs £50k+ – high running costs – need high usage rate to make profit
OPPORTUNITIES	**THREATS**
– add specialist large old US (50s/60s type)	– if competitors move into this product, it could start a price war

Figure 4.27   Prestige Cars SWOT for a product – chauffeur-driven luxury cars

STRENGTHS	WEAKNESSES
– because holidays are pre-booked we can get bookings ahead of time – business travellers will pay more for a reliable service	– competitive market: pricing limited by competition – flight delays add wasted time waiting when other jobs could be taken on
OPPORTUNITIES	THREATS
– school trips – SAGA groups – tie in with wedding car hire to do honeymoon run	– new rail line from town to airport could reduce customers

Figure 4.28   Prestige Cars SWOT for a market segment – travel

STRENGTHS	WEAKNESSES
– mainly affluent customers – not many competitors operate out of town	– many people have their own prestigious cars – some houses are down long unmade up drives/tracks only suitable for 4x4s
OPPORTUNITIES	THREATS
– airport runs – party/Christmas/birthday runs	– many potential customers work in city and may stay overnight when they go for a night out

Figure 4.29   Prestige Cars SWOT for a key sales area – out of town

THEIR STRENGTHS	THEIR WEAKNESSES
– small family-owned flexible company – well established and well known	– concentrate on airport runs to Heathrow, Gatwick, Stansted and Luton, which limits their customer base
OPPORTUNITIES FOR US	THREATS TO US
– they have only standard cars, but we can offer limos or Rolls Royce – we can subsidise airport runs from our leisure and party business	– their ad campaigns could impact on our airport business

Figure 4.30   Prestige Cars – SWOT for a competitor Airport Cars

STRENGTHS	WEAKNESSES
– simple product – a number of completely different markets 　– farmers 　– gardeners 　– leisure	– profit margins are low – product needs to be separately stored
OPPORTUNITIES	THREATS
– to develop more into leisure industries	– more of our competitors may move into this product

Figure 4.31 Global Fuels SWOT for a product – red diesel

STRENGTHS	WEAKNESSES
– sector is subsidised by EU – we deliver any quantity	– farmers want best price – high proportion of sales are red diesel
OPPORTUNITIES	THREATS
– home and barn heating – smallholdings	– more farmers leaving the area – larger farmers with properties around the country may prefer national suppliers

Figure 4.32 Global Fuels SWOT for a market segment – farming

STRENGTHS	WEAKNESSES
– includes major centres of industry 　– Avonmouth/Bristol – major centres of population 　– Bristol, Bath	– very competitive for all of our products
OPPORTUNITIES	THREATS
– new companies moving into the area – leisure in Severn estuary	– many companies are national in operations and may have or may set up deals with national fuel supply companies

Figure 4.33 Global Fuels SWOT for a key sales area – Bristol/Avon

THEIR STRENGTHS	THEIR WEAKNESSES
– multinational company – national supply chain	– large and less flexible – may not be able to react to local requirements
OPPORTUNITIES FOR US	**THREATS TO US**

– we can buy on open market at the best
  price
– we can obtain wide range of lube oil
  products from a wide range of supplier
  companies
	– they can use HP's financial backing
	  to take market share if they decide
	  to do so

Figure 4.34 Global Fuels SWOT for a competitor – HP Fuels

STRENGTHS	WEAKNESSES

– use of glass jars is seen as a sign of a
  quality product
– it fits with our 'up-market' image
– glass can be recycled and this goes
  down well in 'green' countries
	– cost to size ratio is high
	– limited range of flavours available

OPPORTUNITIES	**THREATS**
– sell more as gift packs – target intercity and Eurostar trains	– foil package mini-jams are cheaper

Figure 4.35 The Pure Fruit Jam Company SWOT for a product – mini-pots

STRENGTHS	WEAKNESSES

– high-price 'prestige' market
– they have all-year-round and not just
  seasonal clientele
	– limited number of shops
	– need to contact a lot of individual
	  buyers

OPPORTUNITIES	**THREATS**

– mail-order and Christmas
  catalogues for big name shops
	– all our competitors target them too
	– these specialist shops reduce in
	  numbers every year

Figure 4.36 The Pure Fruit Jam Company SWOT for a market segment – quality shops

STRENGTHS	WEAKNESSES

– affluent market
– high per capita GDP
– every industry is big
    – hotels
    – airlines
    – leisure
	– very price competitive
	– entrenched suppliers

OPPORTUNITIES	**THREATS**
– upmarket stores and mail order	– £/$ exchange rate – 'buy American' bias

Figure 4.37   The Pure Fruit Jam Company SWOT for a key sales area – North America

THEIR STRENGTHS	THEIR WEAKNESSES
– larger company – part of international group – good name	– they lack local coverage in the UK – old-fashioned flavours (raspberry, strawberry, blackcurrant)
OPPORTUNITIES FOR US	**THREATS TO US**
– high value of euro – our new flavours	– they may set up their own company in the UK – they may buy UK producer

Figure 4.38   The Pure Fruit Jam Company SWOT for a competitor – Rein Konfitüre

STRENGTHS	WEAKNESSES
– available in 304 or 316 stainless steels – good range of sizes	– high cost/high price – the product is not yet well established in the water industry
OPPORTUNITIES	**THREATS**
– add control package to valves – use as 'metering product'	– cheap imports from Asia – competing products in special plastics

Figure 4.39   Precision Valves Ltd SWOT for a product – type 'S' valves

STRENGTHS	WEAKNESSES
– a market we all know well – our products are well known and respected in the industry – we have industry experts	– a 'lowest price' market
OPPORTUNITIES	**THREATS**

– new investment programme to meet
  EU directives
– our components now sourced in Far
  East
	– no longer 'buy British' bias
	– some water companies now owned by
	  foreign companies
	  (French/German/US)

Figure 4.40 Precision Valves Ltd SWOT for a market segment – water treatment

STRENGTHS	WEAKNESSES

– large industrial base
– many large-size water and sewage
  plants (London, Reading,
  Southampton, etc)
	– very competitive
	– all major competitors present
	– major plants in Thames Water already
	  upgraded

OPPORTUNITIES	**THREATS**

– water and waste water contractors
  with export work
    – Black & Veach
    – Biwater
    – Veolia
	– framework agreements with suppliers
	  by Thames Water and Southern Water
	– French ownership of some water
	  companies improves access for
	  French competitors

Figure 4.41 Precision Valves Ltd SWOT for a key sales area – South of England

THEIR STRENGTHS	THEIR WEAKNESSES
– larger company – wide product range – good name	– just sacked Scottish distributor – inexperienced own sales force – lack service support – old-fashioned product
OPPORTUNITIES FOR US	**THREATS TO US**
– our new type 'S' valve – our new distributor in Scotland	– high £, low $ – they may set up a service support organisation

Figure 4.42 Precision Valves Ltd SWOT for a competitor – Ace Valve Company

STRENGTHS	WEAKNESSES
OPPORTUNITIES	THREATS

Figure 4.43   SWOT analysis exercise

EXERCISE

Now consider your own sample plan and carry out SWOTs in the same format for:

- your key products;
- your key market segments;
- your key sales areas;
- your major competitors.

With the completion of the situation analysis we are now ready to move on to setting objectives and deciding strategies.

SUMMARY

Completing the market research and collecting the historical data about your company and its products is only the first step. You need to analyse this information and present it in a way that can be used for planning. Before you can decide on your marketing objectives and future strategies, you need to understand clearly the present position of your company and its products in the marketplace. Situation analysis is a process that helps you to do this:

- it reviews the economic and business climate;
- it considers where the company stands in its strategic markets and key sales areas;
- it looks at the strengths and weaknesses of the company – its organisation, its performance and its key products;

- it compares the company with its competitors;
- it identifies opportunities and threats.

The most important process in situation analysis is SWOT analysis, which involves looking at 'strengths' and 'weaknesses' as they relate to 'opportunities' and 'threats' in the marketplace. The strengths and weaknesses refer to the company and its products, whereas the opportunities and threats are usually taken to be external factors over which the company has no control. SWOT analyses should be carried out with regard to your company and its organisation, for all of the products, geographical areas and market segments covered by the plan and also for your main competitors.

The results of this analysis are included in the marketing plan under the headings:

- assumptions;
- sales;
- strategic or key markets;
- key products;
- key sales areas.

5

Setting marketing objectives

Now that we have identified our key strengths and weaknesses, the opportunities and threats to our business, and made assumptions about outside factors that may affect our business, we are in a position to set our marketing objectives. This is the key step in the whole process of preparing a marketing plan.

WHAT IS A MARKETING OBJECTIVE?

Objectives are what we want to achieve; strategies are how we get there. A marketing objective concerns the balance between products and their markets. It relates to *which products* we want to sell into *which markets.*

The means of achieving these objectives, using price, promotion and distribution, are marketing strategies. At the next level down there will be personnel objectives and personnel strategies, advertising objectives and advertising strategies, etc. There will then be tactics, action plans and budgets – all to enable us to achieve our objectives.

Marketing objectives relate to any of the following:

- selling existing products into existing markets;
- selling existing products into new markets;
- selling new products into existing markets;
- selling new products into new markets.

Marketing objectives must be definable and quantifiable so that there is an achievable target to aim towards. They should be defined in such a way that when your marketing plan is implemented, actual performance can be compared with the objective. They should be expressed in terms of values or market shares, and vague terms such as 'increase', 'improve' or 'maximise' should not be used.

The following are examples of marketing objectives:

- To increase sales of the product in the UK by 10 per cent per annum in real terms each year for the next three years.
- To increase sales of the product by 30 per cent in real terms within five years.
- To increase market share for the product from 10 to 15 per cent over two years.

The expression 'in real terms' means that inflation has been taken into account.

It is usual in a marketing plan to set objectives for each of the following:

- sales turnover for the period of the plan by product and market segment;
- gross profit on sales;
- market share for the period of the plan by product and market segment, though this is more difficult.

There may be other objectives that are specific to a particular business. The plan may cover only one product and the market segments could be geographical or by industry. For a small local company, objectives may be more related to the total business than just to parts of it. It could be for a new product that is not expected to break even for several years after its launch. There will also frequently be some marketing objectives that a company will set based on the opportunities identified in the SWOT analyses.

THE PRODUCT PORTFOLIO

Since marketing objectives relate to *products* and *markets* it is important to understand your present position with regard to both before setting the objectives of your marketing plan.

The growth and decline of all products follows a life-cycle curve, which can be represented as in Figure 5.1.

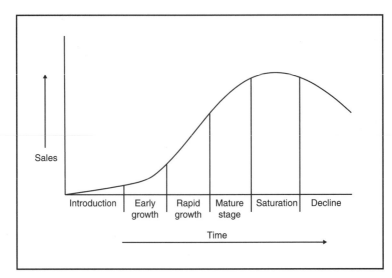

Figure 5.1 Product life-cycle curve

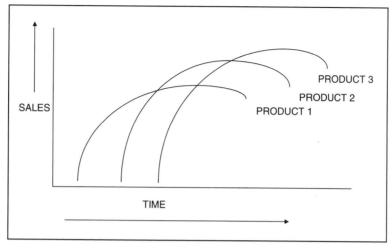

Figure 5.2 A product portfolio

Ideally your company will have a portfolio of products, all at different stages in their life cycle, so that balanced growth can be achieved and risks minimised. Figure 5.2 shows a typical product portfolio.

Figures 5.3 to 5.8 show product portfolio curves for the main products of each of our companies. The arrows show the point on the curve that the product is at.

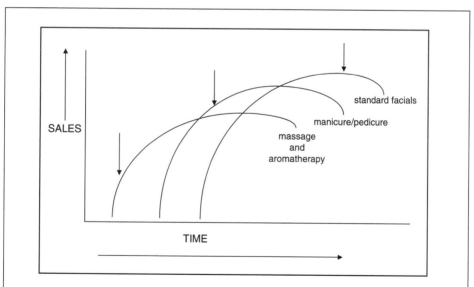

Figure 5.3 Product portfolio for Jane's Beauty & Health

'Standard facials' have reached the 'saturation' stage of their life cycle, 'manicure' is at the 'mature' stage of development even though 'pedicure' is still growing. Massage and aromatherapy are at the 'rapid' stage of growth.

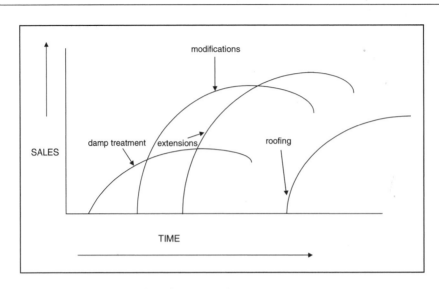

Figure 5.4 Product portfolio for AH Building

'Modifications' are at the mature and almost at the saturation stage of their life cycle, 'damp treatment' is at the mature stage and both 'extensions' and 'roofing' are at different parts of the rapid-growth stage.

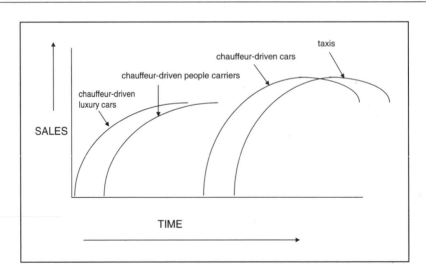

Figure 5.5 Product portfolio for Prestige Cars

'Taxis' are at the saturation stage of their life cycle. 'Chauffeur-driven cars' are mature. Both 'chauffeur-driven people carriers' and 'chauffeur-driven luxury cars' are at the rapid-growth stage of their life cycles.

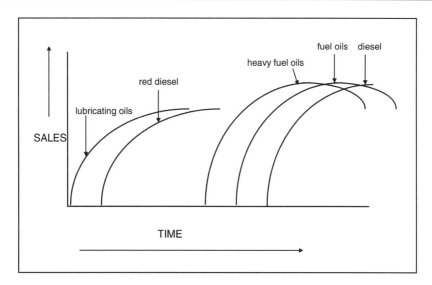

Figure 5.6 Product portfolio for Global Fuels

'Fuel oils', 'heavy fuel oils' and 'diesel' are all at the mature or saturation stage of their life cycle. 'Red diesel' and 'lubricating oils' are both in periods of rapid growth.

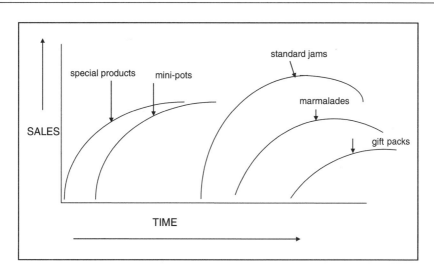

Figure 5.7 Product portfolio for The Pure Fruit Jam Company

The true position with The Pure Fruit Jam Company is more complex, because of the anticipated growth in export business. This means that some products, like 'standard jams', which are at the mature stage of their life cycle in the UK will get a new lease of life in their overseas sales. The same is true to a lesser extent with 'marmalades' and 'gift packs'. 'Special products' and 'mini-pots' are both at the rapid-growth section of their life cycles.

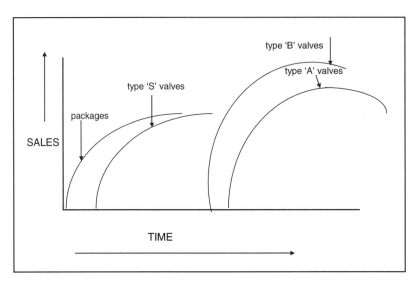

Figure 5.8 Product portfolio for Precision Valves Ltd

Type 'B' valves are at the saturation stage of their life cycle. Type 'A' valves are mature. Both type 'S' valves and packages are at different parts of the rapid-growth section of their life-cycle curves.

EXERCISE

Now construct life-cycle/product portfolio curves (Figure 5.9) for your company's products, indicating where they are currently on these curves.

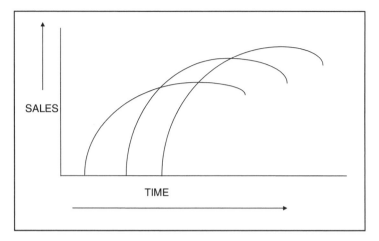

Figure 5.9   Product portfolio exercise

RELATIVE MARKET GROWTH RATE AND SHARE

In any market the price levels of the major players tend to be broadly similar. In a stable market the price levels of the major players will gradually move together. This does not mean that all these companies will make the same level of profit. If one company has a very large market share, it will benefit from economies of scale and will have lower costs. The company with the highest market share is likely to have the highest profit margin. It is therefore more able to withstand a price war. Its market share also indicates its ability to generate cash. Market share is therefore very important and it should be your aim to achieve market dominance wherever possible.

Cash flow is the most important factor in considering your product portfolio, and your company's ability to generate cash will be dependent, to a large extent, on the degree of market dominance that you have over your competitors.

Some years ago the Boston Consulting Group developed a matrix for classifying a portfolio of products based on relative market shares and relative market growth rates. The 'Boston Matrix' is now widely used by companies to consider their product portfolio. The products are colourfully described as:

- *stars* – high market share/high market growth (cash neutral);
- *cash cows* – high market share/low market growth (cash generation);
- *question marks* – low market share/high market growth (cash drain);
- *dogs* – low market share/low market growth (cash neutral).

Relative market share is the ratio of your market share to the market share of your biggest competitor. It indicates the level of market dominance that you have over your competitors.

Market growth rate is important for two reasons. In a fast-growing market the sales of a product can grow more quickly than in a slow-growing or stable market. In increasing sales, the product will absorb a high level of cash to support increasing advertising, sales coverage, sales support and possibly even invest-

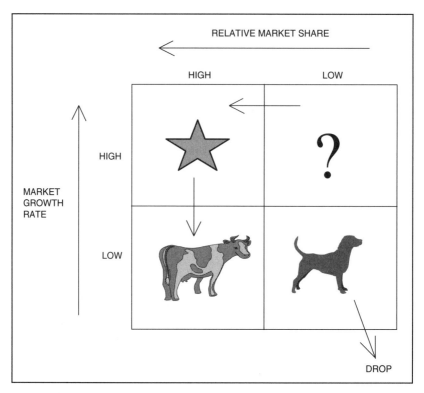

Figure 5.10 Ideal product development sequence

ment in additional plant and machinery. For the purposes of marketing planning, high market growth is normally taken as 10 per cent per annum or more.

The products are entered into the quadrants of the matrix as shown in Figure 5.10.

Question marks can be either newly launched products, which have not yet fulfilled expectations, or products that are declining and need further evaluation as to their long-term viability.

Dogs have low market share and are generally unprofitable. These products would be considered as those that could be dropped from the product portfolio.

Stars have a high cost in spending on marketing and research and development, but also contribute considerably to profits. They are broadly speaking neutral from the point of view of cash generation.

Cash cows are mature products with a high market share, but low market growth. They generate high profits and require only a small amount of marketing investment and no research and development spending to keep them where they are.

Figure 5.11 shows the current position of the product portfolio of Jane's Beauty & Health.

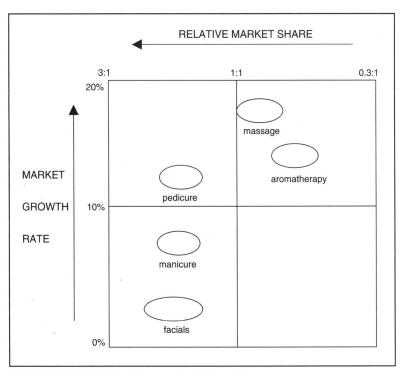

Figure 5.11 Portfolio matrix for Jane's Beauty & Health

'Facials' and 'manicure' are both *cash cows*. Both are still growing, but at a slow rate. 'Pedicure' is already a *star* and although 'massage' and 'aromatherapy' are still *question marks*, they will become *stars* if they continue to grow relative market share as the market for them expands.

'Modifications' are a *cash cow for* AH Building and even if it cannot grow the business, it makes good margins on them. 'Extensions' are *stars* – it is still having to advertise to make the product known, but it is growing rapidly. Roofing is moving from being a *question mark* to becoming a *star*. The *dog* of the pack is 'damp treatment' and AH Building must soon decide whether to drop this product completely.

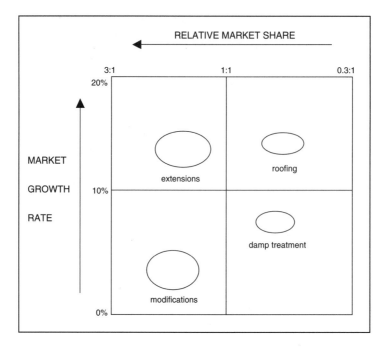

Figure 5.12   Portfolio matrix for AH Building

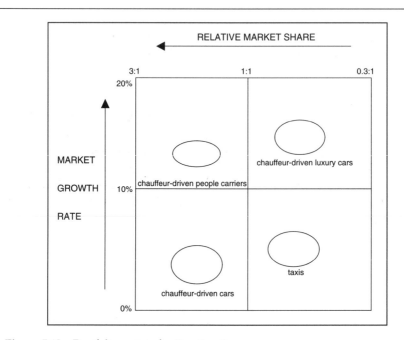

Figure 5.13   Portfolio matrix for Prestige Cars

'Taxis' are fast becoming a *dog for Prestige Cars*, but at the moment are too large a part of the turnover to consider dropping. 'Chauffeur-driven cars' are a good *cash cow*. Prestige Cars is well known for this service, so no advertising is necessary, but margins are fairly good. 'Chauffeur-driven people carriers' are already a *star*, and 'chauffeur-driven luxury cars', although still a *question mark*, are rapidly moving into *star* territory.

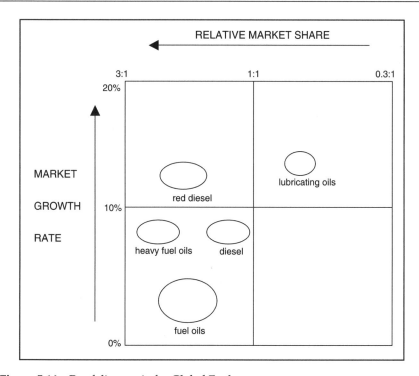

Figure 5.14   Portfolio matrix for Global Fuels

'Fuel oils', 'heavy fuel oils' and 'diesel' are *cash cows for Global Fuels* and bring in the bulk of the company's profits. 'Red diesel' is already a *star*. 'Lubricating oils' have been a *question mark*, but are now moving into the *star* sector.

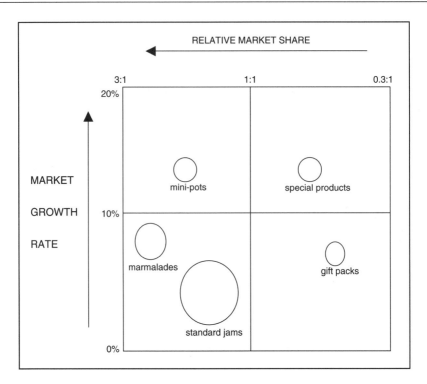

Figure 5.15 Portfolio matrix for The Pure Fruit Jam Company

The Pure Fruit Jam Company is very ambitious with its export plans. It wants to move 'standard jams' and 'marmalades' from their current positions as *cash cows,* towards the area of being *stars.* 'Mini-pots' are already *stars.* It wants to move 'special products' from being a *question mark* to become a *star* and to revive the fortunes of 'gift packs' from being a *dog* to become a *question mark* again.

Figure 5.15 covers the whole product portfolio for the company and sales for all markets. Since the UK sales are such a large part of the overall sales, it would only require slight modification for the company's UK marketing plan. The portfolio matrix, just for export markets, is shown in Figure 5.16. This shows that in export markets, even though growth is rapid, market shares are so low that all products are still just *question marks.*

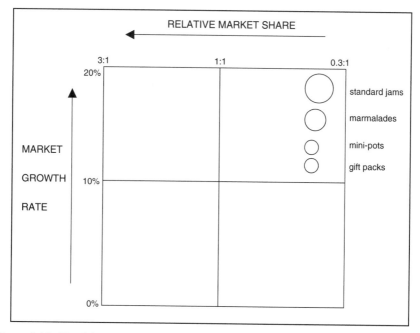

Figure 5.16 Portfolio matrix for The Pure Fruit Jam Company based on export markets only

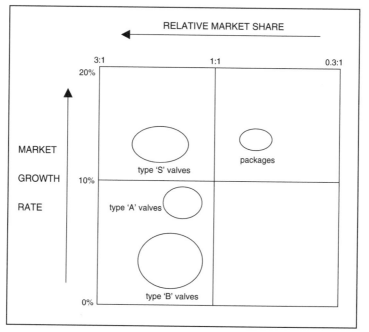

Figure 5.17 Portfolio matrix for Precision Valves Ltd

For Precision Valves both the type 'A' and type 'B' valves are *cash cows*, but are moving towards *dogs*. Type 'S' valves are *stars* and packages are moving from being *question marks* to being *stars*.

EXERCISE

Do similar calculations for the products in your product portfolio and mark them on the matrix in Figure 5.18.

Setting objectives for a marketing plan is not an easy task. Figures for sales turnover or market share cannot just be selected at random. It is an iterative process whereby objectives are set, strategies and action plans are developed, and then it is decided whether the planned objectives are impossible, achievable or easy. The objectives are then reappraised, and should they be changed, the strategies and action plans would also need to be re-examined.

Now that you understand your products better, you can more realistically set the marketing objectives for your plan. This is also an iterative procedure, with preliminary objectives being set and various techniques applied to see how realistic these objectives are.

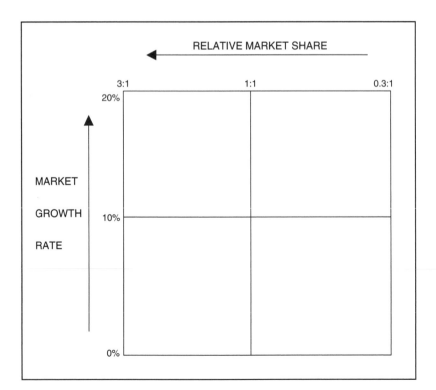

Figure 5.18 Portfolio matrix for your products

Below we list some preliminary objectives for each of our companies. When they state in an objective that an increase is 'in real terms' this means that the amount of growth will be achieved once inflation has been taken into account. In other words, 3 per cent of growth in the first year and 4 per cent of growth in the second and third years needs to be removed from the sales figures to show the 'real growth'.

Jane's Beauty & Health has set the following marketing objectives:

- To increase sales by 15 per cent per year in real terms for the next three years.
- To double our massage business in real terms within three years.
- To increase our aromatherapy business by 70 per cent in real terms within three years.
- To increase 'home visiting' sales from £20,000 to £50,000 within three years.
- To increase margins from 51 to 55 per cent over three years.

AH Building has set itself the following objectives:

- To increase sales by 10 per cent per year for the next three years.
- To increase our extensions business by a third within three years.
- To double our roofing business within two years.
- To increase margins from 43 to 46 per cent over three years.

Prestige Cars has set itself the following objectives:

- To increase sales by 9 per cent per year in real terms for the next three years.
- To increase sales value from people carriers by 60 per cent within three years.
- To increase sales value from luxury car hire by 80 per cent within three years.
- To maintain margins at 38 per cent over three years.

Global Fuels has set itself the following objectives:

- To increase sales by 30 per cent over the next three years.
- To increase sales of red diesel by 250 per cent in volume terms in three years.
- To increase sales of lubricating oils by 250 per cent in three years.
- To increase margins from 33 to 36 per cent over three years.

The Pure Fruit Jam Company has set itself the following objectives for its UK marketing plan:

▪ To increase sales of marmalades by 28 per cent in real terms in three years.
▪ To increase sales of mini-pots by 44 per cent in real terms in three years.
▪ To increase by five times sales of gift packs in three years.
▪ To increase sales of special products by 41 per cent in real terms in three years.

For its export marketing plan the objectives are:

▪ To double sales of standard jams in three years.
▪ To triple sales of marmalades in three years.
▪ To quadruple sales of mini-pots in three years.
▪ To increase by five times sales of gift packs in three years.

Precision Valves Ltd has the following set of objectives for its UK marketing plan:

▪ To increase sales by 40 per cent in real terms in three years.
▪ To increase sales of type 'A' valves by 50 per cent in real terms in three years.
▪ To increase sales of type 'S' valves by 50 per cent in real terms in three years.
▪ To more than double sales of packages in three years.
▪ To increase margins from 38 to 40 per cent in three years.

EXERCISE

Now make a preliminary list of some marketing objectives that you think would be sensible for your sample plan:

▪ ....
▪ ....
▪ ....

In all plans, marketing objectives for the following should be set:

▪ sales turnover for the period of the plan by product and market segment;
▪ gross profit on sales;
▪ market share for the period of the plan by product and market segment, where possible.

We can use gap analysis to decide how realistic our objectives are.

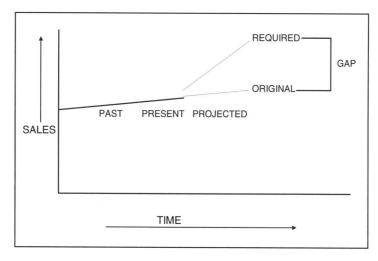

Figure 5.19 A revised sales forecast showing required and originally projected growth

GAP ANALYSIS

Gap analysis is a technique with many uses. From the point of view of setting marketing objectives it can be used to help you analyse and close the gap between what your company needs to achieve and what is likely to be achieved if policies are unchanged.

Figure 5.19 shows the original and required sales forecast for a company with the gap to be bridged.

Let us now look at what the objectives mean in figures for our companies and how big the gap between existing and planned sales will be.

For Jane's Beauty & Health the figures for the last three years have shown real growth of more than 50 per cent or more than 15 per cent a year. In the assumptions, it estimated that inflation will be running at 3 per cent in 20X6, rising to 4 per cent in 20X7 and 20X8. This means that in real terms £410,000 of turnover now will rise to £457,000 in 20X8 just because of inflation (£410,000 x 1.03 x 1.04 x 1.04). So real growth of about 15 per cent per year does not seem unreasonable in theory. So let us look at the 'gap' that has to be filled. Projected sales for 20X8 are £645,000. This is an increase of £235,000 on the current year's £410,000. This 'gap' can be broken down into its constituent parts. First, it is split it into inflationary growth (price increase) and volume growth:

Gap   = £235,000
Price increase   = £46,760
Volume increase   = £188,240

The plan is to double the massage business, which will add about £80,000 in real terms, and to increase the aromatherapy business by 70 per cent, which will add a further £60,000. There will also be increases in other products as a result of the increase in home visiting during the same period.

Table 5.1 Forecast for Jane's Beauty & Health

JANE'S BEAUTY & HEALTH
SALES FIGURES (Historical and Forecast)

SALES AREA: ALL

| | | | | | forecast | |
YEAR	20X3	20X4	20X5	20X6	20X7	20X8
(all values in £k)						
FACIALS	90	100	100	105	110	110
MANICURE	70	80	90	100	110	120
PEDICURE	40	50	60	65	70	75
MASSAGE	20	40	80	120	150	190
AROMATHERAPY	60	70	80	100	120	150
TOTAL	280	340	410	490	560	645

AH Building has grown its business by 34 per cent over the last three years. It is now looking to grow by a further 33 per cent over the next three years. In principle this is no greater growth rate than has been achieved over the last few years. But let us examine the gap.

Projected sales for 20X8 are £930,000. This is an increase of £230,000 over this year's £700,000. As before, we can calculate the amount that inflation will increase the current figure of £700,000:

Gap	= £230,000
Price increase	= £79,834
Volume increase	= £150,166

AH Building is planning to increase sales of extensions by £80,000 (£55,000 of volume growth) and roofing sales by £150,000 (£139,000 of volume growth).

Table 5.2 Forecast for AH Building

AH BUILDING
SALES FIGURES (Historical and Forecast)

SALES AREA: ALL

| | | | | | forecast | |
| YEAR | 20X3 | 20X4 | 20X5 | 20X6 | 20X7 | 20X8 |
(all values in £k)						
EXTENSIONS	120	180	220	250	280	300
MODIFICATIONS	250	220	230	230	230	230
DAMP TREATMENT	90	80	100	100	100	100
ROOFING	20	50	100	150	200	250
OTHER	40	60	50	50	50	50
TOTAL	520	590	700	780	860	930

Prestige Cars has grown its business by 33 per cent over the last three years. It is looking to grow it by a further 38 per cent over the next three years. Again this is not much out of line with past trends.

Projected sales for 20X8 are £1,100,000. This is an increase of £300,000 over this year's £800,000:

Gap	= £300,000
Price increase	= £91,238
Volume increase	= £208,762

The biggest projected increases are £150,000 each in sales turnover of chauffeured people carriers and chauffeured luxury cars. In both cases this is planning to virtually double sales of each product line within three years. This is a tough but hopefully achievable goal.

Table 5.3 Forecast for Prestige Cars

PRESTIGE CARS
SALES FIGURES (Historical and Forecast)

SALES AREA: ALL

| | | | | | forecast | |
| YEAR | 20X3 | 20X4 | 20X5 | 20X6 | 20X7 | 20X8 |
(all values in £k)						
TAXI SERVICE	200	180	200	200	200	200
CARS (WITH DRIVER)	250	220	250	250	250	250
PEOPLE CARRIERS (WITH DRIVER)	100	150	200	250	300	350
LUXURY CARS (WITH DRIVER)	50	100	150	200	250	300
TOTAL	600	650	800	900	1000	1100

Global Fuels has only grown its business by 18 per cent over the last three years, but it is planning to grow by 30 per cent in real terms over the next three years. This is significantly above its trend line.

Projected sales for 20X8 are £2,350,000. This is an increase of £550,000 over this year's £1,800,000. But Global Fuels cannot assume that it can increase prices by the rate of inflation. In fact prices will probably rise anyway, due to inflationary increases in the taxes and duties levied by the government. So in the case of Global Fuels, its whole increase is a volume rise, making its 25 per cent growth an even more significant increase:

| Gap | = £550,000 |
| Volume Increase | = £550,000 |

The whole of this increase is made from more than doubling sales of both red diesel (from £200,000 to £500,000) and lubricating oils (from £100,000 to £250,000). It will need some very good strategies and action plans to support this sales growth, as we will see in the next chapter.

Table 5.4 Forecast for Global Fuels

GLOBAL FUELS
SALES FIGURES (Historical and Forecast)

SALES AREA: ALL

| Net sales after deducting tax & duty | | | | | forecast | |
| YEAR | 20X3 | 20X4 | 20X5 | 20X6 | 20X7 | 20X8 |
(all values in £k)						
FUEL OILS	850	920	900	900	915	930
HEAVY FUEL OILS	300	280	300	300	310	320
DIESEL	270	310	300	300	275	350
RED DIESEL	50	100	200	300	400	500
LUBRICATING OILS	60	80	100	150	200	250
TOTAL	1530	1690	1800	1950	2100	2350

For The Pure Fruit Jam Company we are looking at two separate sets of figures for its UK and export marketing plans.

In terms of its UK sales The Pure Fruit Jam Company has grown its business by 18 per cent over the last three years. It is planning to grow by a further 37 per cent over the next three years, which is twice the trend in recent years.

Projected sales for 20X8 are £2,740,000. This is an increase of £740,000 over this year's £2 million:

Gap	= £740,000
Price increase	= £228,096
Volume increase	= £511,904

It is planning for growth in most of its product lines, including a five-fold increase in the sales of gift packs.

Table 5.5   Forecast for The Pure Fruit Jam Company for UK sales

THE PURE FRUIT JAM COMPANY SALES FIGURES (Historical and Forecast)						

SALES AREA: UK

					forecast	
YEAR (all values in £k)	20X3	20X4	20X5	20X6	20X7	20X8
STANDARD JAMS (340 gm)	1000	1000	1000	1030	1030	1050
MARMALADES (340 gm)	350	350	420	470	520	600
MINI-POTS	100	180	250	320	350	400
GIFT PACKS	90	70	50	100	180	250
SPECIAL PRODUCTS	150	200	280	340	380	440
TOTAL	1690	1800	2000	2260	2460	2740

The Pure Fruit Jam Company only started exporting its products three years ago. Growth has been rapid, from virtually nothing to £500,000 of sales in the current year. It is planning to continue this high rate of growth over the next three years, to more than triple its level of export sales.

Projected sales for 20X8 are £1,650,000. This is an increase of £1,150,000 over this year's £500,000.

Table 5.6   Forecast for The Pure Fruit Jam Company for export sales

THE PURE FRUIT JAM COMPANY SALES FIGURES (Historical and Forecast)						

SALES AREA: EXPORT

					forecast	
YEAR (all values in £k)	20X3	20X4	20X5	20X6	20X7	20X8
STANDARD JAMS (340 gm)	100	200	300	400	500	600
MARMALADES (340 gm)	50	80	100	150	200	300
MINI-POTS	0	20	50	80	150	200
GIFT PACKS	0	30	50	100	180	250
SPECIAL PRODUCTS				100	200	300
TOTAL	150	330	500	830	1230	1650

Gap	= £1,150,000
Price increase	= £57,024
Volume increase	= £1,092,976

It is planning for growth in all of its product lines including a four- or five-fold increase in the sales of some products.

The Pure Fruit Jam Company is highly ambitious in its growth plans. It is planning to double its turnover within three years, with increased sales in its home market as well as its export markets. Can it achieve this? Does it have the sales and marketing resources? Can its manufacturing facilities increase production at this rate? Does it have the financial resources to do it? These are all important considerations that we will look at over the next few chapters.

Precision Valves Ltd has grown its UK business by only 12 per cent over the last three years – in fact this figure falls to 6 per cent when inflation is taken into account. It is now planning to grow its UK sales by 57 per cent over the next three years – 41 per cent in real terms. This is very ambitious and way above the trend based on recent sales growth.

Projected sales for 20X8 are £3,140,000. This is an increase of £1,140,000 over this year's £2 million:

Gap	= £1,140,000
Price increase	= £228,096
Volume increase	= £911,904

The most significant increases are planned for relatively new products – type 'S' valves and packages. But significant increases are proposed for all product lines. Again, we will see how these measure up in the next few chapters.

Table 5.7 Forecast for Precision Valves Ltd

PRECISION VALVES LTD
SALES FIGURES (Historical and Forecast)

SALES AREA: UK

YEAR	20X3	20X4	20X5	20X6	forecast 20X7	20X8
(all values in £k)						
TYPE 'A' VALVES	450	450	400	500	600	700
TYPE 'B' VALVES	1000	900	800	900	950	1000
TYPE 'S' VALVES	100	200	400	500	600	700
PACKAGES	50	100	200	300	400	500
SPARE PARTS	180	180	200	200	220	240
TOTAL	1780	1830	2000	2400	2770	3140

So, do the assumptions pass the test as initial assumptions? In my opinion, the smaller companies are proposing growth that is stretching, and this is good. The two largest companies – The Pure Fruit Jam Company and Precision Valves Ltd – are very ambitious.

Also remember that it is always wise to have something in reserve, since not all strategies and action plans will bring in the full return that we expect from them. It is only when we look in more detail at the strategies in the next chapter that we can get a better feel for how realistic the objectives for any of our companies are.

SUMMARY

Setting marketing objectives is the key step in the preparation of a marketing plan. Marketing objectives are what we want to achieve with our plan; marketing strategies are how we get there.

Marketing objectives relate to any of the following:

- selling existing products into existing markets;
- selling existing products into new markets;
- selling new products into existing markets;
- selling new products into new markets.

Marketing objectives must be definable and quantifiable and should be expressed in terms of values or market shares.

All marketing plans should include objectives for:

- sales turnover for the period of the plan;
- gross profit on sales;
- market share for the period of the plan and gross profit on sales, where possible.

Before setting your marketing objectives it is important to understand your present position in relation to products and markets. You should look at your product portfolio with regard to product life cycles and cash generation. The Boston Matrix is a useful tool for carrying out this analysis.

Although all forecasts are based on an analysis of past sales, they should also take into account the total potential market, the existing market share and the life cycle of the product.

Performance can be increased by considering the total potential market for your products and by using gap analysis to close the gap between what the company needs to achieve and what is likely to be achieved if policies are unchanged.

Marketing objectives ought to be difficult but achievable. The aim is to set objectives that are a challenge, but that can be achieved with effort. They must be motivating rather than discouraging.

6

Devising marketing strategies

Once the initial marketing objectives have been set, it is necessary to consider how they can be achieved. The way that you go about achieving your marketing objectives is through marketing strategies.

It is important to understand what strategy is and how it differs from tactics. *Strategies* are the broad methods chosen to achieve specific objectives. They describe the means of achieving the objectives in the timescale required. They do not include the detail of the individual courses of action that will be followed on a day-by-day or month-by-month basis. These are *tactics*. Strategy is the broad definition of how the objective is to be achieved, the action steps are tactics and the action plans contain the detail of the individual actions, their timing and who will carry them out.

The decision to 'market price' a product is therefore a strategy, but the decisions to decrease prices by a certain percentage in one market and to increase by a certain amount in another are tactics.

Marketing strategies are the means by which marketing objectives will be achieved. They relate to *products, pricing, advertising/promotion* and *distribution*. They do of course also relate to selling, but selling is usually included under the heading of 'promotion'.

Marketing strategies relate to general policies for the following:

■ Products

  - changing product portfolio/mix;
  - dropping, adding or modifying products;
  - changing design, quality or performance;
  - consolidating/standardising.

■ Price

  - changing price, terms or conditions for particular product groups in particular market segments;
  - skimming policies;

- penetration policies;
- discount policies.

▨ Promotion

- changing selling/sales force organisation;
- changing advertising or sales promotion;
- changing public relations policy;
- increasing/decreasing exhibition coverage.

▨ Distribution

- changing channels;
- improving service.

There will undoubtedly be many strategies that could be used and to include all of them in the plan would not be practical. It is, however, possible to narrow down the alternatives by considering only those strategies that offer the greatest chance of success. All of the strategies should be consistent with each other and with the objectives that they are expected to achieve. The strategies of the marketing plan should also be reconciled with those in the corporate or business plan. For example, if an objective in the corporate plan is to change company focus/direction, divest, specialise, retrench, hold/expand existing business, diversify, etc, this would need to be reflected in the proposed marketing plan.

TYPES OF STRATEGY

One way of looking at strategies is to consider whether they are defensive, developing or attacking. All strategies are one of these types or a combination of more than one.

Defensive strategies – designed to prevent loss of existing customers

In your SWOT analyses you will have listed a number of 'weaknesses'. These could relate to the company, its organisation, the products or service offered. A number of strategies would be designed to overcome these weaknesses and to consolidate the company's position in the marketplace.

If one weakness was that the company had a bad reputation for quality, the logical strategy would be 'to improve quality'. If the product was considered to be old-fashioned, the necessary strategy could be to repackage (for a consumer product) or re-engineer (for an industrial product).

Typical defensive strategies would be:

▨ improve company image;
▨ improve quality/reliability of product/service;
▨ improve reliability of delivery promises;

- restyle/repackage product/service;
- improve performance of product;
- improve durability of product;
- overcome product faults.

Developing strategies – designed to offer existing customers a wider range of your products or services

These strategies are based on modifying products or introducing new products to your existing customers in your existing markets. From your SWOT analyses, you will have identified a number of 'opportunities' that can be exploited. Some of these will relate to the market's requirements and how they are being fulfilled by your existing product or product range. If you have a range of four sizes of product, you may have identified a market requirement for another size of the product larger than your largest unit, or smaller than your smallest size. Examples of this are the introduction of bags of 'mini-bars' by chocolate companies and paint in bulk size containers in DIY stores. The introduction of such products can often offer the simplest and least risky strategy to increase turnover.

Typical developing strategies would be:

- increase range of sizes/colours/materials offered;
- increase range of services offered;
- increase range of extra features/options;
- find different uses for product;
- develop new product;
- make product more environmentally friendly.

Attacking strategies – designed to generate business through new customers

This type of strategy involves finding new customers for your product in your existing markets or new customers in new markets. No company has a 100 per cent coverage of its existing market and new customers can be found or attracted from competitors by offering better quality, price or service. Also, new customers can be found in new geographical or industry market segments.

Typical attacking strategies would be:

- change pricing policy;
- use new sales channels;
- find new distribution outlets;
- enter new geographical markets;
- enter new industry sectors.

A useful way of looking at the types of strategy that may be available is to use a matrix that was developed by Ansoff, shown in Figure 6.1.

It can be seen from this matrix that the least risky way to try to expand your business is in the areas you know best – ie, with your existing products in your existing markets.

		LOW RISK	HIGH RISK
		Present product	New product
LOW RISK	Present market	Expand existing market with existing product	Develop new products for existing markets
HIGH RISK	New market	Sell present product in new markets	Develop or acquire new products to sell into new markets

Figure 6.1 Ansoff Matrix – the risks of various strategies

A higher risk strategy is to sell existing products into new markets, which involves the development of market entry strategies. At least with this type of strategy there is only one unknown – the new market – and you are selling something that you know you have sold successfully in your existing markets.

To develop new products for existing markets is an even more risky strategy, but one that most companies have to try at some time or another. If an existing product is reaching the end of its life cycle, there will be no choice but to use a strategy of this type. Many companies have a continuing strategy of introducing one new product every few years to spread the risks.

To develop or acquire new products to sell into new markets is the most risky strategy of all and should not be attempted if other options are available.

DEVISING STRATEGIES

Strategies can come from many different sources and it is wise to consider all possible ways of generating potential strategies. Some strategies may seem to follow logically and obviously from the objectives, but others may evolve in a flash of inspiration. It is a common practice in many companies to have 'brain-storming' sessions to devise a list of strategies. The same approach can also be used to consider possible tactics.

When the list of alternative strategies has been prepared, they should be evaluated to determine which would best satisfy the objectives. You should also determine which strategies could be best implemented with the resources and capabilities that your company has.

If a company only employs 10 people and has a turnover of £0.5 million a year, then a strategy involving 'setting up a subsidiary company in France' would clearly be outside the resources and capabilities at its disposal, whereas in a much larger company with a multi-million pound turnover this may be a logical strategy.

Strategies should be listed under the headings of the four main elements of the marketing mix – product, pricing, promotion and distribution. Examples of specific marketing strategies for these major functions are given below, together with some of the tactics that could be employed.

Products

- Strategy – change product portfolio/mix.
- Tactics

  - offer only one product line;
  - expand your product line to cover a wider market;
  - develop separate products for different markets;
  - make different versions of the product with different names for different markets;
  - acquire new products that complement existing products through the acquisition of new companies.

- Strategy – drop, add or modify products.
- Tactics

  - drop marginal products;
  - develop new products to supersede old products;
  - launch modified product.

- Strategy – change design, quality or performance.
- Tactics

  - establish a quality image through the development of quality products;
  - distinguish your product from your competitors' product in the eyes of your customers;
  - establish a reputation for innovation;
  - create new uses for your existing product by improving performance or by adding exclusive features.

- Strategy – consolidate/standardise the product.
- Tactics

  - rationalise your product line;
  - drop expensive extras/specials.

Pricing

- Strategy – change price, terms or conditions for particular product groups in particular market segments.
- Tactics

  - price product low and obtain maximum profit on spare parts;
  - price product high and use low mark-up on spare parts;

- devise strategy to meet specific pricing policies of competitors;
- set price at 10 per cent below market leader;
- reduce price of product to maximise sales (to allow increased production and reduce unit production cost).

▦ Strategy – skimming policy.
▦ Tactics

- set price of new product at a level 30 per cent above previous products;
- sell on new revolutionary design features and benefits;
- be prepared to reduce price as volume increases if competitors enter market.

▦ Strategy – penetration policy.
▦ Tactics

- set low price for new product to discourage competitors from entering market;
- increase turnover to level where product becomes profitable at this price level.

▦ Strategy – discount policies.
▦ Tactics

- offer quantity discount to encourage larger unit purchases;
- offer retrospective discount based on level of purchases this year;
- offer discount level for next year based on level of purchases this year.

Advertising/promotion

▦ Strategy – change selling/sales force organisation.
▦ Tactics

- strengthen sales organisation;
- reorganise sales force for particular area;
- introduce performance-related bonus scheme for sales force;
- recruit additional sales personnel;
- increase sales effort for most profitable products;
- increase sales effort to increase sales to key/major customers.

▦ Strategy – change advertising/sales promotion.
▦ Tactics

- increase advertising for the product in specific markets;
- start new advertising campaign;
- introduce voucher scheme;
- offer incentive scheme to distributors;
- carry out mailshot;
- increase company image advertising;
- carry out high-key product launch.

▨   Strategy – increase exhibition coverage.
▨   Tactics

  - increase attendance and stand size at major industry exhibitions;
  - use government assistance for overseas exhibitions;
  - encourage overseas distributors to exhibit more and supply equipment and personnel as support.

Distribution

▨   Strategy – change channels.
▨   Tactics

  - set up own distribution direct to stores;
  - change distributor for area;
  - increase number of warehouses for product;
  - reduce to use of only one large warehouse.

▨   Strategy – improve service.
▨   Tactics

  - set up national service network;
  - arrange service through major company with service centres throughout the area.

THE COMPONENT PLANS

To prepare your marketing plan you have to be able to break down individual objectives and strategies into tactics and action plans. A key objective in the planning process is to satisfy yourself that the objectives that you have set are not just achievable, but *profitably* achievable and that the strategies adopted will allow these objectives to be achieved. It is the tactics and the action plans that will allow the plan to be implemented and these need to be decided on and costed. Once you have set your initial objectives and strategies, there are a number of different ways that you can proceed.

You can divide your objectives into sub-objectives for your key products, strategic markets and key sales areas, or you can prepare sub-plans for 'products', 'price', 'promotion' and 'distribution'. In fact, you should adopt both approaches – the sub-objectives and strategies will ultimately be entered into the written plan under the sections 'key products, strategic markets and key sales areas' and the individual plans for the separate parts of the marketing mix will ensure that you are adopting a coordinated approach.

Sub-objectives

If your objective is 'to increase sales of the product by 10 per cent in real terms over two years', this objective will be broken down into a number of component parts. Some of the increase may come from an expected expansion of existing markets, but some will almost certainly be expected to come from expansion into new market segments.

Jane's Beauty & Health has an objective 'to increase our aromatherapy business by 70 per cent in real terms within three years'. A sub-objective could be 'to grow aromatherapy by home visits from zero now to £20,000 a year within three years'. The strategies for this could be:

Product	– package aromatherapy together with massage;
	– expand range of aromatherapy offerings.
Pricing	– discount policy – for multiple sessions.
Promotion/Advertising	– leaflet campaign for home visiting;
	– expand website to allow online home bookings;
	– e-mail offers on aromatherapy to massage customers.
Distribution	– use contract workers.

AH Building has an objective 'to double our roofing business within three years'. It is based in a seaside town and a sub-objective is 'to grow seagull prevention and removal business from £10,000 to £150,000 within three years'. The strategies for this are:

Product	– expand range to include roofing spikes;
	– offer 'filler' cages to block suitable nest sites.
Pricing	– offer discount if ordered at the same time as other
	– roofing work, such as gutter cleaning.
Promotion	– advertise in Yellow Pages;
	– advertise in local paper/free papers.
Distribution	– get supplier of 'seagull spikes' to forward leads in
	– return for using its materials.

Prestige Cars has an objective in its plan 'to increase sales value from people carriers by 60 per cent within three years'. A sub-objective could be 'to expand business with playgroups from £10,000 to £40,000 over the next three years'. The strategies for this could be:

Product	– modify offering to expand into child party and playgroup markets.
Pricing	– offer reduced rate for regular daily runs throughout term time.

Promotion	– mailshot/e-mailshot to playgroups;
	– advertise in Yellow Pages;
	– advertise in local paper/free papers.
Distribution	– expand website to allow online bookings.

Global Fuels has an objective in its plan 'to increase sales of lubricating oils by 250 per cent in three years'. A sub-objective of this is 'to grow sales of lubricating oils into the vacuum industry from £10,000 to £100,000 over three years'. Strategies for this could be:

Product	– increase range of lubricating oils to include special vacuum oils.
Pricing	– offer discount on Fomblin oil if used oil is returned for recovery.
Promotion	– mailshots/e-mailshots to local chemical and food processing companies;
	– take part in Bristol Chemshow.
Distribution	– telesales to chemical and food producers for vacuum oils.

The Pure Fruit Jam Company has an objective in its UK plan to 'increase sales of marmalades by 28 per cent in real terms within three years'. A sub-objective of this is to double sales of breakfast marmalades in Scotland from £50,000 to £100,000 within three years'. Strategies for this could be:

Product	– launch new rum and Cointreau flavoured marmalades.
Pricing	– offer retrospective discount to major outlets based on level of annual purchases.
Promotion	– increase advertising in Scotland;
	– carry out high-key product launch of new breakfast marmalades, including rum and Cointreau flavours.
Distribution	– add distribution outlets in major Scottish cities;
	– expand website to allow online purchases.

For its export plan it has the objective to 'increase by five times our sales of gift packs within three years'. A sub-objective of this is 'to grow sales of gift packs in Japan from £30,000 to £90,000 within three years'. Its strategies for this are:

| Product | – repackage gift packs for the Japanese market: information in Japanese, but retain 'British quality feel'; |
| | – add sake flavoured marmalade to range. |

Pricing
– premium-price alcohol-flavoured marmalades – particularly whisky and brandy.

Promotion
– use government grant to produce Japanese sales literature;
– take part in Nippon Food Show in Osaka as part of the British Pavilion, using government grant support.

Distribution
– use British Embassy commercial section to help find representative in Osaka (for west of Japan).

For its UK marketing plan Precision Valves Ltd has the objective 'increase sales of type "S" valves by 50 per cent in real terms within three years'. A sub-objective is 'double sales of type "S" valves to water-treatment contractors (from £100,000 to £200,000) within three years'. Its strategies for this sub-objective are:

Product
– add control package to type 'S' valve.

Pricing
– offer discount structure to achieve formal supply contracts with key contractors.

Promotion
– mailshot/e-mailshot to water-treatment contracting companies;
– take part in Iwex exhibition in Birmingham.

Distribution
– increase sales coverage by recruiting salesman for the water industry.

Developing individual plans involves looking at your overall approach to a particular part of the marketing mix.

BASIC TYPES OF PRODUCTS

From a marketing point of view there are three basic types of products. These are:

1. consumer goods;
2. industrial goods;
3. services.

There are, of course, some products that could be in all three categories. Paint is an example. It can be purchased by both consumers and industrial companies and it can also be part of the 'service offering' given by a house decorating company. It is also true that not all industrial goods are capital goods and that some consumer goods such as houses or cars are capital items to the purchaser. Nevertheless, these broad definitions hold in most cases and key marketing principles apply equally to the marketing of consumer goods, capital goods and services. It is just the way that the principles are applied that takes a different form.

1. Consumer goods

Consumer markets are characterised by having a large number of customers. By their very nature consumer goods are usually items that are mass-produced in identical form. There are two basic types of consumer goods: fast-moving consumer goods and consumer durables.

Fast-moving consumer goods, sometimes called convenience goods, are items such as food, tobacco, drinks and cosmetics that have a quick turnover and tend to be quickly consumed.

Consumer durables are items such as cars, furniture, clothing and electrical goods which are less frequent purchases that will be used by the customer for a long time.

The consumer is normally taken to be the end-user who may or may not be the actual customer who purchases the goods. A consumer may purchase a television set. Equally, a chocolate bar could just as easily be purchased by a mother to be consumed by her children or for consumption by herself.

Within the consumer goods industry different marketing techniques have been developed for fast-moving consumer goods and for consumer durables. For example, a car manufacturer may wish to get over to the customer the fact that its make of car will not rust for seven years, but a chocolate manufacturer would not want customers to remember that its chocolate bars have a shelf life of seven years. The chocolate manufacturer wants the customer to remember such things as the taste of the bar, the size and the fact that it doesn't melt in your hand. The car manufacturer wants the customer to remember such things as shape, speed and reliability.

Until recently most books on marketing, market research and marketing planning concentrated on the consumer goods industries. Because of the size of consumer markets, consumer data is the most widely collected and analysed type of information available.

Most consumer markets are segmented – ie, there are markets within markets. Consumers can be classified by characteristics such as their age, sex, socio-economic group or occupation. These characteristics will have a bearing on the type of television programmes that they will watch and the newspapers that they will read. Since advertising and selling are expensive, it is important for companies to know which type of customer is likely to buy their product and to target their advertising accordingly. A company selling Rolls Royce cars is more likely to advertise in *The Times* than in the *Sun* newspaper. Equally, a company selling skateboards is unlikely to advertise in the *Financial Times*. Small local businesses are more likely to use local papers and the Yellow Pages than any of these.

In the consumer goods field it is easy to find out what types of customer are likely to buy a particular type of product and to find out what type of advertising is most likely to reach these customers by using market research techniques of the types shown in Chapter 3. The supply chain for consumer goods is often quite long. Figure 6.2 shows the supply chain for a breakfast cereal.

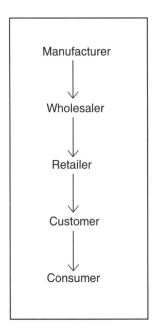

Figure 6.2 Supply chain for breakfast cereal

The bulk of the advertising would be aimed at the customer and the consumer.

In our group of sample companies, only the Pure Fruit Jam Company is selling consumer goods.

2. Industrial goods

Industrial goods are any goods sold by industrial companies to manufacturers, suppliers, contractors or government agencies. The goods would normally be incorporated into other products, used within the company's own business, or resold.

Industrial goods can be raw materials, components or capital goods. The ultimate consumer of the final product probably has little interest in the raw materials or components used in its manufacture. They would include the valves and pipework in a water-treatment plant as well as the chemicals used in the water-treatment process.

The same principles of marketing apply to industrial goods as apply to consumer goods. It is, however, much more difficult to apply these principles in industrial markets, because information about these markets is not so easily available as information about consumer markets. This is because industrial markets are more specific. There will only be a limited number of potential customers for ball bearings and they will probably be different from the potential customers for industrial showers. Companies within these fields would therefore have to commission market research individually. In consumer goods marketing, the customers who buy chocolate bars would be the same customers who buy soap powder, so the same market research information could be of use to companies selling both of these products. The demand for industrial goods ultimately derives from the demand for consumer goods, because the users of industrial goods are usually the manufacturers of consumer goods. Although the connections between the two are complex, nevertheless if sales of dairy products were booming, the industrial companies supplying equipment to the dairy industry would expect their sales to increase as well.

It is a fact that the marketing of industrial goods and *particularly the marketing of capital goods* is more difficult than the marketing of other types of products, because there are less individual customers and each industrial market has its own specific characteristics. A hundred years ago, there were few manufacturers of industrial goods and the products almost sold themselves. There are still many companies selling industrial goods that mistakenly believe that well-engineered quality products will sell themselves. That may have been true 100 years ago but it is no longer the case. There is now fierce international competition and all products – including industrial goods – need to be marketed effectively.

Twenty-five years ago in his book *Marketing Management*, G B Giles stated:

> While there has been a movement on the part of some manufacturers in the consumer goods area to woo the end-consumer – the housewife – there has been almost no effort at all on the part of the manufacturers of capital equipment and industrial material that are produced for use by other manufacturers to discover the needs of the customer. It is not unusual to find top executives in these industries afraid that their customers might think of them as a selling organisation.

There are still unfortunately too many companies even today with the philosophy 'You cannot sell machinery in the same way as soap.' Although the detail would be different, the steps in the preparation of a marketing plan would be similar, whether your product is soap or machinery.

The supply chain in the sale of capital goods is shorter than the supply chain in selling consumer goods and the number of individual customers for the product is considerably less.

Capital goods are often sold directly to the end-user – this is almost never the case with consumer goods, which are usually sold through complex distribution networks. A supplier of chocolate bars could have 30 million final customers, whereas a company supplying capital goods is unlikely to have more than a few thousand customers for its products.

Figure 6.3 shows the supply chain for a manufacturer of capital equipment that supplies components to other companies that build machines, and also complete machines to companies that use these machines to manufacture their products.

Because of the diversity and complexity of markets for industrial goods, there is not as much outside expertise as in the consumer sector and companies need to rely heavily on their own employees for market information or interpretation of outside information. In the industrial sector the number of key players and competitors in any particular industry is usually small.

Of our sample companies only Precision Valves Ltd and Global Fuels are selling industrial goods.

3. Services

The third basic type of product is a service. By this we do not mean the customer service that most reputable companies supply with their products, but a service as a product in its own right.

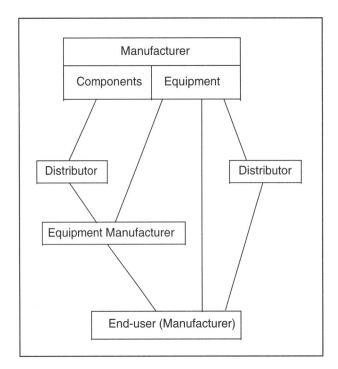

Figure 6.3 Supply chain for capital equipment supplier

Services range from financial services such as banking and insurance to beauty treatment and carrying out roofing repairs. They differ from consumer and industrial goods in that in a service industry there is no tangible product and the product has no shelf life. This is an important fact that influences the way in which services are marketed.

In a service company many of the functional activities are different to those in a manufacturing company. As there is no 'product', there is no need for warehousing or distribution functions. There is also no need for engineering, research and development, purchasing or production departments. Since the 'product' is being sold, a service company must still have finance, operations, quality control and sales and marketing functions.

Since the product has no shelf life, a service organisation must be able to get continuity of work. Because there is no actual product, the advertising used to promote services is different from that used with consumer or industrial goods. Service organisations sell the benefits of their service as their product.

You cannot fail to notice that in any set of Yellow Pages there will be more entries for services than for manufacturers. This is because manufacturers often have more cost-effective methods of advertising. Most services are by their very nature local and the Yellow Pages is the 'buyers guide' to local services.

In a service organisation your marketing needs to at least produce enough sales at the right margins to ensure survival and preferably it should produce better sales to facilitate profits and growth. You need to maximise the volume and quality of customer contacts by attracting more, converting more, satisfying more and making better contacts. The means of achieving this are:

- improve contacts with existing customers;
- improve contacts with known potential customers who do not use your services;
- identify and make contact with new potential customers.

Because a service is not a tangible product it is easy for your potential customers to be confused as to what you are really offering.

You need to consider what your service really is and how it compares with:

- what you currently think your service is;
- what your buyers know your service is;
- what your non-buyers think or know your service to be.

As an example, consider a photographic company offering a 'one-hour film processing service'. If the company does not have the resources to actually provide this service always, at peak times of the year there will be different perceptions of the service that it is offering.

The company thinks that it is offering a one-hour film processing service. It is actually offering a one- to three-hour processing service. Its non-customers know from experience that it cannot guarantee a one-hour service and its customers are prepared to put up with this.

Success in the service sector is dependent on your image and reputation. Advertising, direct mail/e-mail and personal contact are therefore all important.

In your marketing planning you should also bear in mind that it is your total profit and profit margin that is important rather than your turnover. This is true in all industries, but it is particularly important in service industries. Large industrial manufacturing companies have high overheads to be recovered and even marginal business that shows no profit can at least recover overheads. Although there are exceptions such as hotel chains and airlines, which have high overheads, many service companies are relatively small with low overheads and their labour costs make up a large part of their total costs. You should consider ways of turning away marginal business and maximising more profitable business.

The rest of our sample companies – Jane's Beauty & Health, AH Building and Prestige Cars are all selling a service.

THE PRODUCT PLAN

The preparation of the product plan involves looking at your product portfolio and deciding:

- if it should be changed;
- how it should be changed;
- what strategies you can adopt;
- where these strategies will lead you.

In Chapter 5 we looked at the historical and present position of the product portfolio, using the concept of the product life cycle and the Boston Matrix approach.

In preparing the product plan we will use the information already gained from this and will develop it further.

The marketing decisions that we will take for a product will vary, depending on which quadrant of the Boston Matrix it is in. The different quadrants suggest different marketing responses:

question mark	invest heavily in selected products that you believe have good growth potential;
	consider dropping weak or risky products;
star	invest for growth;
	improve competitive position;
cash cow	maintain your competitive market position;
	manage the product to maximise earnings;
dog	minimise investment;
	maximise cash flow short term;
	consider dropping product.

If we now look at the product portfolios from Chapter 5, we have the basis to make decisions about our companies' current product ranges and where they can go.

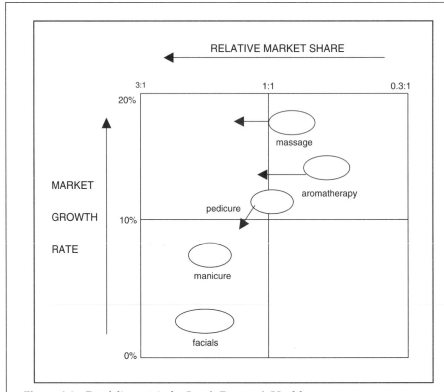

Figure 6.4   Portfolio matrix for Jane's Beauty & Health

Jane's Beauty & Health has been looking at its product portfolio as shown in Figure 6.4. The circles show where its products are now and the arrows show

how it expects the products to move during the course of its marketing plan. In some ways it is lucky, in that it has no products that are *dogs*.

'Facials' and 'manicures' will continue as *cash cows* in a stable market. Their turnover will not grow in real terms, but the products will continue to be profitable. A small level of growth is possible as a spin-off from the home visiting service.

As 'pedicures' have grown to take up a large part of the clientele for 'manicures', the potential for growth in this product is now limited. Over the next three years its growth rate will drop significantly as its relative market share approaches that of 'manicures'.

'Massage' and 'aromatherapy' will become *stars*, as their market growth rate continues to rise and their relative market share increases. Investment in advertising will be necessary to help achieve this level of growth.

This portfolio matrix represents the company's objectives with regard to product, sales turnover and market share. The company will now adopt strategies with regard to price, promotion and distribution that would allow these objectives to be achieved.

The product portfolio matrix for AH Building is shown in Figure 6.5.

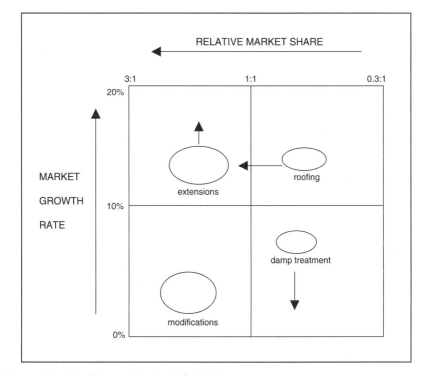

Figure 6.5   Portfolio matrix for AH Building

'Modifications' are a *cash cow* and even if it cannot grow the business, it makes good margins on them and will continue to sell them.

'Extensions' are *stars* – it is still having to advertise to make the product known. It has been growing rapidly but it now expects the growth to slow.

'Roofing' is moving from being a *question mark* to becoming a *star*.

The *dog* of the pack is 'damp treatment' and AH Building must soon decide whether to drop this product completely.

'Chauffeur-driven cars' are a good *cash cow*. Prestige Cars is well known for this service, so no advertising is necessary, but margins are fairly good.

'Chauffeur-driven people carriers' are already a *star*, and 'chauffeur-driven luxury cars', although still a *question mark,* are rapidly moving into *star* territory.

'Taxis' are fast becoming a *dog,* but at the moment are too large a part of the turnover to consider dropping.

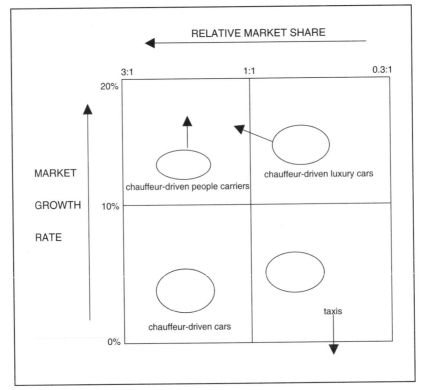

Figure 6.6 Portfolio matrix for Prestige Cars

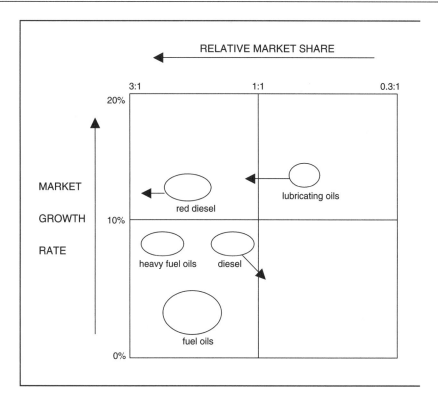

Figure 6.7 Portfolio matrix for Global Fuels

'Fuel oils', 'heavy fuel oils' and 'diesel' are *cash cows* and bring in the bulk of Gobal Fuels' profits. It expects 'fuel oils' to be steady and may see a small level of growth. Heavy fuel oils will not change. There are a fixed number of customers and their requirements do not change. Global Fuels expects sales and market share for 'diesel' to start to decline over the next three years, moving this product into the *dogs* category.

'Red diesel' is already a *star* and further growth is expected from this product.

'Lubricating oils' have been a *question mark,* but are now moving into the *star* sector. It expects dramatic growth in the sales of this product.

'Standard jams' are *cash cows* for The Pure Fruit Jam Company and significant growth is not expected.

'Marmalades' are also *cash cows*, but with the advent of new flavoured marmalades they are moving back towards the *star* quadrant and this is expected to continue over the next three years.

'Mini-pots' and 'special products' are both *stars* or becoming stars and it expects considerable growth in these products over the next three years.

'Gift packs' have been a *dog* – largely because so much of the sales of this product have been as own-label special products. But this has sparked interest from the company's ordinary customers, which has generated demand for this

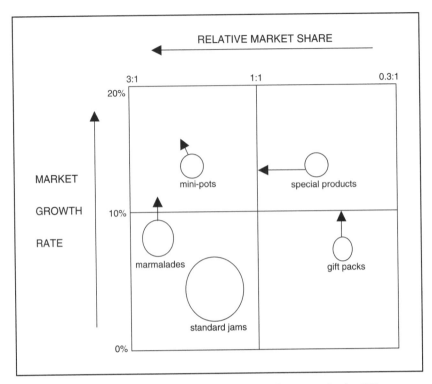

Figure 6.8 Portfolio matrix for The Pure Fruit Jam Company for its UK marketing plan

product under the company's own name. It hopes that this will revive the fortunes of 'gift packs' from being a *dog* to becoming a *question mark* again.

'Special products' are expected to move from being a *question mark* to become a *star*.

The Pure Fruit Jam Company is very ambitious with its export plans; see Figure 6.9.

At present all of the products are so new in export markets that they remain *question marks*. It hopes that during the course of the next three years some if not all of them will move towards the *star* area.

This will have the overall effect of moving 'standard jams' and 'marmalades' from their current positions as *cash cows* in the total company portfolio matrix towards the area of being *stars*.

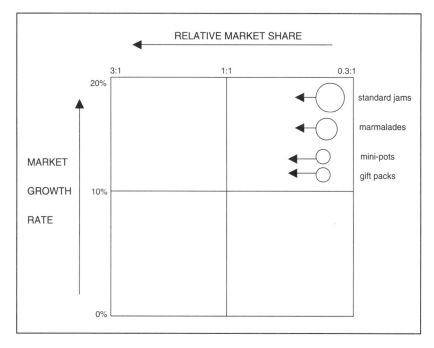

RELATIVE MARKET SHARE

3:1   1:1   0.3:1

20%

MARKET

GROWTH   10%

RATE

0%

standard jams

marmalades

mini-pots

gift packs

Figure 6.9 Portfolio matrix for The Pure Fruit Jam Company for its export marketing plan

Both Precision Valves' type 'A' and type 'B' valves are *cash cows*. They have been moving towards being *dogs,* but the company hopes that with the sales of its new actuators on type 'A' valves and with targeted price reductions on the type 'B' valves (benefiting from reduced costs), these products will start to move back firmly into the centre of the *cash cow* quadrant.

Type 'S' valves are *stars* and this growth is expected to continue as investment in updating water-treatment facilities increases over the next three years.

Packages are based around the type 'S' valve and are moving from being *question marks* to being *stars*. This product is expected to constitute a significant part of the company's UK turnover in three years time.

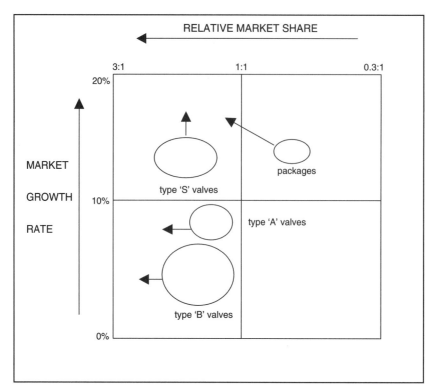

Figure 6.10 Portfolio matrix for Precision Valves Ltd

THE PRICING PLAN

Pricing is a key factor in marketing strategy. It can be a major determinant of whether corporate and marketing objectives will be achieved. Its role needs to be established in relation to the product portfolio, the life cycles of the products and the objectives for sales turnover and market share.

It is generally true to say that the price level of a product will determine the demand for that product. The price that you sell your product at, and the quantity that you sell, will determine the profit you will make from these sales.

If you reduce your price, you would expect to increase the demand for your product. Figure 6.11 shows a typical demand curve.

If you are currently selling your product at price P2 and you are selling a quantity Q2, the total value of sales is P2 x Q2. If you increase your price to P1, the quantity that you sell will reduce to Q1, and if you decrease your price to P3, the quantity that you sell will increase to Q3. The object of the exercise is to increase the value of sales P x Q to the maximum, but to maintain P at a profitable level. If the cost of producing the items is above P3, you cannot justify reducing your price to P3 in the long term, because although you would sell more product, it would be

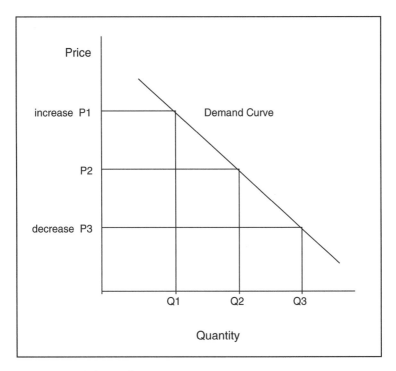

Figure 6.11 A typical demand curve

sold at a loss. There may, however, be good marketing reasons to justify reducing the price to P3 or below as a short-term measure to gain market share.

From an accounting point of view it makes no sense to ever sell a product at a loss. From a marketing point of view, however, you often have to consider the 'chicken and egg' situation. If the product is too highly priced, it may never sell in the quantities necessary for economies of scale to allow the product to be produced profitably. Many large companies, with good financial backing, have seen this and have prepared to initially sell products at the market price, rather than a price based upon initial cost. This has enabled them to build up market share quickly and then to make profits. Pricing must ultimately be related to costs, but cost is not the only factor that must be used to determine price in the marketing environment.

Pricing strategies

There are many types of pricing strategies and tactics that can be considered. Most can, however, be broadly classified as either skimming policies or penetration policies.

Skimming

This involves entering the market at a high price level and 'skimming' off as much profit as possible. As competition enters the market, the price level would be adjusted as necessary.

Penetration

This is the opposite of skimming. With this type of strategy a company sets the price deliberately low. A penetration policy encourages more customers to purchase the product, which increases the company's sales turnover and also its market share.

Premium pricing

Some products sell at a high price because of what they are or because of the reputation of the company that makes them. So Jane's Beauty & Health can sell some aromatherapy products at a much higher price than others. This is also why Prestige Cars can hire out its Rolls Royces at a much higher rate than other cars.

Companies also use specific market pricing against competitors that come into a market at a very low price to try to obtain market share. But bear in mind that in the end nobody wins a price war.

Price leadership

The market leader is in a unique position. It is likely that other companies will set their prices based upon the leader's price and will move prices after it moves – whether up or down. Because of its high market share the market leader is in a strong position to react to price changes from smaller competitors.

The life-cycle effect

The position of a product on its life-cycle curve or in a particular quadrant of the Boston Matrix will also determine the type of pricing strategy that is relevant. If a product is at the saturation stage of its life cycle and is also a 'cash cow' with a high and established market share, it would be illogical to consider price cutting to try to increase market share. It would be far better to keep the price high for as long as possible to milk the product and to provide profits to support newer products. If, on the other hand, a product is at an early stage of its life cycle and is a 'question mark', it may well make sense to consider a penetration policy to increase market share.

Discounting

Pricing policy does not just relate to list prices. Discounting strategies are an integral part of the price equation. They are mainly relevant if you are selling through distribution channels, although even if you are selling directly to end-users, quantity discounts can be used. Discounts can be used to encourage larger individual orders or can be based upon the total amount of business placed in a given period of time. They can be used to encourage customers to buy from your company alone and not to spread their business between you and your competitors.

A company with a portfolio of products has an advantage over a single-product company in terms of its pricing policies. It can gear the pricing strategies for particular products to the position of those products in their life cycles and the overall requirements of the company for profit. It can decide to forego profit today on certain products in order to increase market share and to take its profits on other products that are more established in the marketplace. With a portfolio of products it is possible to have a true pricing plan rather than just a collection of individual pricing strategies.

Further development of the individual plans for distribution and promotion will continue in the next chapter.

We will now consider the strategies that our sample companies intend to adopt in order to achieve the objectives of their marketing plans. Most people tend to mix some tactics in with their strategies and this is not necessarily a bad thing. It is more important to get all the ideas down than to be pedantic about whether an idea should be classified as a strategy or just a tactic.

Jane's Beauty & Health will be using *developing strategies* to offer existing customers a wider range of products and also *attacking strategies* by targeting a new market – customers who want the service to be offered at home. It will be developing its product offering, by offering a wider range of aromatherapy treatments. The company will be adding 'web analytics' software to its website that will tell it who has logged on to the site and what products they have looked at. It will use this information to prepare targeted e-mails to specific customers with special offers. The company will use questionnaires and e-mail questionnaires to get a better feel for additional products that its existing customer base would be prepared to pay for. It will be looking at its workforce and using additional staff for home visits as well as contract staff to cope with peaks and troughs in demand.

The key strategies that it will adopt are listed below.

Products

Package products	– manicure + pedicure; – massage + aromatherapy;
develop new products	– expand range of aromatherapy offerings.

Pricing

Discount policy	– for multiple sessions; – for students with student card.

Promotion

Change advertising/sales promotion	– leaflet campaign for home visiting; bonus scheme for frequent users; – e-mail offers on aromatherapy to massage customers;
Increase web coverage	– expand website; – add 'web analytics' for e-marketing. – weblinks from suppliers' sites.

Distribution

Increase sales channels
— expand home visiting;
— use contract workers.

AH Building Ltd will be using *developing strategies* to offer existing customers a wider range of products and *attacking strategies* by targeting a new market – seagull prevention and removal. AH Building is based on the coast and seagulls nesting on the roofs of houses is a big problem.

Products

Develop new product
— expand Monarch home extensions to include brickwork;
— extend roofing range to include seagull removal.

Pricing

Discount policy
— for repeat orders within nine months.

Promotion

Change advertising/sales promotion
— advertise in Yellow Pages;
— increase advertising in local paper/free newspapers;
— set up a website;
— take part in local 'Ideal Homes' show.

Distribution

Increase sales channels
— get supplier of 'seagull spikes' to forward leads in return for using its materials;
— train key workers to give budget pricing.

Prestige Cars will be adopting *developing strategies*. It will be finding additional uses for its chauffeur-drive product (supermarket runs for older people) and its luxury chauffeur-drive (children's parties).

Products

Modify products
— modify offering to expand people carriers and luxury cars into the children's party and playgroup markets.

Pricing

Discount policy   – offer discounts for 'supermarket runs' out of peak hours.

Promotion

Change advertising/sales promotion
– increase coverage in Yellow Pages
– add 'web analytics' for e-marketing
– mailshots/e-mailshots to playgroups and businesses
– give new leaflets/cards to each customer with their bill.

Distribution

Expand website   – to allow online bookings.

Global Fuels will be using *defensive strategies* to protect its existing sales of heating oils and *developing strategies* to expand its sales of red diesel in the leisure industries. It will be using *developing strategies* with existing customers (who purchase other products) and *attacking strategies* (to find new customers) for a range of lubricating oils used in vacuum applications. It has identified the chemical industry around Bristol as a target with the introduction of ATEX regulations for explosive atmospheres. It sees good potential to expand lubricating oil sales into this sector.

Products

Expand product range
– increase range of lubricating oils on offer to include special vacuum oils.

Pricing

Discount policy
– for summer deliveries (heating oil)
– for winter deliveries (red diesel for leisure use).

Promotion

Change advertising/sales promotion
– take part in local exhibitions
– mailshots/e-mailshots to local chemical and food-processing companies
– mailshots/e-mailshots to boat clubs add 'web analytics' for e-marketing.

Distribution

Telesales	– to chemical and food producers for vacuum oils;
	– to promote red diesel through garden centres.
Expand website	– to take orders online.

For its UK plan The Pure Fruit Jam Company will be using mainly *defensive strategies* and *developing strategies*. It will be repackaging a number of products and relaunching its new-look gift packs and additions to its range of alcohol-flavoured marmalades. It will be trying to build distributor loyalty by offering retrospective discounts based on the level of annual purchases. It will be adding distribution channels in Scotland and the North of England.

Its strategies for the UK market are listed below:

Products

Add/modify products	– launch new-look gift packs;
	– launch rum and Cointreau flavoured marmalades;
	– drop 'bulk' jams – strawberry, raspberry.

Pricing

Discount policies	– offer retrospective discount to major outlets based on level of annual purchases.

Promotion

Change advertising/sales promotion	– carry out high-key product launch for rum and Cointreau flavoured marmalades;
	– increase advertising in Scotland;
	– add 'web analytics' for e-marketing.

Distribution

Add distribution channels	– expand outlets in major cities in North and Scotland;
	– sell mini-pots through Hotel Catering Services Ltd;
Expand website	– to allow online purchases.

For its export plan The Pure Fruit Jam Company has a very ambitious marketing plan with the intention of tripling its export sales within three years. It is adopting a mix of *developing strategies* and *attacking strategies*. It has a new sales manager with a lot of export experience and intends to use government grants and support as well as its own resources to help expand its sales. It will be concentrating particularly on the USA, Canada and Japan and will be introducing 'local' products and 'local' packaging in a number of key markets.

Products

Change product	– make different versions of the product with different names for different markets.

Pricing

Change pricing	– introduce new discount structure for distributors;
premium pricing	– for alcohol based marmalades.

Promotion

Restructure sales management	– new sales manager will take over responsibility for export sales; – increase exhibition coverage; – use government assistance for exhibitions; – add 'web analytics' for e-marketing.

Distribution

Change channels	– appoint new distributors for North America; – appoint new distributor for West of Japan.
Expand website	– to allow online purchases.

In the scope of its UK plan, Precision Valves Ltd intends to concentrate mainly on expanding its existing markets with its existing products. It will also expand the sales of the new product packages and type 'A' valves with new actuators into existing markets. These are low-risk strategies. It will be increasing advertising and taking part in a major water exhibition. It intends to recruit a new salesman to help develop its sales in the water industry still further. The strategies being adopted are mainly *developing* and *attacking* strategies.

Products

Develop new products	– new activator for type 'A' valves – expand range of packages; – add control package to type 'S' valves.

Pricing

Penetration policy	– offer lower pricing for type 'B' valves to achieve framework agreements (favoured supplier) with water companies.
Discount policy	– offer discount to new distributors for initial stock orders.

Promotion

Change sales force organisation	– recruit salesman for the water industry.
Change advertising/sales promotion	– increase advertising;
	– use mailshots/e-mailshots;
	– increase exhibition coverage;
	– add 'web analytics' for e-marketing.

Distribution

Change distribution	– appoint new distributor in Scotland.
Increase sales coverage	– recruit salesman for the water industry.

EXERCISE

Now prepare a list of strategies for your marketing plan.
    Our preliminary strategies are:

Products

....
....
....

Price

....
....
....

Promotion

....
....
....

Distribution

....
....
....

ACTION PLANS

Once you have selected the outline strategies and tactics to achieve your marketing objectives, you need to turn these strategies into programmes or action plans that will enable you to give clear instructions to your staff. If you will be carrying out the work yourself, you still need a clear listing of the actions and timescale to work to.

Each action plan should include:

- current position – where you are now;
- aims – what to do/where do you want to go;
- action – what you need to do to get there;
- person responsible – who will do it;
- start date;
- finish date;
- budgeted cost.

Each action plan would need to be broken down into its component parts. I have prepared some action plans for each of our sample companies.

Table 6.1 shows a suggested layout for an action plan for Jane's Beauty & Health. This plan is for the strategy of 'carry out a leaflet campaign for home visits'.

The £800 to prepare the leaflet is the only actual money that Jane's Beauty & Health will have to spend. The other costs are the nominal cost of people's time.

Each of the actions on this action plan could be broken down into a number of parts. In the preparation of the leaflet there would be a number of stages, including:

- having photographs taken;
- preparation of information to go into leaflet;
- preparation of preliminary layout;
- writing copy;
- preparation of artwork;
- final checking;
- printing.

Table 6.1 An action plan for Jane's Beauty & Health

ACTION PLAN – leaflet campaign for home visiting
DEPARTMENT: SALES

Aim	Current position	Action	By	Start	Finish	Cost
Carry out leaflet campaign	Address list out of date	Update list	Jane	1.1.X6	1.3.X6	£50
	No leaflet	Prepare initial text	Jane	1.1.X6	1.1.X6	£25
	No leaflet	Prepare new leaflet	Ace Ads	1.2.X6	1.3.X6	£800
		Deliver leaflet to address list	Jane and Sue	1.3.X6	1.4.X6	£50

AH Building prepares an action plan for advertising, which is shown in Table 6.2. Ian is making the decisions about the advertising, but Janice will prepare the text and book the adverts with the local paper. The cost of preparing the text is just the internal cost of Janice's time.

Table 6.2 An action plan for AH Building

ACTION PLAN – advertise
DEPARTMENT: SALES

Aim	Action	By	Start	Finish	Cost
Advertise in local paper	Decide dates for advertising	ILH	1.1.X6	12.1.X6	
	Prepare text for advert	JDT	12.1.X6	31.1.X6	£25
	Book adverts	JDT	1.2.X6	1.2.X6	£200
	Send text to paper	JDT	5.2.X6	5.2.X6	

Several of our companies have decided to do mailshots, but they are also looking at the alternative of doing e-mailshots. Prestige Cars decided to look at the alternatives of doing a mailshot or an e-mailshot to local businesses. The action plans and costs are shown in Tables 6.3 and 6.4.

For the mailshot, it already has a mailing list, but it has not been updated for two years, so it needs to update it to avoid letters and brochures going astray.

Table 6.3 An action plan for Prestige Cars for a mailshot

ACTION PLAN – mailshot to local businesses
DEPARTMENT: SALES

Aim	Current position	Action	By	Start	Finish	Cost
Carry out mailshot	Mailing list out of date	Update list	ALT	1.1.X6	1.3.X6	£200
		Prepare text	JDT	1.2.X6	1.3.X6	£25
	No brochure	Prepare new brochure	NBF	1.11.X5	1.3.X6	£3000
		Send out	ILH	1.3.X6	1.4.X6	£700

Table 6.4 An action plan for Prestige Cars for an e-mailshot

ACTION PLAN – e-mailshot to local businesses
DEPARTMENT: SALES

Aim	Current position	Action	By	Start	Finish	Cost
Carry out e-mailshot	Need 'opt-in' e-mail list of local companies	Purchase list	ALT	10.1.X6	10.1.X6	£200
		Prepare text	JDT	10.1.X6	20.1.X6	£25
	Need link to website	Create link on e-mail	JDT	20.1.X5	20.1.X6	£10
		Send out	ILH	1.2.X6	1.2.X6	£100

The £200 cost for updating the mailing list is the internal cost of the time for someone to do this. The cost of the brochure is the price to be paid to an agency that will produce the artwork and print the brochure. The cost of sending out is the cost of envelopes and postage stamps, but there is also time involved in filling and sealing the envelopes.

Prestige Cars contacted an e-marketing company. It downloaded information from the website and was impressed by statistics showing that using precision 'opt-in' e-mail gives responses of 5 to 15 per cent of those contacted compared to only 1 to 3 per cent responses from traditional direct mail.

It contacted the e-marketing company by phone and discussed what it wanted to do. It was able to purchase a B2B opt-in e-mail list covering three local postcode areas. It was advised not to prepare a brochure, but instead to include a link to its website in the e-mail that was being sent out. Not only was the total cost of the e-mailshot less than 10 per cent of the cost of doing the mailshot, but it could also be completed in a fraction of the time. Needless to say Prestige Cars decided to do an e-mailshot.

Global Fuels is planning to expand its website to take orders online and also to add 'web analytics' software for e-marketing. This system will allow it to analyse hits on the site and help it to prepare its own lists of who visits the site and the products they are interested in. Its action plan is shown in Table 6.5. This is just the initial action plan. When the order is placed with the supplier, a schedule of the work together with key dates must be prepared by the supplier. This should tie in with the dates that have been shown in the action plan.

Table 6.5 An action plan for Global Fuels

**ACTION PLAN – expand website to take orders online
and add 'web analytics' software for e-marketing
DEPARTMENT: SALES**

Aim	Action	By	Start	Finish	Cost
Expand website to take orders online and add 'web analytics' software for e-marketing	Select company to carry out work	DFL	1.1.X6	1.3.X6	£200
	Place order	DFL	1.3.X6	1.3.X6	£8000
	Test site	DFL/NAF	1.4.X6	1.6.X6	£2000
	Go live	NAF	1.6.X6		

The Pure Fruit Jam Company is preparing an action plan for the product launch of its new range of specialist marmalades. This is shown in Table 6.6. This action plan is only a summary of the key overall tasks. 'Prepare launch package' is in itself a complex job with a number of constituent parts that all have to be produced before the launch:

❚ press release;
❚ leaflet;
❚ letter to key customers;
❚ letter to distributors;
❚ press advert;
❚ jam 'kits' – including a sample of each jam.

Similarly, 'book venues' involves booking venues for an internal company launch, press launch, a launch to key customers and a launch to key distributors. 'Send out invitations' also includes actions to update the list of who should be invited – from the press, from customers and from distributors.

It also prepares an action plan for producing a Japanese brochure for its export marketing plan; this is shown in Table 6.7. In this plan it does not show one single order with the agency, because payments are made on completion of individual parts of the work.

Table 6.6 An action plan for The Pure Fruit Jam Company for its UK plan

ACTION PLAN – product launch for specialist marmalades
DEPARTMENT: SALES

Aim	Action	By	Start	Finish	Cost
Carry out product launch	Prepare launch package	JAW	1.1.X6	1.6.X6	£5000
	Manufacture samples	AKH	1.3.X6	15.5.X6	£3000
	Book venues and hotels	EBG	1.11.X5	1.1.X6	£3000
	Book advertising	EBG	1.3.X6	1.4.X6	£15000
	Send out invitations	EBG	1.3.X6	1.4.X6	£300

Table 6.7 An action plan for The Pure Fruit Jam Company for its export plan

ACTION PLAN – produce Japanese brochure
DEPARTMENT: SALES

Aim	Action	By	Start	Finish	Cost
Produce Japanese brochure	Meet with agency for kick-off meeting	AHF/IGT	15.1.X6	15.1.X6	£200
	Prepare text – UK text with changes for Japanese market	IGT	15.1.X6	31.2.X6	£100
	Get text translated at Nippo	IGT	31.2.X6	22.3.X6	£850
	Get photography done	AHF	1.2.X6	1.3.X6	£800
	Check initial artwork	AHF/IGT	1.3.X6	1.4.X6	£500
	Check final artwork	AHF/IGT	15.4.X6	30.4.X6	£2500
	Print	AHF	15.5.X6	30.5.X6	£2500

Prestige Valves Ltd is taking part in the Iwex exhibition in November 20X6. Its action plan for this is shown in Table 6.8. To get a good position it has to book its stand a year ahead. It also has to book hotels well in advance to avoid being too far away from the exhibition site. Most of the actions shown on the action plan will again be broken down into a list of sub-actions with dates and responsibilities.

Table 6.8 An action plan for Prestige Valves Ltd

ACTION PLAN – IWEX exhibition
DEPARTMENT: SALES

Aim	Action	By	Start	Finish	Cost
Exhibit at IWEX	Book exhibition stand	BNK	1.11.X5	1.11.X5	£8000
	Place order for stand design and build	ANT	1.2.X6	1.3.X6	£10000
	Agree artwork	BNK	1.6.X5	1.6.X6	£5000
	Book hotels	ANT	1.2.X6	1.2.X6	£2000
	Book carpets, furniture, lighting	BNK	1.6.X6	1.6.X6	£3000
	Final approval meeting	BNK	1.7.X6	1.7.X6	

After scheduling your activities on the basis of action plans you should combine the individual action plans and programmes into larger functional programmes (product, pricing, promotion, distribution). These functional programmes would appear in the marketing plan. They would then be developed into an overall schedule – a master programme that can be used for controlling the implementation of the plan. This is the schedule of what/where/how in the written plan. Although it would only be the larger functional programmes and the master programme schedule that would appear in the written plan, each of the smaller plans and programmes would need to be communicated to those who have to carry them out.

SUMMARY

Marketing strategies are the methods by which you achieve your marketing objectives. They are the broad methods chosen and they describe the means of achieving the objectives in the timescale required. The individual courses of action that are followed on a day-to-day basis are tactics.

Marketing strategies relate to *products, pricing, advertising/promotion* and *distribution*. They can be categorised as 'defensive', 'developing' or 'attacking' strategies.

As there will always be a huge range of potential strategies available to any company, those that will best satisfy your objectives and which can be effectively implemented using the resources and capabilities of your company should be selected.

Objectives should be divided into sub-objectives for your key products, strategic markets and key sales areas and sub-plans should be prepared for 'products', 'price', 'promotion' and 'distribution'.

The product plan involves looking at your product portfolio and deciding:

∎ if it should be changed;
∎ how it should be changed;

■ the strategies you can adopt;
■ where these strategies will lead you.

The pricing plan determines pricing policy and tactics. It determines the mix of pricing and discount policies that best suits your product portfolio.

Strategies must be converted into programmes or action plans in order that they can be carried out. Each department and member of staff needs to know their responsibilities and the timetable for carrying them out.

These individual action plans are then combined into larger functional programmes, which in turn are combined in the master programme schedule. It is the larger functional programmes and the master programme schedule that appear in the written marketing plan.

7

Distribution, advertising and sales promotion

Promotion means getting the right message to the right people. It involves personal selling, advertising and sales promotion. But before you can plan your advertising and sales promotion you need to select the right channels for your product and your business from those available. This is part of the distribution plan, which will always be part of any marketing plan.

THE DISTRIBUTION PLAN

The physical distribution of goods is only one aspect of distribution as defined by marketing planners. Distribution involves:

- marketing channels;
- physical distribution;
- customer service.

Marketing channels

Marketing channels are the means that a company can select to get into contact with its potential customers. If its potential customers are unaware of the product, they will not buy it. There are a wide variety of different channels that a company can use. Figure 7.1 shows a typical selection of available marketing channels.

Direct sales is an expensive channel to operate and is mainly restricted to high-value industrial goods. The bulk of advertising expenditure is used on consumer goods, particularly low-value-repeat buy items such as food and household consumables. Consumer goods are usually sold through distributors, wholesalers and retailers rather than through direct selling, but it is usually still necessary for

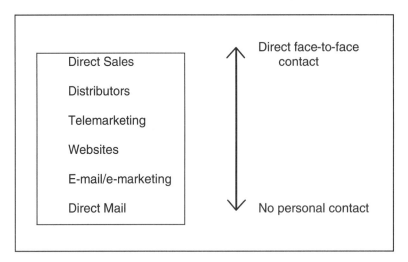

Figure 7.1 Marketing channels

the company to have a salesforce to sell to these distributors, wholesalers and retailers. Small businesses operating in a local environment will normally carry out direct sales, whether they are offering a service or a commodity.

The mix of objective and subjective needs will vary considerably from market to market. In the case of consumer goods the buyer is concerned largely with subjective needs such as emotional satisfaction, although he or she will also consider objective needs such as quality and price.

The industrial buyer will make his or her purchasing decision mainly on the basis of objective considerations – product performance, price, delivery, and the quality of manufacture. There will, however, also be subjective considerations such as the image of the product and the confidence that he or she has in the supplying company and the salesperson. Services come somewhere in between.

Figure 7.2 shows how objective and subjective needs influence purchasing decisions for consumer goods, industrial goods and services.

It follows that although personal contact selling can influence the clients' subjective as well as objective considerations, it is more effective in industrial selling where objective considerations and technical understanding of the product have greater importance. The buyer of a fast sports car is more likely to have been influenced in his or her choice by the prestige of the product and media advertising than by the salesperson in the showroom, who is only reinforcing the advertising message.

The characteristics of the product you are selling will have a considerable influence on the mix of marketing channels that you finally select; see Figure 7.3. The number of channels of distribution will also affect prices because of the level of discounts that will need to be built into the price structure.

Direct sales

In a perfect world direct selling with the salesperson face-to-face with the customer would give a company the maximum possibility of getting the message

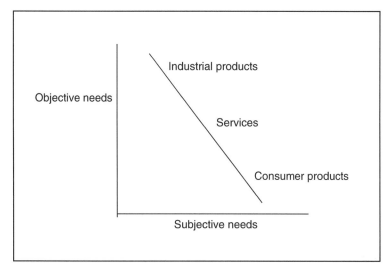

Figure 7.2 The affect of 'needs' on purchasing decisions

across and closing the sale. In the real world this is just not cost-effective for large and medium-sized companies, which all employ a mixture of direct and indirect sales techniques.

For the small local business, direct selling either in person or by phone is the only option open to it. In most cases the 'salesperson' is the owner or partner in the business. The advantages of personal selling are:

▓ It allows two-way communication between the buyer and seller.
▓ The salesperson can tailor the presentation to the individual needs of the customer.

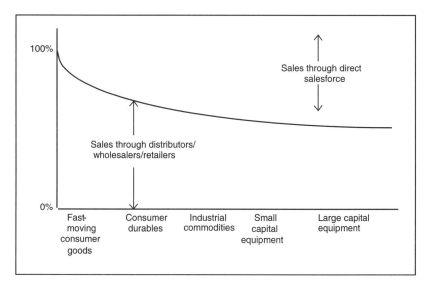

Figure 7.3 The influence of product characteristics on distribution channels

- The salesperson comes to know and be known by the customers.
- The salesperson can negotiate directly on price, delivery and discounts.
- The salesperson can close the sale.
- The salesperson can monitor customer satisfaction levels.

Distributors

In consumer goods industries distributors could be retailers, wholesalers, or even companies that sell to wholesalers. For industrial goods, it is not usual to use wholesale/retail outlets in the same way. Direct sales to customers generally make up a larger proportion of sales than with consumer goods, but the use of commission agents and distributors is widespread. A distributor takes over the selling role of the manufacturer and most distributors have their own salesforce dealing with customers.

Distributors would normally be expected to hold enough stock to service the geographical area for which they are responsible. Most distributors sell a range of products, so a product will not get the exclusive treatment through a distributor's salesforce that it would through a company's own salesforce.

A direct salesforce can be structured:

- by product;
- by area;
- by account.

Distributors can also be appointed on the same basis.

Telemarketing

Telemarketing involves selling and marketing by telephone rather than by direct physical contact. Generally, it has been found that telemarketing is most effective when it supplements the field salesforce activity rather than completely replacing it. It is cost-effective because 40 to 50 telephone calls can be made per day, whereas 6 to 10 personal visits per day is normal for direct sales calls. The main advantages of telemarketing are:

- lower cost than a direct salesforce;
- it frees up the salesperson's time by reducing routine calling activity;
- it increases frequency of customer contact;
- it allows dormant accounts to be revived.

Websites

The internet provides a major new sales channel for all types of products. Most of the major supermarket chains have online purchasing, where customers can order their weekly shopping and have it delivered to their door. Hotel rooms and packaged holidays can also be booked online, either directly with the hotel/package tour provider, or at specialist sites such as www.travel.telegraph.co.uk. Books and

CDs can be purchased from a number of sites including www.amazon.co.uk. Computers, cars and electrical goods can all now be ordered online.

One effect of these websites is to drive down prices, because the consumer can now surf the web and compare prices from different suppliers. But there is an additional advantage to companies in terms of getting the best out of their websites and in using them for sales promotion. The use of web analytics software means that companies can now track which pages of their website are most popular, which promotions are clicked on most – basically which parts seem to attract users and which parts don't. They can track where users enter and where they leave, where they come from (which search engines, etc), where they go next, how long they stay on the site and how many pages they look at while they are there. This is far more detailed feedback than is available in other media.

E-mail/e-marketing

E-marketing and web analytics have brought about big changes in marketing tactics. E-mail is the perfect vehicle to build lifetime relationships with customers. There are a large number of e-marketing companies that can supply permission-based technology to help businesses communicate and build or add to their existing database of potential and existing customers, creating targeted direct e-marketing campaigns with information and offerings specific to each customer's interests. Permission marketing can turn online visitors into lifetime customers by allowing regular communication with both existing and prospective customers. Giving consumers total control of messages they receive is the future of direct marketing on the internet. Permission marketing is the ideal solution to personalise relationships and secure continued customer support.

With opt-in e-mail, responses (5 to 15 per cent) are far greater than those from banner advertising (0.5 per cent) or traditional direct mail (1 to 3 per cent). In addition to a greater response rate, a direct e-mail marketing campaign costs only a fraction of the cost of more traditional methods of marketing.

E-mail bulletins can even track how many users open the e-mails, and what if anything they click on in the bulletin. This is far more effective at collating customer information than direct mail.

Direct mail

Direct mail includes mail-order business and the use of mailshots. Mailshots involve sending information on a specific product by mail to potential customers on a mailing list. They rely for their success on the accuracy of the mailing list used, and a small return rate (1 to 3 per cent) is considered quite normal. They are still very popular, but in many cases are being superseded by e-mailshots on the grounds of cost and efficiency.

Physical distribution, warehousing and factory location

Physical distribution involves not only the holding of stock, but also communicating within the distribution network and the way that the product is packaged for distribution. The proximity of the factory to its markets is more important with

high-bulk, low-value goods than with sophisticated capital goods, but stocking at
the factory, at warehouses or at logistics centres is an important part of distribution strategy that will determine whether you can give as good a service as your
competitors – or better.

Customer service

For the distribution plan we are only interested in the aspects of customer service
that affect distribution. This really relates to the level of availability of the product
to the customer. Distribution is about getting the product to the right place (for the
customer) at the right time. Theoretically you want to offer your customers 100
per cent availability of the product. In practice this is not possible. It is necessary
to find a balance between the costs and benefits involved . The costs of extra availability cannot exceed the extra revenue that will be gained as a result.

Below, we consider the *marketing channels* and *physical distribution* used by our
sample companies.

Like most small local businesses, Jane's Beauty & Health, AH Building and
Prestige Cars all use direct selling. A lot of their business comes in because of
'word of mouth' and adverts locally in the press and Yellow Pages. Much business
is repeat business from existing customers. All of these companies either have a
website or are developing a website so that potential customers can view products
or even place orders online.

Since Jane's Beauty & Health and Prestige Cars have their products on site,
physical distribution is not a problem. AH Building orders in materials, before
committing a date to carrying out a job.

The situation with Global Fuels is a little more complicated.

Marketing channels

Global Fuels uses a mixture of direct sales and distributors or agents. In the
Bristol/Avon area and Somerset/Wiltshire, most of its sales are direct to end-
customers. But in Devon and Cornwall it also has a number of
distributors/agents in major towns. (These are small fuel suppliers, which do
not stock the range of products that Global Fuels can provide). Global Fuels
also uses a number of specialist distributors for farm sales and one ship's chan-
dler company that sells to the boating industry.

Physical distribution

The company keeps a reasonable level of stock for most major products. For
some of the specialist lubricating oils, it purchases from the manufacturer and
arranges direct shipment to its end-customers. Heavy fuel oils are also delivered direct from the manufacturers. In summer it occasionally gets large heating oil shipments for farms delivered direct.

Its own deliveries of bulk products are made by its own fleet of road tankers. Lubricating oils are in their own separate containers and when they are delivered from the company's warehouse it uses local haulage contractors, or for more urgent deliveries it uses overnight delivery services from companies such at TNT or DHL.

For the UK market The Pure Fruit Jam Company uses the following.

Marketing channels

The Pure Fruit Jam Company does not consider tele-marketing or direct mail as these are not applicable channels for this type of product. It uses a mix of direct sales (to the wholesale buyers) and distribution (distributors will sell to the small retailers). It carries out limited nationwide advertising of the products to support these channels. It is in the process of expanding its website to allow orders to be placed directly with the company for gift packs and specialist products.

Physical distribution

The company manufactures its product in one factory only. It has a contract with a haulage contractor to deliver the product to major wholesalers, distributors and large retailers. The company has an integrated live computer database showing stocks at all these warehouses at all times. The product is packed in boxes – 30 jars to a box. The boxes are packed 12 to a pallet and shrink wrapped on the pallet.

For export markets The Pure Fruit Jam Company uses local distributors in individual countries. The product is packed in the same way as for delivery in the UK market.

Precision Valves Ltd uses a different mix of marketing channels.

Marketing channels

Precision Valves Ltd uses a mixture of direct sales (to large key accounts and contracting companies) and distributors (which hold stock of valves and spares). It has recently started to use telemarketing to follow up dormant accounts.

Physical distribution

The company manufactures valves at its factory in the South of England and holds a stock of components and spare parts at the factory. It does not stock finished valves and only supplies to order. The company's distributors operate on a discount level of 30 per cent from the company's list price and this finances the stocks of equipment that they hold in stock. The company uses local haulage contractors for deliveries of finished goods. More urgent deliveries are made using nationwide overnight services such as DHL, UPS and TNT. The company operates an MRP (Materials Resource Planning) system with a computer database that includes order processing and invoicing. In addition the company operates a computer database for its distribution network and can advise one distributor where it can find a component (with another distributor) if it does not have it in stock.

EXERCISE

Now consider the marketing channels and distribution used by your own company for the products and areas covered by your marketing plan. Detail these below:

Marketing channels

....

....

....

Physical distribution/logistics

....

....

....

In the distribution plan it is necessary to consider if a change in marketing channels or physical distribution is necessary.

All of our companies have decided to do more with the internet. Those that do not have websites intend to get them set up and those that already have them intend to expand and in many cases get them set up to take orders online. Most will be adding software to their website that will tell them who has logged on to the site and what products they have looked at. They will use this information to prepare targeted e-mails to specific customers with special offers.

Viral or 'word of mouth' marketing works very well for small businesses. It works on the basis that it is only human nature when you hear of a good deal to want to share it with others. So our smaller companies are also intending to use targeted viral marketing to sell their products. As an example, Jane's Beauty & Health will be e-mailing offers on aromatherapy to customers who already use its massage service. AH Building and Prestige Cars will also be using targeted mailshots or e-mailshots.

Global Fuels intends to use telesales to promote its vacuum oils to chemical and food producers and also for red diesel to garden centres. It intends to expand its website to allow online purchases. The company will also add 'web analytics' for e-marketing. It will be using e-mailshots to the chemical industry, food-processing industry and to boat clubs. The company also intends to appoint more local agents/distributors in the parts of its area that are more distant from its base. It has decided to increase its stocks of lubricating oils so that it can deliver them from its own warehouse.

The Pure Fruit Jam Company intends to expand its website to allow online purchases. It will also add 'web analytics' for e-marketing. It intends to expand its distribution outlets in the North of England and Scotland and to set up a distribution deal for its mini-pots for the hotel trade. For export markets, it will continue to expand distribution, particularly in the USA and Canada.

Precision Valves Ltd intends to expand its website to allow online purchases. It will also add 'web analytics' for e-marketing.

It has its highest sales in the South, where it is based, and in the Midlands and the North of England, where the company's distribution is strong. Its sales in Wales, Scotland and Northern Ireland are minimal. It is in the process of appointing a new distributor for Scotland and will be evaluating and possibly replacing its distribution in Wales and Northern Ireland.

THE ADVERTISING AND PROMOTIONS PLAN

The advertising and promotions plan involves personnel, advertising and promotions.

Personnel

Once you have selected your mix of distribution channels you can decide on the personnel requirements of the plan. As shown in Figure 7.3, your product will determine to some extent the channels that you use. The channels will determine to some extent the type of sales organisation that you need. In the situation analysis in Chapter 4 we carried out a SWOT analysis for the sales organisation of our sample companies. This indicated the weaknesses that need to be addressed and the opportunities that they can take.

We now need to detail the existing sales structure and the proposed structure for the plan. In doing this we need to indicate which personnel are existing and which are additional (or replacements!).

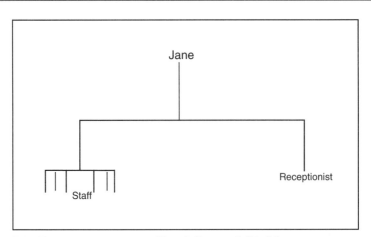

Figure 7.4   Existing organisation of Jane's Beauty & Health

At Jane's Beauty & Health only Jane and Jenny are involved in sales. Jenny is the receptionist.

The existing organisation is shown in Figure 7.4.

With this structure only Jane and the receptionist are able to take orders. This means that both Jane and Jenny can only fit in half a day working on beauty treatments, since they must spend half of the day on reception.

Jane intends to change this structure. She intends to train up two other members of staff to take phone calls and look after the reception area. There will be a general roster, but if one of the four of them does not have a client they will take over reception. At the busiest times of the day or week, they will use the answerphone so that all eight employees can be working with clients. The new structure is shown in Figure 7.5.

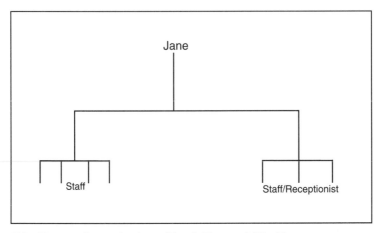

Figure 7.5   Proposed organisation of Jane's Beauty & Health

Figure 7.6 Existing organisation of AH Building

There is a similar situation at AH Building, where only John James, the owner, does the selling. So there is no real sales structure – just a company structure as shown in Figure 7.6.

John has decided to train up his two senior foremen so that they can give budget quotations. They will also feed these to Susan in the office, who will prepare and send out the written quotation. The new organisation is shown in Figure 7.7.

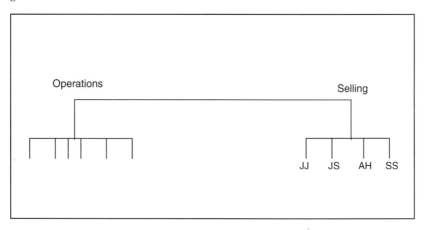

Figure 7.7 Proposed organisation of AH Building

Prestige Cars has a full-time receptionist, who is in effect *the* salesperson. The structure is shown in Figure 7.8.

The owner now intends to get involved in selling and to give responsibility to the senior drivers in luxury cars, people carriers and chauffeur cars for promoting and selling their products (Figure 7.9).

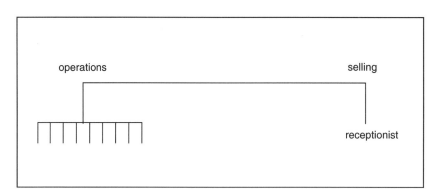

Figure 7.8   Existing organisation of Prestige Cars

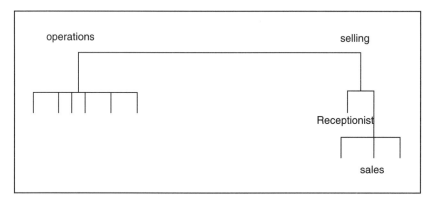

Figure 7.9   Proposed organisation of Prestige Cars

In Global Fuels, the managing director manages the major distributors and the sales manager manages direct sales and minor distributors (Figure 7.10).

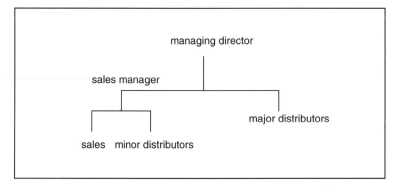

Figure 7.10   Existing sales organisation for Global Fuels

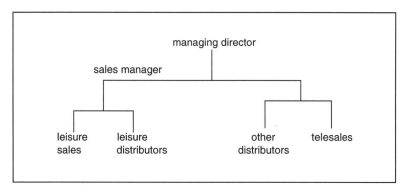

Figure 7.11 Proposed sales organisation for Global Fuels

In its marketing plan Global Fuels has decided that the sales manager should concentrate on the leisure market, which he knows well. He will take over managing distributors for the leisure industry and the managing director will manage the others. The managing director will also manage the telesales, for which he will use Gillian, the accounts clerk, two hours a day. The new structure is shown in Figure 7.11.

The Pure Fruit Jam Company has a sales director, a new sales manager, and a marketing assistant who handles advertising, publicity and exhibitions. Its existing sales structure is shown in Figure 7.12.

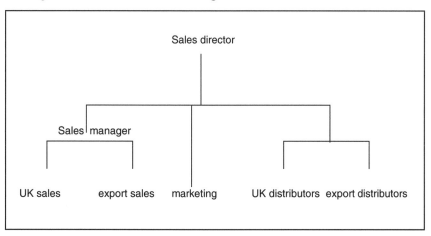

Figure 7.12 Existing sales organisation at The Pure Fruit Jam Company

The new sales manager has a lot of experience in export sales, so the intention is to give him full responsibility for export sales. The sales director will concentrate mainly on UK sales and overall marketing (Figure 7.13).

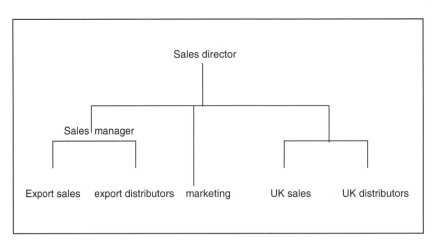

Figure 7.13 Proposed sales organisation at The Pure Fruit Jam Company

The existing UK sales organisation of Precision Valves Ltd is shown in Figure 7.14.

At present there is only one person doing the selling in the UK (the sales and marketing director is handling the export business and marketing). In its plan it intends to recruit a sales engineer to handle the water and waste water industries. It will then change the sales structure to that shown in Figure 7.15.

This structure adds one person to the company's overall sales organisation. This change is shown in Table 7.1 and will be included in the budgeting part of the plan.

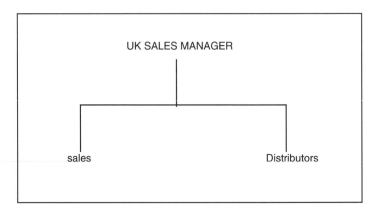

Figure 7.14 Existing UK sales organisation for Precision Valves Ltd

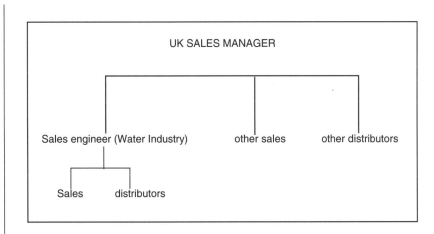

Figure 7.15 Proposed UK sales organisation for Precision Valves Ltd

Table 7.1 Proposed UK sales organisation for Precision Valves Ltd

Position	Existing Personnel	New Personnel	Total
Sales Director	1		1
Water Industry Manager	1		1
Sales Engineer		1	1
Total	2	1	3

EXERCISE

Now consider the sales organisation for your plan. Draw up the existing organisation structure, detail its strengths and weaknesses, analyse the focus that you have and the focus that you need. Draw up your new structure and if it is different from the existing structure, note the new personnel required.

....
....
....
....

Advertising and promotions

The purpose of advertising is to get a message across to the customer. Advertising operates at three levels – it informs, persuades and reinforces. Advertising to inform normally relates to the promotion of new products and services. Advertising to persuade is what most people understand as advertising. There is also the public relations side of advertising – promotional public relations. This includes media relations and exhibitions.

Because advertising on television and in the national press is very expensive, most television and national press advertising relates to consumer goods with large annual sales or services such as banking and insurance. The advertising of industrial and capital goods uses much narrower and more specific outlets such as industry-specific magazines. Repeat advertising is more effective than one-off advertisements. The same advert repeated every week or every month in a limited number of outlets is more effective than different one-off adverts in a wide range of outlets.

Service products sold through local outlets would use advertising in local papers and Yellow Pages. Similarly, industrial products are normally promoted at exhibitions that are specific for that industry rather than general trade fairs.

Many companies, particularly small businesses, are now using viral or 'word of mouth' marketing concepts as one of their main methods of sales promotion. There are many specialist e-marketing companies that offer tailored packages to be used for this. Typically an offer might involve sending a customised e-mail message to subscribers of a mailing list, offering them a chance to win a prize, small gift certificate or even the chance to try out a product or service free of charge. The key to viral marketing is exposure. You want potential clients to visit your website and see what you have to offer. The prize is to make their visit worthwhile. Customised software allows you to select recipients who would be most likely to respond well to your product, based on stated preferences and mailing list subject matter. You can also personalise each message with each client's name.

Jane's Beauty & Health intends to carry out a leaflet campaign for home visiting as well as some local press advertising. Table 7.2 shows its press advertising schedule.

It will be expanding its website to take orders online. It will also be adding 'web analytics' software to enable it to analyse hits on its website and to use this information to prepare targeted e-mail campaigns to specific customers with specific offers. It intends to use this particularly to offer aromatherapy to customers who purchase or are interested in massage.

Table 7.2 Press advertising schedule for Jane's Beauty & Health

PRESS ADVERTISING																
YEAR:20X6																
MEDIA	No	Rate per insertion	Total cost	J	F	M	A	M	J	J	A	S	O	N	D
		£	£												
Gazette (Wednesday)	4	50	200			x		x		x					x
Herald (Friday)	4	50	200	x		x		x		x			x		
Friday Ad	6	40	240	x		x		x		x		x		x	x

AH Building will be advertising in Yellow Pages and in the local press. It will also be taking part in the 'Ideal Homes' show in town. Details of its exhibition costs are given in Table 7.3.

It also intends to set up a website for which it is budgeting £5,000.

Table 7.3 Exhibition costs for AH Building

EXHIBITION COSTS	
Name of exhibition:	Ideal Homes
Location:	Downtown Sports Arena
Date:	8–10 June 20X6
Stand size:	6m² (2m × 3m)
COSTS	**£**
Stand space rental	120
Artwork, photographic panels	500
Rental of table/chairs	200
TOTAL	**880**

Prestige Cars will also be advertising in the local press and will be increasing its coverage in Yellow Pages with a block advert. Its main promotions will be by means of various mail shots/e-mail shots that it is planning to local playgroups and local businesses. It also intends to expand its website to allow online booking of car hire and 'web analytics'. The action plan for its e-mail shot to local businesses is shown in Table 7.4.

Table 7.4 Action plan with costs for email shot for Prestige Cars

ACTION PLAN – e-mail shot to local businesses

DEPARTMENT: SALES

Aim	Current position	Action	By	Start	Finish	Cost
Carry out e-mail shot	Need 'opt-in' e-mail list of local companies	Purchase list	ALT	10.1.X6	10.1.X6	£200
		Prepare text	JDT	10.1.X6	20.1.X6	£25
	Need link to website	Create link on e-mail	JDT	20.1.X5	20.1.X6	£10
		Send out	ILH	1.2.X6	1.2.X6	£100

Global Fuels intends to take part in two local exhibitions – the Bristol Chemshow and the West of England Agricultural Show. It will also be carrying out separate mailshots/e-mailshots for the boating, chemical and food industries. It will be revamping its website and adding in the facility to take orders online and 'web analytics' for e-marketing. It will be spending about £10,000 each on the exhibitions and its website project. The schedules for exhibition expenditure are given in Tables 7.5 and 7.6.

Table 7.5 Expenditure schedule for exhibition for Global Fuels: the Bristol Chemshow

EXHIBITION COSTS

Name of exhibition:	Bristol Chemshow
Location:	Avon Exhibition Centre
Date:	4–6 October 20X6
Stand size:	9 m² (3 m × 3 m)
Stand and artwork:	Riverside Design

COSTS	£
Stand space rental	800
Shell scheme rental	2,000
Artwork, photographic panels	2,000
Rental of carpets, furniture, lights	800
TOTAL	**5,600**

Table 7.6 Expenditure schedule for exhibition for Global Fuels: West of England Agricultural Show

EXHIBITION COSTS

Name of exhibition:	Agricultural Show
Location:	West of England Showground
Date:	18–22 June 20X6
Stand size:	6 m² (2 m × 3 m)

COSTS	£
Stand space rental	600
Artwork, photographic panels	2,000
Rental of furniture, lights	400
TOTAL	**3,000**

During 20X6 in the UK, The Pure Fruit Jam Company will be carrying out a high profile product launch for its new range of breakfast marmalades with a press launch on 26 June and a trade launch on 27 June. It will also be relaunching its gift packs at the Foodex exhibition in March. It will be adding distribution channels in Scotland and the North of England and will be carrying out a press advertising campaign to support that. It will also be adding 'web analytics' for e-marketing to its website.

Details of its product launch and exhibition expenditure are given in Tables 7.7 and 7.8.

Table 7.7 Product launch costs for The Pure Fruit Jam Company for its UK plan

PRODUCT LAUNCH COSTS

Name of product:	New marmalade range
Location:	Cumberland Hotel
Date:	26–27 June 20X6
Agency:	Top Notch Advertising

COSTS	£
Hire of hotel room and facilities	3,000
Design, supply and build launch stand	8,000
Artwork, photographic panels	5,000
Launch video	10,000
Sample packs	3,000
Launch dinner	3,000
Hotel bills/expenditure for launch staff	2,000
TOTAL	**34,000**

Table 7.8 Exhibition costs for The Pure Fruit Jam Company for its UK plan

EXHIBITION COSTS

Name of exhibition:	Foodex
Location:	NEC Birmingham
Date:	6–8 March 20X6
Stand size:	32 m² (4 m × 8 m)
Stand contractor:	Top Notch Advertising

COSTS	£
Stand space rental	4,000
Design, supply and build	8,000
Artwork, photographic panels	4,000
Rental of carpets, furniture, lights, phone, etc	2,000
Hotel bills/expenditure for stand staff	2,000
TOTAL	**20,000**

There will also be separate schedules for its press advertising campaigns for Scotland and England, together with individual action plans.

For its export plan The Pure Fruit Jam Company will be concentrating particularly on North America and Japan and will be introducing 'local' products and 'local' packaging in a number of key markets.

For the Japanese market it will be repackaging gift packs and adding a sake flavoured marmalade range. It is using government grants to produce Japanese sales literature and also to support taking part in the Nippon Food Show in Osaka as part of the British Pavilion.

For the North American market it will take part in Hotel Suppliers 20X6 in Chicago and will support local distributors with targeted advertising

Details of exhibition expenditure are shown in Table 7.9.

A similar table of costs would also be prepared for the US exhibition.

Table 7.9 Exhibition costs for The Pure Fruit Jam Company for its export plan

EXHIBITION COSTS

Name of exhibition:	Nippon Food Show
Location:	International Exhibition Centre, Osaka
Date:	12–14 May 20X6

Stand size:	32 m^2 (4 m × 8 m)
Stand contractor:	Brit-Ex Contracting

COSTS	**£**
Stand space rental	6,000
Design, supply and build	10,000
Artwork, photographic panels	6,000
Rental of carpets, furniture, lights, phone, etc	3,000
Hotel bills/expenditure for stand staff	3,000
Air fares	3,000
TOTAL	31,000
less government grants of £3,000 **TOTAL COST**	**28,000**

Precision Valves Ltd is targeting the water industry. Tables 7.10 and 7.11 show a press advertising schedule and exhibition cost schedule that it has prepared. It will also be carrying out some targeted mail/e-mail shots and expanding its website to include 'web analytics' for e-marketing. The costs of these items will go into the advertising and promotions plan.

Table 7.10 Schedule of press advertising for Precision Valves Ltd

PRESS ADVERTISING

APPLICATION: WATER INDUSTRY   **YEAR 20X6**

Media	No	Rate per insertion £	Total cost £	J	F	M	A	M	J	J	A	S	O	N	D
Water & Waste Treatment	2	1800	3,600						x				x		
Water Services	2	1500	3,000							x				x	
Water Bulletin	3	800	2,400				x				x			x	
Water Yearbook	1	2,000	2,000	x											
TOTAL COST			11,000												

Table 7.11 Schedule of expenditure for a major exhibition for Precision Valves Ltd

EXHIBITION COSTS	
Name of exhibition:	Iwex
Location:	NEC Birmingham
Date:	6–8 November 20X6
Stand size:	64 m^2 (8 m X 8 m)
Stand contractor:	Exhibition Contractors Ltd

COSTS	£
Stand space rental	8,000
Design, supply and build	10,000
Artwork, photographic panels	5,000
Rental of carpets, furniture, lights, phone, etc	3,000
Hotel bills/expenditure for stand staff	2,000
TOTAL	**28,000**

EXERCISE

Prepare similar schedules and costs for promotions that you intend to include in your plan.

....
....
....

SUMMARY

Implementing a marketing plan requires communication, which means getting the right message over to the right people. This involves personal selling, advertising and sales promotion.

Before you can put together your advertising and promotions plan, you need to select the right marketing channels for your product and your business from those available. This is a part of the distribution plan and you will need to decide the mix of direct sales and distribution through distributors, wholesalers, retailers, etc. The characteristics of the product will influence the mix of channels used.

As well as the selection of marketing channels, the distribution plan also includes the physical distribution of goods and customer service.

Once the distribution plan is complete, advertising and sales promotion can be planned and personnel requirements can be decided. The advertising and promotions plan should include details of the present structure of your sales organisation and any changes proposed for the implementation of the marketing plan.

Advertising informs, persuades and reinforces ideas about products. As well as pure advertising, it includes promotional public relations activities such as media relations, exhibitions and company websites. It is expensive and must be used as an integral part of the whole marketing effort. It needs to be targeted effectively and the results monitored.

The same is true of sales promotions. These are special offers either to the customer or to the salesperson to help to promote sales of a specific product.

The advertising and promotions plan should include the details, schedules and costs of the advertising and sales promotion campaigns that are included in the marketing plan.

8

Planning for a new product and developing new sales areas

When planning for a new product or a new sales area you will probably not have any historical data yourself that can be used for planning purposes. That does not mean that no useful data exist. There are many external sources that you can use – particularly if your new sales areas will be export markets.

PLANNING FOR A NEW PRODUCT

When preparing a marketing plan for a completely new product, it is likely that there will be no historical data at all. There is, of course, the situation where the product is superseding another product and in such cases historical data for the superseded product should be used. Due note should, however, be taken of changes to the specification of the new product which may broaden its application.

Even if there were no historical data relating to the product, some market research would have been carried out to determine market size, competition, etc, and to estimate the potential market for the product. The methods are the same as those used for making projections of the potential market for any product, covered in Chapter 5.

There is also a difference between planning for a new product for a manufacturing company such as Precision Valves Ltd or The Pure Fruit Jam Company, where they will probably be manufacturing the product themselves, and planning for small service companies, like our other sample companies, where a new product will be something bought in that they add to the range of products that they have on offer.

Below, we look at new products that our sample companies are considering and show how they would plan for these in their marketing plans. Some of these are really extensions of existing products, but some are brand new products that have not been offered so far.

Jane's Beauty & Health is considering adding arm and hand massage and foot and leg massage to its range and would offer these to customers for manicure and pedicure as well as other massage customers.

Its plan for this is included in its marketing plan. The figures are quite small, so it does not really merit a separate plan. It has projected what they will do in the following section: 'We are planning to expand our massage options to include arm and hand massage and foot and leg massage. We will offer these to clients who currently take manicure and/or pedicure and also to other clients interested in massage for stress relief.'

The increased turnover from arm/hand massage and foot/leg massage is shown in Table 8.1.

'This is a new product that we have not been offering so far. We see the customer base as being primarily "mature business" and "young singles". Some of this will be offered in our city centre salon, but we will also offer it for "home visits", together with our other massage options.'

Table 8.1 Additional turnover from new product, Jane's Beauty & Health

JANE'S BEAUTY & HEALTH
SALES FIGURES (Historical and Forecast)

SALES AREA: ALL

				← forecast →		
YEAR (all values in £k)	20X3	20X4	20X5	20X6	20X7	20X8
ARM/HAND + FOOT/ LEG MASSAGE	0	0	2	10	20	30

AH Building is based in a seaside town and in its plan it is including a new product – seagull prevention and removal.

'We see a need in the town for "seagull prevention and removal systems". During the summer months seagulls set up home on the roofs of residents' houses to breed. They are large and aggressive birds and once they have young they attack anyone in the vicinity. They also leave mess on the roofs of houses.

'We see our target markets as being "affluent retired" and "expanding families". The key sales areas are "Seaside' and "Old Town", but we also expect to find a smaller number of customers in the "town centre" and the "suburbs".'

The target turnover from this application is shown in Table 8.2.

Marketing objectives

'We plan to double our roofing business in real terms within three years. A key part of this plan is to grow our "seagull prevention and removal" business from £10,000 now to £150,000 within three years.'

Marketing strategies

Product	– expand range to include roofing spikes;
	– offer 'filler' cages to block suitable nest sites;
Pricing	– offer discount if ordered at the same time as other roofing work, such as gutter cleaning.
Promotion	– advertise in Yellow Pages;
	– advertise in local paper/free papers.
Distribution	– get supplier of 'seagull spikes' to forward leads in return for using its materials.

Table 8.2 Extra turnover from seagull protection application, AH Building

AH BUILDING

SALES FIGURES (Historical and Forecast)

SALES AREA: ALL

					forecast	
YEAR (all values in £k)	20X3	20X4	20X5	20X6	20X7	20X8
SEAGULL PROTECTION	0	0	10	50	75	150

Prestige Cars is looking at the possibility of adding electric cars and possibly including electric cars for the disabled. This would be a completely new product separate from its existing products. It has done some work on this to see if it would be viable. This constitutes a separate marketing plan parallel to its main plan. If it decides to proceed with this new product, the plan will need to be integrated into its overall plan.

'Our mainstream business has been with petrol or diesel cars. It was suggested to us that we should consider the market for electric cars and appliances (including those for the disabled). In examining this we have split the market into three:

1. electric cars for use by local residents;
2. electric cars for use by tourists;
3. buggies for the disabled.'

Key products

1. Electric cars for use by local residents

'For this application area, we would act as a franchise, selling new electric cars to local residents and providing them with a recharging facility open during our normal office hours. For use of the recharging facility we would charge an annual rate to cover for one recharge per week and individual charges above this level of usage.'

2. Electric cars for use by tourists

'Here we would have to invest in cars ourselves. We estimate usage would require a total of 10 cars to be available for use mainly during the summer months. We would consider hiring out these cars on short-term hire to local residents during the winter months, so that they can try the idea and see if they like it.'

3. Buggies for the disabled

'These units would need to be available in the centre of town and we would need to hire premises either in the Arndale Shopping Centre or nearby. The units would be completely different from the standard electric cars and would require their own charging unit at the hire site.

'For all of these products we would need to invest in the cars themselves and also in the equipment for recharging the batteries. From information that we have received from the suppliers, we see that a full recharge would give 100 miles of travel for an electric car and 10 miles for a disabled buggy.'

Based on a fleet of 10 electric cars and 10 disabled buggies Prestige Cars see, potential turnover as shown in Table 8.3.

Marketing objectives

- To generate £150,000 of turnover within three years.
- To generate an addition profit of £75,000 from this project.
- To pay back our investment within five years.

Marketing strategies

Product	– offer new energy-efficient range of electric cars and sell on basis of reduced running costs compared to petrol/diesel.
Pricing	– offer short-term hire during winter to allow people to try out the product.
Promotion	– advertise in Yellow Pages; – advertise in local paper/free papers.
Distribution	– sub-contract buggy hire to town centre cycle shop.

Table 8.3 Turnover for electric cars project, Prestige Cars

	PRESTIGE CARS					
				SALES FIGURES (Historical and Forecast)		
SALES AREA: ELECTRIC CARS						
				◄──── forecast ────►		
YEAR	**20X3**	**20X4**	**20X5**	**20X6**	**20X7**	**20X8**
(all values in £k)						
LOCAL RESIDENTS				10	25	50
TOURISTS				15	30	60
DISABLED				20	30	40
TOTAL	0	0	0	45	85	150

Budgets and P&L account

Total capital investment for this project would be £150,000 (£130,000 for the cars/buggies and £20,000 for the recharging facility). Depreciated over seven years, this would cost about £20,000 per year. The P&L account for the extra business is shown in Table 8.4.

Table 8.4 P&L account for electric car project, Prestige Cars

	PRESTIGE CARS		
		PROFIT & LOSS ACCOUNT	
ELECTRIC CARS PROJECT			
	20X6	**20X7**	**20X8**
(all values in £k)			
SALES TURNOVER	50	100	150
less COST OF SALES	10	20	25
GROSS PROFIT	40	80	125
ADMINISTRATION	5	5	5
RENT	5	5	5
RATES	5	5	5
ADVERTISING	5	5	5
OVERHEADS	10	10	10
DEPRECIATION	20	20	20
TOTAL OPERATING EXPENSES	50	50	50
OPERATING PROFIT	−10	30	75

Global Fuels has decided to enter the market for lubricating oils for the vacuum industry. This will be part of its overall plan.

'We have been expanding sales of lubricating oils over the last three years. We see this as an area for growth and in particular we want to target the market for specialist oils for the vacuum industry.'

The target turnover for this application is shown in Table 8.5.

Marketing objectives

To grow sales of lubricating oils for use in the vacuum industry from £10,000 to £100,000 over three years.

Marketing strategies

Product   – increase range of lubricating oils to include special vacuum oils.
Pricing   – offer discount on Fomblin oil if used oil is returned for recovery.
Promotion   – mailshot/e-mailshot to local chemical and food-processing companies take part in Bristol Chemshow.
Distribution – telesales to chemical and food producers for vacuum oils.

Table 8.5 Extra turnover from the sale of vacuum lubricating oils, Global Fuels

GLOBAL FUELS
SALES FIGURES (Historical and Forecast)

SALES AREA: ALL
Net sales after deducting tax & duty   ◀——— forecast ———▶

YEAR (all values in £k)	20X3	20X4	20X5	20X6	20X7	20X8
VACUUM OILS			10	30	70	100

The Pure Fruit Jam Company is adding rum and Cointreau flavoured marmalades – it already has whisky and brandy flavours. This is included in its main marketing plan and the key information is given below.

'We entered the field of flavoured marmalades two years ago and immediately saw growth in our marmalade products. Our initial launch was with whisky and brandy flavoured brands. We have carried out market research and now intend to launch two new products next year – Cointreau flavoured and rum flavoured marmalades.'

The sales (history/budget) are shown in Table 8.6.

Table 8.6 Sales of flavoured marmalades, The Pure Fruit Jam Company

THE PURE FRUIT JAM COMPANY						
SALES FIGURES (Historical and Forecast)						

SALES AREA: ALL

← forecast →

YEAR (all values in £k)	20X3	20X4	20X5	20X6	20X7	20X8
WHISKY MARMALADE		15	65	85	110	140
BRANDY MARMALADE		10	52	70	100	130
RUM MARMALADE				20	40	60
COINTREAU MARMALADE			20	40	60	
TOTAL	0	25	117	195	290	390

Strategic markets

Quality shops

'We have found a ready market for our flavoured marmalades in quality shops and expect the bulk of the product to sell through these.'

Hotels

'Jarvis and MacDonalds hotels have taken well to mini-pots with our whisky and brandy flavoured marmalades. We expect them also to take our new flavours.'

Marketing objectives

- To grow sales of flavoured marmalades from £117, 000 now to £390,000 within three years.
- To grow sales of rum flavoured marmalade to £60,000 within three years.
- To grow sales of Cointreau flavoured marmalade to £60,000 within three years.

Marketing strategies

Product   – launch rum and Cointreau flavoured marmalade;
     – launch new look gift packs.

Pricing   – offer retrospective discount to major outlets based on level of annual purchases.

Promotion   – carry out high-key product launch for rum and Cointreau flavoured marmalades.

Distribution	– expand outlets in major cities in North and Scotland; – sell mini-pots through Hotel Catering Services Ltd; – expand website to allow online purchases.

Precision Valves Ltd wants to consider adding a range of filters for the water-treatment industry.

'Our main business is in selling valves to the water industry. We know this market very well and have been considering manufacturing and selling filter packages. The advantage is that we would be selling to the same customers who buy our valves. We could also build packages with filters and valves. On the downside we have to consider that we have never manufactured filters before and that we would need to invest to do this.

'We have carried out research of the market and estimated what we could achieve if all of our existing customers took only 10 per cent of their filter requirements from us in three years time.'

Key products

Cartridge filters

'We envisage that the bulk of the product we would offer would be cartridge filters. We would buy the cartridges from AMF Cuno and manufacture the housings ourselves.'

Sand filters

'We would only supply small units (up to 1 cubic metre in size). We believe we could be competitive with these sizes of vessel.'

Packages

'Many of our customers are not interested in building up units and would prefer to take filter packages. This would help us to sell our valves together with the filters.'

Marketing objectives

- Grow sales of filters to £150,000 within three years.
- Grow sales of filter packages to £200,000 within three years.

Table 8.7   Projected sales of filters, Precision Valves Ltd

<table>
<tr><td colspan="7" align="center">PRECISION VALVES LTD
SALES FIGURES (Historical and Forecast)</td></tr>
<tr><td colspan="7">SALES AREA: UK</td></tr>
<tr><td></td><td></td><td></td><td></td><td colspan="3" align="center">◄——— forecast ———►</td></tr>
<tr><td>YEAR
(all values in £k)</td><td>20X3</td><td>20X4</td><td>20X5</td><td>20X6</td><td>20X7</td><td>20X8</td></tr>
<tr><td>FILTERS</td><td></td><td></td><td></td><td>20</td><td>70</td><td>150</td></tr>
<tr><td>PACKAGES</td><td></td><td></td><td></td><td>20</td><td>100</td><td>200</td></tr>
<tr><td>TOTAL</td><td>0</td><td>0</td><td>0</td><td>40</td><td>170</td><td>350</td></tr>
</table>

Marketing strategies

Product	– produce cartridge filters and also small sand filters; – produce packages including these filters.
Pricing	– offer discount structure to key contractors.
Promotion	– mailshot/e-mailshot to water companies and water-treatment contractors; – take part in Iwex exhibition at NEC.
Distribution	– increase sales coverage by recruiting salesman for the water industry.

DEVELOPING NEW SALES AREAS

Just as basic marketing principles need to be adapted to the differences between consumer goods, industrial goods and services, consideration also needs to be given to regional and geographical differences.

We will now look at new sales areas for our sample companies and see if and how new areas can be developed.

Very small local service businesses would certainly not be thinking of expanding into export markets. However, small manufacturing units may well get a level of overseas exposure by means of their website. Even a company based in a small town could sell 'home-made English Christmas cakes' over the internet. But Jane's Beauty & Health has little interest in expanding its activity outside its home town. Its limits are expanding into different areas of the town, where it is not presently active.

The situation with AH Building is a little different. Because its service is provided at its customers' homes, it would be able to expand its activities to neighbouring towns. In considering this, it would first decide whether its local market in its own town is relatively saturated. A good example of how it might expand geographically would be with its home extensions. If there is no agent for these in neighbouring towns, and since this is a more up-market product, it could easily offer it more widely. This would involve some logistical expansion and it might need to increase its ability to deliver goods itself.

Before embarking on such an expansion AH Building would:

▦ Check the contractual position with its supplier of home extensions;
▦ Get agreement from the supplier to operate in a wider area;
▦ Work out the additional costs of travelling to the next town (say 20 miles each way) in terms of travelling costs and also travelling time that it would have to pay its workers;
▦ Decide if the margins it would make would cover these additional costs.

Prestige Cars is already operating in a wider area than its local town – though most of its business is local or is generated locally. There are only a few ways that it could consider expanding geographically, because a large part of its costs are related to the distance it has to travel on any job. It could expand in terms of 'reverse activities'. An example of this would be with regard to airport runs. It already takes people to the airport and collects them. It could try to set up business arrangements with companies at the airport for 'reverse travel', such as having a contract with various airlines to collect 'lost luggage' from the airport and return it to the owners in the area of its base.

Although we have covered a small amount of expansion, none of our companies so far has really been interested in expanding geographically.

A company like Global Fuels is likely to be more adventurous than this. Global Fuels already operates in the counties of Cornwall, Devon, Somerset, Wiltshire, Bristol and Avon. There are a number of peripheral counties such as Dorset, Gloucestershire, Hereford and Worcestershire where it doesn't currently operate. In deciding whether it would be worthwhile to expand into these new counties, there are a number of factors it would take into account:

▦ What is the mix of key industries/customer groups in these areas?
▦ Does this fit in with its target customer base?
▦ What competition will it encounter?
▦ Will the competition have advantages (near to the market) that it will not have?
▦ How near is it to each market compared to its existing markets?

When it looks at this, it can see that Dorset borders onto its existing markets of Somerset and Wiltshire. In additional to farming customers, it also sees the opportunity here of selling into the leisure industry around Corfe, Poole and Bournemouth. Gloucestershire also looks promising – very near to its home base – for farming and industrial customers. But Herefordshire and Worcestershire look less promising. They are also not far away, but are dominated by major large competitors based in the Birmingham area.

But in looking at what Global Fuels could do to expand geographically, we are covering a lot of the criteria that all companies should use when thinking of expanding – whether it is just into the next town, into the next county or into a different country.

It is important when considering expanding your business that you first of all consider the easiest and least risky ways to expand. In Chapter 6, Figure 6.1, we considered the Ansoff Matrix. We learnt that the option with the least risk is to sell your existing products into your existing markets and use your experience of both to grow market share and find new applications. The next level of risk is selling new products into existing markets or selling existing products into new markets – whether these markets are geographical or by application.

So before considering selling into any new geographical market you should carry out an audit of that market and see how it fits in with your product, your capabilities and your existing markets.

Product

- Is your product suited to this market without changes?
- Will modifications be required?
- Will you need to expand your range?

Capabilities

- Are you well placed geographically to tackle this market?
- Do you have the resources – sales, admin, service?
- What will be the impact on your cash flow?

Market characteristics

- What are the market characteristics – size, customer base, customer type?
- How do these fit with markets you cover already?
- Will you need to train your staff in new techniques to tackle this market?

Local markets

If you are a small local service company, then the next small town is not likely to be significantly different from your own town. But if you are based in a small town and your next town is a major city (or vice versa), there could be significant differences, both in the customer base and in the level of competition.

REGIONAL DIFFERENCES

Even within the UK, there can be significant differences between regions. Areas such as Cornwall or the North East have a few major areas of population and industry and many smaller towns and villages. Population density is much lower that in the South East of England or in the industrial conglomerations of Birmingham, Manchester or Leeds. This produces two opposing factors. Because of the isolation, many people prefer to deal with local businesses or distributors rather than dealing with companies a hundred miles away. But because population density is lower, a smaller number of such companies can survive and make a decent living. People often have considerable loyalty to their local community and a Southerner selling in the North of England could have just as many problems as someone from Yorkshire selling in London. Scotland and Northern Ireland are also areas with their own traditions and, in many parts, a different pace of life than that of the big industrial cities of Northern England.

The Pure Fruit Jam Company is planning to increase its UK sales by 23 per cent over the next three years. Only 10 per cent of its sales are in Scotland and it plans to double this level of sales over the next three years. It is also looking to expand sales in Wales and Northern Ireland.

All of these three areas have differences from other parts of the UK and a local patriotism with regard to their region. For the scope of this plan, we will just consider Scotland.

The company's sales in Scotland have grown over the last three years, mainly as a result of signing up supply deals with the hotel chains Jarvis and MacDonald's. Sales are entirely in the markets of 'quality shops' and 'hotels'; see Table 8.8.

Both of the hotel chains have said that they are very pleased with the quality and price of the product being supplied and the forecasts are based on those figures. The company will also be targeting quality shops. It has had success with specialist marmalades and gift packs in quality food stores in England and believes that it can repeat this success in Scotland. It will be increasing advertising and in-store promotions to help to develop the market further.

Table 8.8 Historical and forecast sales in Scotland for The Pure Fruit Jam Company

THE PURE FRUIT JAM COMPANY
SALES FIGURES (Historical and Forecast)

SALES AREA: SCOTLAND

				◄——— forecast ———►		
YEAR (all values in £k)	20X3	20X4	20X5	20X6	20X7	20X8
HOTELS	32	72	145	180	240	270
QUALITY SHOPS	35	42	51	75	100	120
OTHER	2	8	10	10	10	10
TOTAL	69	122	206	265	350	400

Precision Valves Ltd is also looking at Scotland. This has been a difficult market, mainly because it has failed to find good local distribution. It has found that the local water and waste-water companies want to deal locally with a company 'just down the road'. It now has an opportunity: its main competitor, Ace Valve Company, has just sacked its Scottish distributor, because it has purchased a small Scottish valve manufacturer and intends to use that company to sell its products in Scotland. Precision Valves has already had preliminary discussions with the distributor, based on the outskirts of Glasgow, and is optimistic of signing it up as a distributor from the start of the following year, when its contract with Ace Valve Company terminates.

OVERSEAS MARKETS

It is not possible to give detailed information on all geographical markets, but the following notes give some guidelines on the major industrial markets.

Some differences are obvious – more chocolate is sold in cold and temperate countries than in hot countries and more ice cream is sold in hot countries than in cold countries. Other differences are not so obvious. The differences between various regions of the same country are not usually as marked as those between different countries.

In marketing planning it is important to consider the suitability of a product for a particular type of market. Simple agricultural tools may find a ready market in developing and developed countries alike, but sophisticated capital equipment is more likely to find a market in developed markets. Even though luxury goods will be sold in developing countries, the size of the market for them will be proportionately larger in the richer industrialised countries.

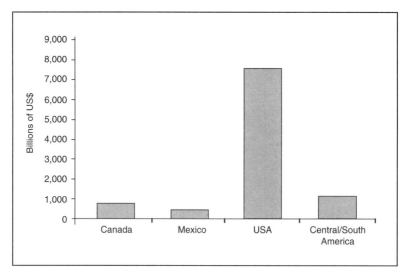

Figure 8.1 GDP data for the Americas

The measure of a country's wealth is its gross national or gross domestic product (GNP or GDP). Figures 8.1 to 8.3 show GDP at market exchange rates for 1999 for major countries and regions. It may come as a surprise to find that the GDP of Spain is as big as the GDP of the whole of Africa or that the GDP of Italy is bigger than the GDP of the whole of Central/South America.

When you consider selling to export markets, it is important to consider the cost-effectiveness of building up sales in one market rather than another. You need

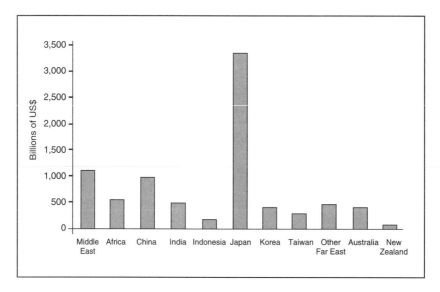

Figure 8.2 GDP data for Africa, the Middle East, Asia and Australasia

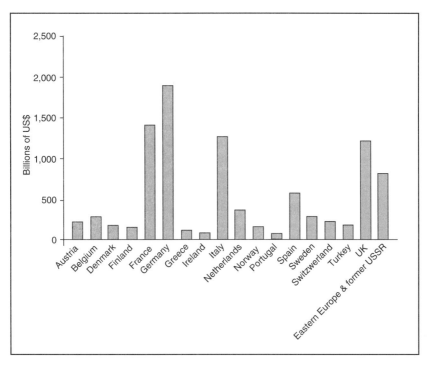

Figure 8.3   GDP data for Europe

very good reasons for developing the African or South American markets before you develop your sales in Western Europe or the USA.

The European Union (EU) and other blocs

Britain does more trade now with Europe than with any other trading bloc.

There are three major trading blocs in the world, which together account for nearly three-quarters of world trade. These are North America (USA/NAFTA), Asia Pacific (Japan/ASEAN) and the European Union (EU). Even the external trade of the EU is greater than the external trade of the USA and Japan combined. Its population is larger than that of the USA and its combined gross national product is larger than that of Japan and about the same as that of the USA. Table 8.9 shows comparative data for the EU, NAFTA and Asia Pacific.

The European Community (EC) was founded in 1957 when the Treaty of Rome was signed by West Germany, France, Italy, Holland, Belgium and Luxembourg. These countries were joined by the UK, Ireland and Denmark in 1973, Greece in 1981, Spain and Portugal in 1986, Austria and Sweden in 1995 and by Poland, Hungary, Slovenia, the Czech Republic, the Slovak Republic, Lithuania, Latvia, Estonia, Cyprus and Malta in 2004.

In 1991 in Maastricht, EU leaders agreed on the texts of a Treaty on European Union, Economic and Monetary Union (EMU) and associated protocols. The

Table 8.9 Comparative data for major trading blocs

	EU	NAFTA	Asia Pacific
Population (millions)	454	401	1750
GDP (billion $)	9053	8744	5913
Monthly car sales	1224	822	654
% of world exports	34.6	19.3	26.4

EU came into force in November 1993 and economic and monetary union with a single currency was introduced (for 12 participating nations) on 1 January 2002.

There are now 25 separate countries in the EU, ranging from Luxembourg with a population of less than half a million to Germany with a population of more than 80 million.

With the creation of the single market in 1992, the expansion into the EU in 1995 and EMU in 2002, the EU is now the 'home market' for every company operating within it. Companies based in Manchester can sell directly to customers in Rome or Frankfurt and French companies can bid for refuse collection contracts in London. There are still some obstacles, but there is now an ever-increasing move towards European rather than national standards throughout the EU.

The North American Free Trade Agreement (NAFTA) was ratified in 1993, but it is far less far-ranging than the EU treaties. It is an agreement to gradually eliminate almost all trade and investment restrictions between the USA, Canada and Mexico over 15 years. Whereas the EU is a single market, NAFTA is far less integrated. Workers cannot move freely between NAFTA countries; members of NAFTA still, unlike EU countries, take anti-dumping actions against each other; and the USA, Canada and Mexico set their own tariffs, while there is a common tariff on imports to the EU.

The Asia Pacific grouping is even looser, and whereas the EU and NAFTA are based on treaties, in Asia, economic integration is based on market forces.

Although there is talk of widening free trade areas between NAFTA and the EU, the real trend is towards regionalisation of trade, with rapid growth forecast in intra-regional trade. Many companies are responding to this trend by regionalising their sales and marketing approach into the three areas of the Americas, Europe and Asia Pacific.

China and India are also becoming of interest to all types of businesses, including small manufacturing companies. A recent report by Goldman Sachs projects that China's gross domestic product will have overtaken that of all European countries by 2010, Japan by 2016 and the USA by 2041. Over the same period it is projected that the Indian economy will also overtake the European countries, putting it fourth in size after the USA, China and Japan by 2030.

ASSISTANCE FOR EXPORTERS

During 1999, following a government review, a new organisation was established to assist UK exporters. Now called UK Trade & Investment, this organisation has developed a national export strategy that for the first time consolidates all government support for exporters under one organisation, integrating the activities of the Department of Trade and Industry, the Foreign and Commonwealth Office, overseas embassies and regional and local providers of export services in the UK. New arrangements have been established with Business Links and Chambers of Commerce.

A vast array of information on exporting and export markets is available on the UK Trade & Investment website (www.uktradeinvest.gov.uk). Information can also be accessed via Business Links (www.businesslink.gov.uk). UK Trade & Investment trade teams are available in your local Business Link, and if you enter your postcode on the UK Trade & Investment website, it will bring up the name, contact telephone number and e-mail address of an international trade adviser in your nearest Business Link. You can then contact this adviser for specific information and guidance.

Exporting can extend your available markets, boost your turnover and avoid you having too great a dependence on your UK-based customers. But moving into export is a large step for any business – so it's important that you honestly assess if you are ready and able to take on the challenge.

Here are the UK Trade & Investment's 10 key steps to successful exporting:

1. Research your market.
2. Implement an export strategy.
3. Construct an export plan.
4. Choose your sales presence.
5. Promote your product.
6. Get the legal side right.
7. Get paid on time.
8. Choose your distribution methods.
9. Transport goods effectively.
10. Have a good after-sales policy.

UK Trade & Investment has an interactive assessment tool on its website. This is a questionnaire that will help you recognise your strengths and isolate your weaknesses as you get ready to break into export markets. You can find it on the UK Trade & Investment website in the section 'Trade' under 'Are you ready to Export?'

Also to be found on the website is information about UK Trade & Investment's assessment and skills-based programme, 'Passport', which provides new and inexperienced exporters with the training, planning and ongoing support that they need to succeed overseas. It offers a business health check, mentoring from one of its local export professionals, an individual export plan and a range of developmental training from which to choose.

Before entering export markets you also need to assess the suitability of your product and decide on which markets to try to enter. Again, there is a wealth of country and sector information on the UK Trade & Investment website.

UK Trade & Investment offers a service where, for a competitive fee, you can commission research into a particular market. This can include preparation of a list of potential distributors in the country and even help in setting up meetings with these potential distributors.

UK Trade & Investment also provides support for participants in overseas exhibitions, sector-focused missions and seminars. Grants are available to help small businesses with the cost of overseas exhibitions, paying up to 50 per cent of 'eligible costs' up to a maximum of £2,500. Sector-focused trade missions last between three and eight days. Small businesses taking part in these trade missions are eligible for travel grants to cover up to half the cost of the visit. The missions are often specific to a particular industry or event.

UK Trade & Investment publishes a magazine, *Overseas Trade*, 10 times a year. This is free and an application form can be downloaded from the UK Trade & Investment website. The magazine is also available online at www.overseas-trade.co.uk.

In addition to government assistance, the independent company British Exporters (www.export.co.uk) produces a UK Exporters CD ROM and also offers a service where it publishes information on your company and its products on an export website. The service includes up to four scanned brochure pages. It also runs Supercatex low-cost catalogue exhibitions – particularly in new or emerging markets. This is a cheap way for exporters to dip their toe in the water in markets that for cost reasons they would not consider visiting, even on a trade mission. Participation costs can be as low as £100 or up to £500, depending on whether there is any government funding and the number of venues covered in a particular country. The principle of the exhibition is simple. Companies supply a company profile and a specific amount of brochures. These brochures are then exhibited in the exhibition, which is often supported by personnel from the local British Embassy or Consulate. On completion of the exhibition, a detailed report is provided on those visitors who requested each exhibitor's catalogue.

INDIVIDUAL EXPORT MARKETS

The approach to export markets is completely different to selling in your home market. Apart from distance, there are different cultures, different languages and different currencies to be dealt with. A lot of information on individual countries is available on the website of UK Trade & Investment and also on www.world atlas.com.

Key characteristics of some major export markets are given below.

Germany

Germany has the largest economy in Europe. It has a very wide industrial base, so it is extremely unlikely that you will not have any local competition. Its trading practices are open and there is therefore competition from all over the world.

Although there are a number of specific 'industrial areas' such as the Ruhr where heavy industry tends to predominate, you will find quite large industrial concerns all over Germany in towns and villages as well as in the big cities. It is quite common to find a factory almost in the middle of nowhere in a small village. There are still a large number of family-owned businesses in Germany; this is the case even with some very large organisations.

Germany is a federal republic consisting of 16 Länder or states. The distribution system reflects both the size and the federal structure of the country. Agents or distributors covering the whole country are rare and most are still regional, with the bulk of their business in either the north or the south. They may insist that they can cover the whole of Germany, but unless they have at least three or four branch offices they will not give you effective coverage. Typical distribution would be based in Hamburg, Düsseldorf, Frankfurt, Stuttgart, Munich and Berlin.

In development terms, the old 'East Germany' is still behind the west, and in spite of massive investment, it will still be at least 10 years before it really catches up. You cannot expect distribution in the east to be as comprehensive or sophisticated as in the west, but in the long term the opportunities are just as great.

For most products, the German market is at least twice as large as the UK market. There is also considerable potential to sell components to German companies that are exporting equipment or plant. In particular, Germany is very strong in mechanical engineering and the export of industrial plant. These exports have traditionally been strong in Eastern Europe and this will continue.

The Germans have a well-deserved reputation for efficiency and quality. To get into the German market you must be good at what you do and to stay there you must be able to stay ahead technically. You must be prepared to meet buyers' requirements in design, price, delivery and standards, and your literature must be available in German.

In business the Germans tend to be formal (particularly in the south of the country) and people who have been working together for 20 years will still refer to each other as 'Herr Schmidt' or 'Doctor Schmidt'. You should do the same. The US style of using first names at initial meetings is not acceptable in Germany.

France

France is the largest country in Western Europe. Twenty per cent of the population live in Paris, which has assumed an economic and commercial importance greater than that of any other city in France. Paris is the centre of industry, banking, insurance and foreign trade. Most French companies of any size have an office in Paris, whether or not this is the head office. But if your product is to be sold all over France, your distributor should have branch offices in cities such as Lyons, Marseille, Bordeaux and Nantes, otherwise you should consider appointing local agents or distributors in the regions. It is often the case that although a company has an office in Paris, the main factory is out in the provinces.

France has nearly 30 per cent of the EU's usable farmland and agriculture is a major industry occupying about 8 per cent of the working population and contributing some 6 per cent of GNP. French industrial development since 1945 has tended to favour the consumer goods industries and vehicle production. France also has well-developed defence and nuclear industries. Nevertheless, it suffers (in the same way as the UK) from a narrow industrial base. This means that although in many industries there is stiff local competition, there are many gaps that offer potential to companies with the right type and quality of product.

A knowledge of the French language is essential if you want to do business in France. This knowledge can come from a French-speaking member of your company or from English-speaking members of the staff of your distributor in France.

There are regional differences between Paris, the west and the south of the country and business tends to be conducted in a more formal manner in Paris than in the provinces. In business the French tend to be distant rather than formal. They may not be punctual themselves, but they will expect you to be punctual. If you are late for an appointment, you will be received coolly – if at all. It is true that you will be expected to shake hands at the start and end of meetings, but this is just a habit. It takes a long time to build up personal relationships when conducting business in France.

Italy

The GNP of Italy now equals or exceeds that of the UK and the importance of this market should not be underestimated.

Although Rome is the official capital of Italy, Milan is the commercial capital. Industry is concentrated in the large cities in the north of the country and the south is predominantly agricultural. A distributor or local company should therefore be set up in the north, where most industry is situated.

Engineering, construction and textiles are Italy's three biggest industries. Italian industry is well known at home and abroad for the design and style of its products.

The Italians are less formal than the Germans and less distant than the French. They are very conscious of their level and status within their company and titles are very important. They can be volatile in temperament, but are always charming – even when saying no. They are well known for their lack of punctuality and it is wise to check by telephone beforehand that your arranged meeting is still scheduled to take place. The Italians love to haggle, especially over price, and they are not well known for prompt payment. Nevertheless there are plenty of business opportunities in Italy and perseverance pays dividends in the long run.

Other European countries

None of the other European countries, with the possible exception of Russia, can compare with the UK, Germany, France and Italy in population and industrial size. The most common way of selling into the smaller countries is therefore through a local distributor. There is much French influence in Belgium. Holland and the Scandinavian countries have their own individual styles, with which the British and the Germans are familiar. The Scandinavians in particular buy and sell high-quality state-of-the-art products. The cost of doing business in these countries reflects the high cost and standard of living their citizens enjoy. Of the old Eastern European countries, Poland, Hungary and the Czech Republic have now developed into market economies. There are also good possibilities in neighbouring countries such as Romania and Bulgaria, where the infrastructure is not so well developed; this may deter your competitors and give you opportunities if you are prepared to persevere.

The USA

The USA is the world's largest economy and the GNP of just one state – California – would rank it in the top 10 nations of the world if it were a separate country. As the US market is so large in itself, many companies can make a perfectly good living without ever getting involved in exporting. Many US companies are only active in one state or one area of the USA.

In a country where individual states are often larger than several European countries, distance is a problem. You cannot deal with a company in New Jersey and assume that this company will be able to sell your product throughout the USA. Any company is only as good as its distribution network and it is quite common for a company to be 'big on the East coast but unknown on the West coast'. If you choose to sell in the USA through a local company, you will probably find that this restricts your business to the geographical areas where this company is strong.

Distributors in the USA tend to be successful in specific industries such as aerospace, chemicals, pulp and paper, and water treatment. If your product is sold into two completely different industries, you would probably have to run two completely separate sets of distributors for these industries.

Japan

Japan's economy is second only to that of the USA in size. It accounts for about two-thirds of the total GDP of the Asia Pacific region.

After the dramatic growth and yen appreciation of the 1980s, the bubble burst and through the 1990s Japan was almost continuously in recession or stagnation. This has brought about many changes within Japan and Japanese industries. The country was already moving out of the old smokestack industries and into higher-technology industries. The recessionary environment has seen the demise of the 'job for life' concept and many major Japanese companies have been forced to restructure and shed labour. Takeovers and partial takeovers of Japanese companies, such as Renault taking a major stake in Nissan, would have been unheard of only a few years earlier. Another impact of difficult times has been a greater willingness to consider importing goods and components to reduce costs. So prospects are good for companies manufacturing quality goods and components at reasonable prices. Japan is the world's largest manufacturer of motor vehicles and is a major force in semiconductors, electronic goods, machine tools and industrial robots.

Tokyo is the commercial and financial centre of Japan. The headquarters of most Japanese corporations are in the greater Tokyo area. The bulk of Japanese industry and population is situated in the coastal plain from Tokyo to Osaka.

The pace of doing business in Japan is much slower than in the USA or Europe. Much store is placed on personal relationships and doing things in the proper manner. Unless you have visited Japan it is difficult to understand how totally different it is to any other country. For 300 years until 1868 Japan was completely isolated from the outside world. In that time it developed different solutions to many problems and these were often different to the solutions adopted in the rest of the world. Over the last hundred years the Japanese have modernised by keeping the best of the old and incorporating the best of the new from outside.

If you want to do business with Japan you need to understand Japanese business etiquette. There are many books dealing with this complex subject and you should read one before starting to deal with the Japanese. In Japan, 'face' is all important. The Japanese language is very complicated and it takes at least a year of full-time study to achieve a reasonable conversational ability. The Japanese will be extremely pleased if a foreigner makes an attempt to learn a few simple words, but attempts to use a limited knowledge of the language for business conversation will normally be counterproductive. Interpreters should be used in all business dealings. It follows that you cannot just get onto a plane and set off to do business in Japan. UK Trade & Investment, through its Japan Unit, can provide a wealth of information and support materials to UK exporters entering the Japanese market. Also, the Japan External Trade Organisation (Jetro) has offices in most major industrialised countries to help promote imports to Japan (see www.jetro.go.jp).

There are still barriers to doing business in Japan, but these are coming down all the time. The biggest barrier to trade is the complex distribution system and this is a problem to new Japanese companies as well as to exporters to Japan. To do anything in Japan you need a local presence – whether this is a distributor or a local company. The most common way of dealing with Japan is to find a distributor and, as business grows, to consider setting up a joint venture company.

Initial contacts in Japan can be made through UK Trade & Investment, the British Embassy in Tokyo (Commercial Section) or by taking part in exhibitions. Many companies have been surprised at how quickly they have made progress in the Japanese market in recent years.

China and Asia Pacific

There certainly has been a dramatic shift in manufacturing eastwards – and that does not just mean Japan. Hong Kong and Singapore have already moved from the developing to the developed world. Taiwan and South Korea are not far behind.

But China is by far the biggest prize and has the biggest potential. Since Hong Kong returned to China, it continues to be a way of accessing the Chinese market, but more and more Western (and Japanese) companies are going direct, setting up joint venture companies with local partners. China will become the largest economy in the world by the middle of the 21st century. It already accounts for 3.9 per cent of the world's merchandise exports – about half the level of exports of Germany or Japan.

Although there have been sporadic problems in the upward growth of many Asia Pacific nations, most continue to show average growth rates of easily double those achieved by Western economies.

After Japan, China is the largest economy in the region. But many Western companies find it easier to get started in the more developed economies of Singapore, Taiwan or South Korea. Hong Kong is still used as a springboard for mainland China and it is the overseas Chinese who are pushing much of the development in the whole region.

The Indian sub-continent should also not be forgotten. India will be one of the top four world economies by the middle of the 21st century.

MARKETING PLANS FOR EXPORT MARKETS

Of our sample companies, only The Pure Fruit Jam Company and Precision Valves Ltd are involved in exporting their products. We have been working through an export plan for The Pure Fruit Jam Company as we have worked our way through this book, and we will now look at a sub-part of its export marketing plan. It wants to grow sales in a number of export markets, but the Japanese market is of particular interest. As part of its export plan, its sales manager has prepared a sub-plan for the Japanese market, which is shown below.

'We have been working at the Japanese market for three years and have made some progress with sales of our gift packs and mini-gift packs through the Seikokku Group. Seikokku is an 'up-market' department store with in-house food markets. We have also had success with the Golden Apricot hotel chain with our mini-pots.

'We will be repackaging gift packs and adding a mandarin orange marmalade and a sake flavoured marmalade range. These products will be packaged with local style packaging and may be sold as own label products through prestige stores such as Seikokku.

'We are using government grants to produce Japanese sales literature and also to support taking part in the Nippon Food Show in Osaka as part of the British Pavilion.

'Our contracts with Golden Apricot and Seikokku have given us good experience of how business is carried out in Japan. The Japanese like UK quality food products, which are considered to be very chic. With the 'prestige' of British quality products we are confident of major expansion here. We consider there to be considerable potential for our products and plan to increase sales from £50k to £300k within the next three years.'

Assumptions

Japanese GDP will continue to grow at a rate of 2 per cent per year over the next three years. The pound sterling will not strengthen against the yen during the timescale of the plan

The sales (history/budget) is shown in Table 8.10.

Key products

Gift packs

'Gift packs consist of either two specialist standard size jars of jam or marmalade or a gift pack of six mini-pots of different flavours. This business has really taken off with Seikokku and we hope to secure other major contracts shortly.'

Mini-pots

'We sell mini-pots mainly to hotels and airlines. Golden Apricot Hotel Group has started taking significant amounts of this product and we are near to securing a contract with the No Vacancies Group. We are also optimistic about securing contracts with major airlines. Our discussions with Japan Airlines are well advanced.'

Marmalades

'We have had no success with our full size jars of our standard marmalades, but Seikokku has expressed an interest in our whisky flavoured marmalades and we have also agreed to manufacture mandarin orange marmalade and sake flavoured marmalade for it.'

Strategic markets

'Our strategic markets are supermarkets/department stores and hotel chains. We are also optimistic about selling to Japan Airlines and All Nippon Airlines for their first-class cabins.'

Sales in these markets for 20X5 and forecasts for 20X6 to 20X8 are given in Table 8.11.

Supermarkets/department stores

'This is a major market for us in the UK and in Japan it was our first success with the Seikokku chain taking our gift packs and mini-gift packs. We are optimistic that we can sign up other chains that operate more in the west of Japan.'

Table 8.10 Sales to Japan, The Pure Fruit Jam Company

THE PURE FRUIT JAM COMPANY
SALES FIGURES (Historical and Forecast)

SALES AREA: JAPAN

YEAR (all values in £k)	20X3	20X4	20X5	20X6	20X7	20X8
					forecast	
STANDARD JAMS (340 gm)						
MARMALADES (340 gm)				15	40	60
MINI-POTS			20	60	105	150
GIFT PACKS			30	45	80	90
SPECIAL PRODUCTS						
TOTAL	0	0	50	120	225	300

Table 8.11 Sales in Japan by market, The Pure Fruit Jam Company

THE PURE FRUIT JAM COMPANY
SALES FIGURES (Historical and Forecast)

SALES AREA: JAPAN

YEAR (all values in £k)	20X3	20X4	20X5	20X6	20X7	20X8
					forecast	
QUALITY SHOPS/SUPERMARKETS			30	60	120	150
HOTELS			20	40	70	100
AIRLINES				20	35	50
TOTAL	0	0	50	120	225	300

Hotel chains

'The Golden Apricot Hotel Group has started taking significant amounts of our mini-pots and we are near to securing a contract with the No Vacancies Group.'

Airlines

'We have no business at present with Japanese airlines, but we are optimistic about selling to Japan Airlines and All Nippon Airlines for their first-class cabins.'

Key sales areas

Key sales areas are shown in Table 8.12.

East Japan

'This area encompasses greater Tokyo and most of the eastern side of Japan. Our main contacts are in Tokyo and we have had major success with Seikokku, whose head office is there. We want to find other business through companies with their head offices and central purchasing in the Tokyo area. We are hoping to conclude a deal with the No Vacancies Group based in Shinagawa.'

West Japan

'This area is based on Osaka and covers the area also to the west. We have had success here with the Golden Apricot Hotel Group.'

Hokkaido

'We have been contacted by a chain of 'hot springs' on the northern island of Hokkaido. We have sent samples and are waiting to see the results.'

Marketing objectives

- To grow sales in Japan from £50,000 to £300,000 within three years.
- To increase our sales of mini-pots to hotels from £20,000 to £100,000 within three years.
- To gain £50,000 a year of sales of mini-pots to airlines within three years.
- To increase sales to quality shops/supermarkets to £150,000 within three years.
- To grow sales of gift packs from £30,000 to £90,000 within three years.
- To sell £60,000 a year of specialist marmalades in Japan within three years.

Marketing strategies

Product	– repackage gift packs for the Japanese market – information in Japanese, but retain 'British quality feel'; – add sake flavoured marmalade to range.
Pricing	– premium price alcohol flavoured marmalades – particularly whisky and brandy.
Promotion	– use government grant to produce Japanese sales literature; – take part in Nippon Food Show in Osaka as part of the British Pavilion, using government grant support.
Distribution	– use British Embassy (Commercial Section) to help find representative in Osaka (for west of Japan).

Table 8.12 Sales into key market areas, The Pure Fruit Jam Company

THE PURE FRUIT JAM COMPANY
SALES FIGURES (Historical and Forecast)

SALES AREA: JAPAN

				← forecast →		
YEAR (all values in £k)	20X3	20X4	20X5	20X6	20X7	20X8
EAST JAPAN			35	80	150	200
WEST JAPAN			15	40	75	100
HOKKAIDO				5	10	20
TOTAL	0	0	50	125	235	320

SUMMARY

There are three basic types of products. These are consumer goods, industrial goods and services. There may also be an element of service in consumer or industrial goods. Although the key marketing principles apply to all of these types of products, they are applied differently.

Consumer markets are characterised by being large markets with a high number of individual customers. Because of the size of the markets, consumer data is widely collected and analysed and readily available.

Industrial goods are normally sold to companies that incorporate them into other products, use them in their business, or resell them. Information about industrial markets is not so easily available as consumer information, because industrial markets are more specific with less individual customers.

Services differ from other types of product in that there is no tangible product to sell and the product has no shelf life. Service organisations sell the benefits of their service as their product.

Just as basic marketing principles need to be adapted to the differences between consumer goods, industrial goods and services, regional and geographical differences must be catered for. When planning for a new product or new sales area you will probably not have any historical data yourself that can be used for planning purposes. That does not mean that no useful data exists. There are many external sources that you can use – particularly if your new sales areas will be export markets. Consideration should be given to the size and importance of different geographical markets. North America (USA/NAFTA), Asia Pacific (Japan/ASEAN and the European Union (EU) are the major trading blocs, accounting for nearly three-quarters of world trade between them.

9

Budgets and income statements

In carrying out the marketing planning process and preparing your plan, you have already seen how to decide on strategies and to prepare the action plans to enable you to carry out your strategies and achieve your objectives. You have seen how realistic objectives can be set. But what about your strategies and action plans? They may be feasible, but are they cost-effective? If the cost of implementing your strategies and carrying out your action plans is greater than the contribution to company profits resulting from the additional sales forecast in the plan, you might as well forget the plan now – unless you can devise other strategies to achieve the same objectives.

How can you decide if your marketing plan is viable? By preparing a partial profit and loss account. For sales personnel, this can be the most difficult part of the whole process. All companies have a particular way of putting together the financial data that goes into their profit and loss account. It is wise to involve someone from your finance and accounting department to help you to prepare the partial profit and loss account that you need for your plan.

PROFIT AND LOSS ACCOUNT

The profit and loss account is a summary of the success or failure of the transactions of a company over a period of time. It lists income generated and costs incurred. From the point of view of our marketing plan, we are not interested in anything below the line of operating profit, because our marketing activities will only affect items reported above this line in the profit and loss account. Basic profit and loss accounts for our sample companies, down to the operating profit level, are shown below (Tables 9.1 – 9.6).

FileMaker Pro 7: why a database is the best way to communicate, implement and monitor your marketing plan

By now you will have gained a very good insight into what is required to create your marketing plan. But this is only the beginning of your journey to success. Once the plan is written, you need to communicate the plan – to those who must approve it and to those who will implement it. Moreover, your plan needs to be flexible and dynamic in order to allow for inevitable changes to both internal and external business conditions.

Technology clearly has a role to play in a modern business. Many people will use a product such as Microsoft PowerPoint to present the initial plan. Financial information may be kept in a spreadsheet. These tools may help at the original planning and communication phase, however, all too often, people make the mistake of thinking that they are appropriate in the execution phase. The key point to bear in mind when executing your marketing plan is to realize that it is a dynamic process. Spreadsheets, word processing and presentation software are essentially static tools. With the plan agreed and communicated, you really need to be able to monitor, analyse and report on the progress you are making. Ideally, you want to have a near real-time view of your entire business.

The judgments and assumptions that your original marketing plan was based on will change. If you record your actual and planned marketing activities you will have a clear picture of your marketing mix by product and by market sector, allowing you to react to the changing conditions.

How do you achieve this? Fortunately, there is a type of software package that lends itself very well to providing a dynamic means of monitoring, analyzing and reporting on the progress of your plan. And because of its inherent flexibility, reworking your plan to take account of changing conditions is easy to achieve in minutes rather than weeks.

Using modestly-priced database software, you can have a very tight handle on the health of your business. For example, with software such as FileMaker Pro 7, it's simple to convert spreadsheet information into a database format that gives new life and possibilities to the information you've already entered. With the information in a database, you have far more flexibility in terms of sharing and communicating your marketing plan.

Another vital feature of FileMaker Pro 7 is that it allows you to start with a basic approach and then build and refine your application as you go forward.

Perhaps the most important part of the marketing planning process is how the plan is to be implemented – and how the implementation is to be monitored and measured. Unless you have a very firm grip on who is responsible for doing what and when, as well as whether you are achieving the objectives you set yourself, the best written marketing plan in the world will fail.

Ultimately, writing the marketing plan is merely the start of an ongoing iterative process. With FileMaker Pro, you can track every activity related to your marketing plan – as well as help execute the plan in the most efficient manner. For example, if your plan included an advertising campaign, you'd be able to record the costs associated with buying advertising space, track information about how many responses were generated and compare which titles perform best for you. You would be able to carry out a similar exercise with a direct marketing campaign or indeed any other element of the marketing mix. Perhaps most crucially, because all of your information is being held in one place, it is possible to review everything at one time – giving you the big picture of how your marketing plan is performing. FileMaker is also incredibly flexible when it comes to creating reports – different people, with different responsibilities, can see what they need to know about the performance of the marketing plan.

Longer term, FileMaker Pro can be used to run virtually every aspect of your business. It not only allows you to track the time, cost and resources of customer events, it can even help you organise the event itself – right down to creating forms, checklists and printing delegate badges.

In summary, the marketing plan is merely the beginning of your journey. The key to success is being able to control and adapt to the inherently dynamic nature of the business environment. Ultimately, FileMaker Pro 7 is the ideal tool for communicating, implementing and monitoring the success of your marketing plan – or indeed, your entire business.

Why not see for yourself how FileMaker Pro could make a real difference to the success of your marketing. You can obtain a free 30-day trial version from **www.filemaker.co.uk**. *Or call for more information on* **01628 534158**.

Table 9.1 Basic P&L account for Jane's Beauty & Health

	Profit and Loss account	
		£000
	Turnover	410
less	Cost of Sales	200
	Gross Profit	210
less	Operating Expenses	160
	Operating Profit	50

Table 9.2 Basic P&L account for AH Building

	Profit and Loss account	
		£000
	Turnover	700
less	Cost of Sales	400
	Gross Profit	300
less	Operating Expenses	250
	Operating Profit	50

Table 9.3 Basic P&L account for Prestige Cars

	Profit and Loss account	
		£000
	Turnover	800
less	Cost of Sales	500
	Gross Profit	300
less	Operating Expenses	250
	Operating Profit	50

For Global Fuels and our other companies an additional expense is 'distribution costs'.

Table 9.4 Basic P&L account for Global Fuels

	Profit and Loss account	
		£000
	Turnover	1800
less	Cost of Sales	1200
	Gross Profit	600
less	Distribution Costs	100
	Operating Expenses	350
	Operating Profit	150

Table 9.5 Basic P&L account for The Pure Fruit Jam Company

	Profit and Loss account	
		£000
	Turnover	2500
less	Cost of Sales	1200
	Gross Profit	1300
less	Distribution Costs	100
	Operating Expenses	600
	Operating Profit	600

Table 9.6 Basic P&L account for Precision Valves Ltd

	Profit and Loss account	
		£000
	Turnover	2500
less	Cost of Sales	1400
	Gross Profit	950
less	Distribution Costs	50
	Operating Expenses	400
	Operating Profit	500

It is important to understand the key items reported in the profit and loss account.

Turnover

The turnover represents the total amount of revenue earned during the year from the company's normal trading operations.

Cost of sales

This represents the direct costs of making the product that is sold. The costs are primarily labour and materials.

Gross profit

When the cost of sales is removed from the turnover, the resultant figure is the gross profit. This gives a direct comparison between what the 'product' can be sold for and what it costs to make. This 'margin' has to be sufficient to cover all of the costs and overheads incurred in running the business.

Other costs

These would include distribution costs, administration and operating expenses. This includes the cost of running the sales and marketing department together with advertising and promotional costs. It would also include salary costs (that are not part of the cost of sales), rates, electricity, telephone costs, heating, and depreciation of any capital equipment.

Operating profit

This is the key figure in the accounts as far as we are concerned. It is the net result of trading for the year, when total sales revenue is compared with the expenses incurred in earning that revenue. It is the ultimate measure of whether it has been worthwhile staying in business.

EXERCISE

Before you start budgeting for your marketing plan you need to familiarise yourself with the accounting practices used within your own company or business unit. If you do not already have them, you should obtain copies of your company's profit and loss account and get your accountant to explain how the distribution costs and operating expenses are calculated and allocated.

BUDGETING THE COST OF A MARKETING PLAN

Your marketing plan is part of your company business plan. The principles are the same whether you are preparing the sales budget for the overall company marketing plan or calculating the effect of an individual marketing plan (such as the UK marketing plan for Precision Valves Ltd). However, in budgeting and evalu-

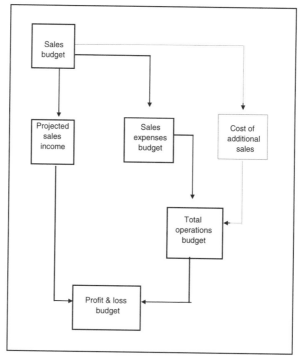

Figure 9.1 Budgeting for additional sales

ating individual marketing plans, we only need to consider part of the company budgeting process. This is shown in Figure 9.1.

It is only if your product is a new one or if you are forecasting considerable increases in business from your plan that major capital investment may also be required. Obviously, if your plan includes an increase in personnel, there will be additional requirements for office space, furniture, PCs and other equipment, which must also be budgeted for.

With our companies we are considering an increase in turnover in the plan. With a marketing plan for an individual product or market, we would not be considering the total company turnover and costs, but only the additional turnover generated by the plan and the costs associated with its implementation. Either way, it is best initially to look at the extra business separately.

There are a number of techniques that allow you to predict whether the extra business that you will generate from your plan will be profitable or not. One of the simplest is to cost up all of the expenses that you intend to incur in implementing your plan and to compare these with the contribution that will be generated by the additional sales turnover that will result from your plan. For individual plans this method is quite adequate and we will use it here. (When a new product is being introduced, more complex techniques such as break-even analysis or payback analysis can also be used. These techniques are explained further in *The Marketing Plan*, also published by Kogan Page.)

It is necessary to cost up all of the action plans for all of the different strategies through which you intend to achieve your objectives.

First let us look at the profit and loss account including operating expenses for Jane's Beauty & Health for this year before the implementation of the marketing plan. This is shown in Table 9.7.

Now let's look at a partial profit and loss account for Jane's Beauty & Health based on the additional costs of implementing its marketing plan.

In preparing this profit and loss account budget, we start at the top with the forecast sales. Here we are only showing the additional sales. The cost of sales is the direct cost, in materials and labour, of making the budgeted amount of sales. The gross profit is the 'margin' to cover other costs and to contribute to profits. In its plan, it is including taking on one additional person every year. These additional people will be mainly carrying out 'home visiting', so apart from their salary and related costs, the company will have to invest in portable packs of materials to allow them to work in people's homes. In carrying out the marketing plan, the operating expenses incurred will include administrative charges for the management of company equipment, allocation of office space (rent/rates/heating/lighting), and computer management and maintenance. In a small local company like Jane's Beauty & Health, the sales and marketing costs are limited to the preparation of leaflets for the home visiting campaign, local press advertising, the cost of the expansion of the website and the cost of the bonus scheme for frequent users.

It can be seen from Table 9.8 that the plan shows a loss in its first year and only breaks even in year two. This is quite normal. It would be nice if we could always plan to break even straight away, but in the real world it is often necessary to invest first and reap the rewards later. It would be of concern if break even was later than the second year because it would then become a vanishing horizon. In this case it would be wise to reconsider the plan.

Table 9.7 Example of P&L account including operating expenses budget, Jane's Beauty & Health

JANE'S BEAUTY & HEALTH	
PROFIT & LOSS ACCOUNT (all values in £k)	**20X5**
SALES TURNOVER	410
less COST OF SALES	200
GROSS PROFIT	210
ADMINISTRATION	15
RENT	50
RATES	20
TELEPHONE	10
ADVERTISING/MARKETING	10
OVERHEADS	35
DEPRECIATION	20
TOTAL OPERATING EXPENSES	160
OPERATING PROFIT	50

The company can now add this partial profit and loss account to its current profit and loss account to prepare a forecast of the total profit and loss account for the next three years; see Table 9.9.

Table 9.8 Partial P&L account for the additional sales included in the marketing plan, Jane's Beauty & Health

JANE'S BEAUTY & HEALTH			
EFFECT ON PROFIT & LOSS ACCOUNT OF EXTRA SALES			
(all values in £k)	20X6	20X7	20X8
SALES TURNOVER	80	150	235
less COST OF SALES	30	60	90
GROSS PROFIT	50	90	145
ADMINISTRATION	5	10	15
RENT	5	5	5
RATES	5	5	5
TELEPHONE	7	10	15
ADVERTISING/MARKETING	20	13	16
OVERHEADS	5	10	15
DEPRECIATION	5	10	15
TOTAL OPERATING EXPENSES	52	63	86
OPERATING PROFIT	−2	27	59

Table 9.9 The effect on the P&L account of the additional sales and operating expenses for implementing the new marketing plan, Jane's Beauty & Health

JANE'S BEAUTY & HEALTH			
PROFIT & LOSS ACCOUNT			
(all values in £k)	20X6	20X7	20X8
SALES TURNOVER	490	560	645
less COST OF SALES	230	260	290
GROSS PROFIT	260	300	355
ADMINISTRATION	20	25	30
RENT	55	55	55
RATES	25	25	25
TELEPHONE	17	20	25
ADVERTISING/MARKETING	30	23	26
OVERHEADS	40	45	50
DEPRECIATION	25	30	35
TOTAL OPERATING EXPENSES	212	223	246
OPERATING PROFIT	48	77	109

The complete profit and loss account for AH Building for this year is shown Table 9.10.

In its partial profit and loss account for implementing its plan (Table 9.11), AH Building is also taking into account staff changes. Jim Smith will be retiring in the first year of the plan, but the company intends to take on two apprentice bricklayers. The costs of the two new apprentices will be the same as the current costs of Jim Smith, so there are no additional labour costs in the plan.

Again there is additional investment in the first year of the plan, in marketing costs with setting up the website and administration and overhead costs are also rising. So the plan is only going to break even in the first year and major profits will come in the second and third years.

The full profit and loss account for AH Building is given in Table 9.12.

Table 9.10 P&L account for AH Building

AH BUILDING	
PROFIT & LOSS ACCOUNT	**20X5**
(all values in £k)	
SALES TURNOVER	700
less COST OF SALES	400
GROSS PROFIT	300
ADMINISTRATION	40
RENT	65
RATES	30
TELEPHONE	15
ADVERTISING/MARKETING	10
OVERHEADS	60
DEPRECIATION	30
TOTAL OPERATING EXPENSES	250
OPERATING PROFIT	50

Table 9.11   Partial P&L account for AH Building for the additional sales included in its marketing plan

AH BUILDING

EFFECT ON PROFIT & LOSS ACCOUNT OF EXTRA SALES

(all values in £k)	20X6	20X7	20X8
SALES TURNOVER	80	160	230
less COST OF SALES	45	90	102
GROSS PROFIT	35	70	128
ADMINISTRATION	5	10	15
RENT	5	5	5
RATES	2	3	5
TELEPHONE	5	8	12
ADVERTISING/MARKETING	10	5	5
OVERHEADS	5	10	15
DEPRECIATION	0	0	0
TOTAL OPERATING EXPENSES	32	41	57
OPERATING PROFIT	3	29	71

Table 9.12   The effect on the P&L account of AH Building of the additional sales and operating expenses for implementing its marketing plan

AH BUILDING

PROFIT & LOSS ACCOUNT

(all values in £k)	20X6	20X7	20X8
SALES TURNOVER	780	860	930
less COST OF SALES	445	490	502
GROSS PROFIT	335	370	428
ADMINISTRATION	45	50	55
RENT	70	70	70
RATES	32	33	35
TELEPHONE	20	23	27
ADVERTISING/MARKETING	20	15	15
OVERHEADS	65	70	75
DEPRECIATION	30	30	30
TOTAL OPERATING EXPENSES	282	291	307
OPERATING PROFIT	53	79	121

The complete profit and loss account for Prestige Cars for 20X5 is shown in Table 9.13.

Because of the cost of its car fleet and in particular the value of the luxury cars, Prestige Cars' biggest expense is depreciation. In its partial profit and loss account for implementing its plan (Table 9.14), it has added in extra money for advertising, mailshots/e-mailshots and expanding its website. During the course of the plan it does not intend to purchase any additional cars, but will just replace vehicles that have reached their replacement date. It will also be continuing its move to contract employees for the taxi side of the business.

Prestige Cars has looked at the idea of introducing electric cars as a special project, but has decided against it for now.

The full profit and loss account for Prestige Cars is shown in Table 9.15.

Table 9.13 P&L account for Prestige Cars

PRESTIGE CARS	
PROFIT & LOSS ACCOUNT	**20X5**
(all values in £k)	
SALES TURNOVER	800
less COST OF SALES	500
GROSS PROFIT	300
ADMINISTRATION	30
RENT	50
RATES	20
TELEPHONE	10
ADVERTISING/MARKETING	5
OVERHEADS	40
DEPRECIATION	95
TOTAL OPERATING EXPENSES	250
OPERATING PROFIT	50

Table 9.14 Partial P&L account for Prestige Cars for the additional sales included in its marketing plan

PRESTIGE CARS			
EFFECT ON PROFIT & LOSS ACCOUNT OF EXTRA SALES			
(all values in £k)	20X6	20X7	20X8
SALES TURNOVER	100	200	300
less COST OF SALES	62	125	187
GROSS PROFIT	38	75	113
ADMINISTRATION	10	15	20
RENT	5	5	5
RATES	2	3	5
TELEPHONE	5	8	12
ADVERTISING/MARKETING	10	10	10
OVERHEADS	5	10	15
DEPRECIATION	10	20	20
TOTAL OPERATING EXPENSES	47	71	87
OPERATING PROFIT	−9	4	26

Table 9.15 Full P&L account for Prestige Cars for implementing its plan

PRESTIGE CARS			
PROFIT & LOSS ACCOUNT			
(all values in £k)	20X6	20X7	20X8
SALES TURNOVER	900	1000	1100
less COST OF SALES	562	625	687
GROSS PROFIT	338	375	413
ADMINISTRATION	40	45	50
RENT	55	55	55
RATES	22	23	25
TELEPHONE	15	18	22
ADVERTISING/MARKETING	15	15	15
OVERHEADS	45	50	55
DEPRECIATION	105	115	115
TOTAL OPERATING EXPENSES	297	321	337
OPERATING PROFIT	41	54	76

With our three largest companies, the detail on the profit and loss account is expanded. This is because each of these companies has a separate sales department, and sales and marketing costs are more significant than with our smaller companies. For this reason the sales costs including salaries and promotional costs are listed separately.

The first spreadsheet that Global Fuels has prepared shows the operating expenses for its sales department (Table 9.16).

This shows the sales expenses for the current year and extra costs for the first year of the plan. The figure for the following year includes an inflation element and also figures based on the growth of the business or other factors. Under 'sundry items, other' is included the £10,000 to expand its website. An additional £5,000 to support mailshots/e-mailshots is shown under 'advertising'.

The partial profit and loss account for the three years of the plan is shown in Table 9.17.

Global Fuels can now add this partial profit and loss account to its current profit and loss account to prepare a forecast of the total profit and loss account for the next three years (Table 9.18).

Table 9.16   Operating expenses budget for sales department, Global Fuels

GLOBAL FUELS

OPERATING EXPENSES BUDGET FOR 20X6

Department: Sales

Item	20X5 expenses £k	Inflation %	Inflation £k	Growth £k	Other £k	20X6 expenses £k
Salaries	55	3	1.65			56.65
Recruitment	8	3	0.24			8.24
Travel/entertaining	14	3	0.42	5		19.42
Car costs	11	3	0.33	3		14.33
Advertising	19	3	0.57		5	24.57
Exhibitions	9	3	0.27	2		11.27
Literature	20	3	0.6			20.6
Sundry items	12	3	0.36		10	22.36
		3	0			0
Total	148	3	4.44	10	15	177.44

Table 9.17 Partial P&L account for the additional sales included in the marketing plan, Global Fuels

GLOBAL FUELS			

EFFECT ON PROFIT & LOSS ACCOUNT OF EXTRA SALES			
	20X6	**20X7**	**20X8**
(all values in £k)			
Invoiced sales	150	300	550
less Cost of sales	100	200	304
Gross profit	50	100	246
Sales & Marketing costs			
Salaries	2	2	3
Recruitment	0	3	0
Travel/entertaining	5	5	5
Car costs	3	5	7
Advertising	6	7	9
Exhibitions	2	5	8
Literature	1	3	5
Sundry items	10	5	5
Total sales costs	29	35	42
Administration costs	5	5	6
IT costs	2	2	3
Distribution costs	3	4	5
Total operating expenses	39	46	56
Operating profit	11	54	190

Table 9.18 P&L account projection for Global Fuels

GLOBAL FUELS			

PROFIT & LOSS ACCOUNT	20X6	20X7	20X8
(all values in £k)			
Invoiced sales	1950	2100	2350
less cost of sales	1300	1400	1504
Gross profit	650	700	846
Sales & Marketing costs			
Salaries	57	57	58
Recruitment	8	11	8
Travel/entertaining	19	19	19
Car costs	14	16	18
Advertising	25	26	28
Exhibitions	11	14	17
Literature	21	23	25
Sundry items	22	17	17
Total sales costs	177	183	190
Administration costs	160	160	161
Data processing costs	49	49	50
Distribution costs	103	104	105
Total operating expenses	489	496	506
Operating profit	161	204	340

The Pure Fruit Jam Company has two plans – one for its UK business and one for its export business. It is therefore important that in budgeting it takes into account the different costs and different margins related to each section of its business. It has therefore prepared operating expense budgets separately for both its UK and export plans.

Included in the UK figures (Table 9.19) are the salary and other costs of the sales director and marketing assistant. Advertising for 20X6 includes the cost of increased advertising in Scotland. Exhibition costs are to cover the Foodex Exhibition and also the cost of the product launch for the new marmalade range. The costs of expanding the website are also being charged to the UK sales department budget under 'sundry items'.

The partial profit and loss account for the first three years of the UK plan is shown in Table 9.20.

In its export plan, the same information is included for the export sales activities.

Table 9.19   Operating expenses budget for UK sales department, The Pure Fruit Jam Company

THE PURE FRUIT JAM COMPANY

OPERATING EXPENSES BUDGET FOR 20X6

Department: UK Sales

Item	20X5 expenses £k	Inflation %	Inflation £k	Growth £k	Other £k	20X6 expenses £k
Salaries	80	3	2.4			82.4
Recruitment	0	3	0			0
Travel/entertaining	14	3	0.42	5		19.42
Car costs	11	3	0.33	3		14.33
Advertising	30	3	0.9		30	60.9
Exhibitions	10	3	0.3	2	54	66.3
Literature	20	3	0.6		10	30.6
Sundry items	12	3	0.36		20	32.36
		3	0			0
Total	177	3	5.31	10	114	306.31

Table 9.20   Partial P&L account for the additional sales included in The Pure Fruit Jam Company's UK plan

THE PURE FRUIT JAM COMPANY

EFFECT ON PROFIT & LOSS ACCOUNT OF EXTRA UK SALES

(all values in £k)	20X6	20X7	20X8
Invoiced sales	260	460	740
less Cost of sales	130	230	370
Gross profit	130	230	370
Sales & Marketing costs			
Salaries	2	2	3
Recruitment	0	0	10
Travel/entertaining	5	7	9
Car costs	3	5	7
Advertising	31	20	25
Exhibitions	56	25	30
Literature	11	15	18
Sundry items	20	5	5
Total sales costs	129	79	107
Administration costs	10	5	6
IT costs	5	5	5
Distribution costs	5	5	5
Total operating expenses	149	94	123
Operating profit	−19	136	247

Table 9.21 Operating expenses budget for export sales department, The Pure Fruit Jam Company

THE PURE FRUIT JAM COMPANY

OPERATING EXPENSES BUDGET FOR 20X6

Department: Export Sales

Item	20X5 expenses £k	Inflation %	Inflation £k	Growth £k	Other £k	20X6 expenses £k
Salaries	50	3	1.5			51.5
Recruitment	12	3				
Travel/entertaining	20	3	0.6	20	10	50.6
Car costs	5	3	0.15	3	6	14.15
Advertising	19	3	0.57		5	24.57
Exhibitions	10	3	0.3	2	50	62.3
Literature	10	3	0.3		30	40.3
Sundry items	12	3	0.36		10	22.36
		3	0			0
Total	138	3	3.78	25	111	265.78

Table 9.22 Partial P&L account for additional sales included in the export marketing plan of The Pure Fruit Jam Company

THE PURE FRUIT JAM COMPANY

EFFECT ON PROFIT & LOSS ACCOUNT OF EXTRA EXPORT SALES

(all values in £k)	20X6	20X7	20X8
Invoiced sales	330	730	1150
less Cost of sales	198	438	690
Gross profit	132	292	460
Sales & Marketing costs			
Salaries	2	2	3
Recruitment	0	3	0
Travel/entertaining	31	5	5
Car costs	9	5	7
Advertising	6	7	9
Exhibitions	52	5	8
Literature	30	3	5
Sundry items	10	5	5
Total sales costs	140	35	42
Administration costs	5	5	6
IT costs	5	5	5
Distribution costs	5	5	5
Total operating expenses	155	50	58
Operating profit	−23	242	402

Table 9.23 Total P&L account for The Pure Fruit Jam Company for the period of its plans

THE PURE FRUIT JAM COMPANY

PROFIT & LOSS ACCOUNT

(all values in £k)	20X6	20X7	20X8
Invoiced sales	3090	3690	4390
less Cost of sales	1528	1868	2260
Gross profit	1562	1822	2130
Sales & Marketing costs			
Salaries	134	134	136
Recruitment	12	15	22
Travel/entertaining	70	46	48
Car costs	28	26	30
Advertising	85	76	83
Exhibitions	129	50	58
Literature	71	48	53
Sundry items	55	34	34
Total sales costs	584	429	464
Administration costs	235	230	232
Data processing costs	75	75	75
Distribution costs	110	110	110
Total operating expenses	1004	844	881
Operating profit	558	978	1249

Included in the export figures (Table 9.21) are the salary and related costs for the sales manager. Increased travelling costs are shown under 'growth' for the sales manager's costs and under 'other' for travel costs for the sales director to support major overseas exhibitions. Exhibition costs are for the Nippon Food Show in Osaka, Japan and Hotel Suppliers 20X6 in Chicago, USA. Literature costs include the provision of Japanese literature and also the cost of specific materials for the USA exhibition.

The partial profit and loss account for the first three years of the export plan is shown in Table 9.22.

Although The Pure Fruit Jam Company is producing two separate plans, what is important is the overall company profit and loss account. This is shown in Table 9.23.

Precision Valves Ltd has prepared a spreadsheet showing the operating expenses for its UK sales department for its UK plan (Table 9.24).

This shows the sales expenses for the current year and the extra costs for the first year of the plan. Salary costs for this year include the sales manager's salary and related costs. In 20X6 a new sales engineer will be recruited for water industry sales. Under 'other' are included salary and related costs and also costs for a company car and for travel and entertaining. Under 'advertising' it has included the cost of its advertising campaign and mailshots/e-mailshots for the water industry and under 'exhibitions' it has included the costs of the Iwex exhibition in Birmingham.

In addition it has prepared a partial profit and loss account for the three years of the plan; see Table 9.25.

Precision Valves Ltd can add this to its current profit and loss account for its UK operations to produce a forecast profit and loss account for the plan (Table 9.26).

Table 9.24   Operating expenses for UK sales department, Precision Valves Ltd

PRECISION VALVES LTD

OPERATING EXPENSES BUDGET FOR 20X6

Department: Sales

Item	20X5 expenses £k	Inflation %	Inflation £k	Growth £k	Other £k	20X6 expenses £k
Salaries	45	3	1.35		25	71.35
Recruitment	2	3	0.06		9	11.06
Travel/entertaining	9	3	0.27		7	16.27
Car costs	11	3	0.33		8	19.33
Advertising	19	3	0.57		11	30.57
Exhibitions	9	3	0.27		28	37.27
Literature	20	3	0.6		7	27.6
Sundry items	6	3	0.18		5	11.18
		3	0			0
Total	121	3	3.63	0	100	224.63

Table 9.25 Partial P&L account for the additional sales included in the marketing plan, Precision Valves Ltd

PRECISION VALVES LTD			
EFFECT ON PROFIT & LOSS ACCOUNT OF EXTRA SALES			
	20X6	20X7	20X8
(all values in £k)			
Invoiced sales	400	770	1140
less Cost of sales	240	462	684
Gross profit	160	308	456
Sales & Marketing costs			
Salaries	26	2	3
Recruitment	9	3	0
Travel/entertaining	7	5	5
Car costs	8	5	7
Advertising	12	7	9
Exhibitions	28	5	8
Literature	8	3	5
Sundry items	5	5	5
Total sales costs	104	35	42
Administration costs	10	20	30
IT costs	15	15	15
Distribution costs	20	38	57
Total operating expenses	149	108	144
Operating profit	11	200	312

Table 9.26 P&L account projection for UK operations of Precision Valves Ltd

PRECISION VALVES LTD			
PROFIT & LOSS ACCOUNT (UK operations only)			
	20X6	20X7	20X8
(all values in £k)			
Invoiced sales	2400	2770	3140
less Cost of sales	1440	1662	1884
Gross profit	960	1108	1256
Sales & Marketing costs			
Salaries	71	47	48
Recruitment	11	5	2
Travel/entertaining	16	14	14
Car costs	19	16	18
Advertising	31	26	28
Exhibitions	37	14	17
Literature	28	23	25
Sundry items	11	11	11
Total sales costs	225	156	163
Administration costs	158	168	178
Data processing costs	62	62	62
Distribution costs	120	138	157
Total operating expenses	565	524	560
Operating profit	395	584	696

This is only a forecast for UK operations and would need to be combined with the profit and loss account for its export sales to produce a total company profit and loss account. In terms of the company's published accounts, it is the total profit and loss account that is important, but separating out into the UK and export plans and UK and export accounts allows the management to see how profitable the two parts of the business are.

EXERCISE

Now detail the initial operating expenses budget for the sales department in your plan. Also prepare a partial profit and loss account for the additional sales and additional costs included in your plan.

....

....

....

SUMMARY

Because there is no point in proceeding with your marketing plan unless it is going to increase company profits, you need to be able to evaluate its cost-effectiveness. You need to budget for the extra costs of your plan and to confirm that the return in increased contribution and profit justifies the expenditure involved.

In the preparation of marketing plans for individual products or markets, you need to consider the additional turnover and contribution generated by the plan and the costs associated with its implementation. A partial profit and loss budget should be prepared.

In preparing the overall company marketing plan you must prepare the sales budget, which consists of the projected sales income, and the selling expenses budget. These are then fed into the overall company budget, to be included in the company business plan.

10

Writing and presenting your plan

Now that you have collected all of the information for your plan, you can prepare the written document and set about communicating it effectively to the relevant people in your company and to other interested parties such as your financial advisers or bank.

The written plan should only contain the key information that needs to be communicated – it should be clear and concise, and excessive or irrelevant detail should be excluded. The bulk of the internal and external market research information collected in the course of the preparation of the plan should not be included in the written plan since this would only confuse the reader. The detail of all of the individual action plans would also be excluded from the main document, although a summary of very important action plans may be included. Other key information that you want to include should be put in appendices and not in the main document. The scope and length of the written document will also depend on the type and size of company preparing the plan and the depth of products and markets covered.

The written plan must be clear, concise and easy to read. The following points give some guidelines:

- Start each complete section on a new page – even if this means that some pages have only five or ten lines of text on them.
- When listing key points, use double spacing.
- Do not try to cram too many figures onto one page.
- Do not reduce the size of documents used in the plan to a point where they become difficult to read.
- Use a reasonable font size when printing the document.
- If the plan is too long it will just not be read, so be ruthless and cut out unnecessary text.
- Do not use jargon that may not be understood by all those who will receive the plan, and be sure to expand any abbreviations to their full form at their first appearance.

CONTENTS

Section		Page
1	INTRODUCTION	2
2	EXECUTIVE SUMMARY	3
3	SITUATION ANALYSIS	
	3.1. Assumptions	4
	3.2. Sales (History/Budget)	5
	3.3. Strategic Markets	7
	3.4. Key Products	9
	3.5. Key Sales Areas	11
4	MARKETING OBJECTIVES	13
5	MARKETING STRATEGIES	14
6	SCHEDULES	18
7	SALES PROMOTION	19
8	BUDGETS	20
9	PROFIT AND LOSS ACCOUNT	22
10	CONTROLS	23
11	UPDATE PROCEDURES	24
	APPENDIX 1	26
	APPENDIX 2	32

Figure 10.1   Contents list of a complete marketing plan

If you are careful in the way that you write the plan, you can use many of the individual sections as presentation slides.

You should start with a table of contents, which will enable the reader to quickly locate the various sections of the plan. Figure 10.1 shows how the table of contents should be set out.

Depending on the scope of your plan, you may need to omit or combine certain sections.

INTRODUCTION

This gives the background to the plan and the reasons for its preparation, and outlines its purposes and uses.

Our sample companies have prepared introductions to their plans.

The introduction to the plan for Jane's Beauty & Health is as follows:

'We have grown the business steadily since we started out five years ago. We feel that we have reached the limits that we can with our current set-up at our City Centre shop. We therefore decided to analyse our business to decide how we could best carry out our next stage of expansion.'

AH Building starts its plan:

'After the stagnation of two to three years ago, we have made significant sales growth in the last year – principally with our home extensions. We have now decided to analyse our business to decide how we can grow it further in a profitable way.'

For Prestige Cars:

'Prestige Cars started off as a taxi company. With the transfer of the business to new owners three years ago, we have moved the business rapidly into a chauffeur hire company. This plan analyses our business and recommends ways to expand from our present customer base.'

The introduction for Global Fuels is:

'Global Fuels is a supplier of bulk oil products in the South West of England. We have a mix of customers varying from individual homes and farms, to large industrial companies. We started in home heating oils, but have expanded into diesel and lubricating oils.'

The Pure Fruit Jam Company begins both its UK and export plans with the following introduction:

'The Pure Fruit Jam Company is a manufacturer of specialist jams and conserves. The company uses only fresh fruits and ingredients and we have had considerable success with the trend towards organic and "non-synthetic" products. We intend to build on our success.'

The introduction to the UK plan for Precision Valves Ltd is:

'UK sales have stagnated in recent years. The water industry has always been our main industry. After privatisation of the Water Authorities the company did well. But the private water companies have cut back on investment in recent years. With the enforcement of EU directives for water treatment and sewage disposal, the industry is now again carrying out a major capital improvement programme. It was therefore felt by the sales and marketing director that we needed to analyse our position in the market and prepare for growth to take advantage of the increased level of spending by the industry.'

EXERCISE

Now prepare an introduction for your plan:

....
....
....

EXECUTIVE SUMMARY

The summary should present the key points of the plan in a clear and concise form. It should not be too long or verbose. All personnel reading the plan should be able to understand the essence of the plan from this summary.
    The summary should always include:

∎   the underlying assumptions on which the plan is based;
∎   the objectives of the plan;
∎   the timescale over which the plan will be implemented.

Although you can draft out an executive summary at any time, you cannot finalise the text until the plan is complete.

The executive summary for the marketing plan of Jane's Beauty & Health is given below:

'Although our sales have grown steadily over the last five years, we have seen a plateau in our standard treatments of facials, manicure and pedicure. Massage and aromatherapy have been our biggest growth areas in recent years. We believe that we can grow this business further, both from our existing premises and also by providing a 'home-visiting' service. We also believe that we can expand our traditional business by means of 'home-visiting', without the need to expand our premises or take on the heavy financial commitment of additional premises.

'The objective of this plan is to grow the business by 15 per cent a year in real terms over the next three years. If we are successful, we will consider opening new outlets as the second stage of our expansion plan.'

AH Building summarised its plan in the following way:

'The company is now solid and has started to grow since we took on the Monarch range of home extensions and conservatories. We see further potential to grow this side of the business and also to expand our roofing business, which we only started two years ago.

'The objective of this plan is to grow the business by about 10 per cent a year in real terms over the next three years.'

Prestige Cars' executive summary is:

'Four years ago, the company was a small taxi firm competing with many other taxi companies in the locality. Over the last three years we have not tried to expand this part of the business. Instead we have expanded our chauffeur hire business. Recently we have put significant additional effort into two new areas – people carriers and luxury cars.

'Our business with people carriers is growing steadily, but our chauffeur luxury car hire has expanded rapidly. We see scope to develop both of these parts of our business further – particularly the luxury car hire.

'The objective of this plan is to grow the business by 9 per cent a year in real terms over the next three years.'

Global Fuels has the following summary:

'Our business was stagnating until we decided to move into related products. We are now making a good return with red diesel and lubricating oils and see great possibilities to grow our business with these products.

'The objective of this plan is to grow the business by 25 per cent over the next three years.'

The Pure Fruit Jam Company has the following executive summary for its UK plan:

'Sales growth in the UK has been sporadic, with stagnation in the sales of standard jams and marmalades. But our mini-pots have been well received by hotel chains and airlines. We have also seen growth in our special products, particularly the whisky and brandy "Scottish" and "French" breakfast marmalades. With added sales from our website and the relaunch of our gift packs, we are confident of a rapid rise in sales over the next three years. The objective of this plan is to increase UK sales by 23 per cent over the next three years, from an estimate of £2 million this year to £2,740,000 in 20X8.'

For its export plan the summary is considerably different:

'We only started in the export market five years ago and have made considerable progress, so that export sales now represent 20 per cent of our total sales. Our marmalades are selling well in the USA and Europe and our mini-pots are well received by hotel chains and airlines. Our website is also progressing well and with the introduction of our online purchasing service we expect to increase sales of our gift packs and special products.

Our new sales manager has experience of export markets and will help us in our growth.

The objective of this plan is to triple our export sales from an estimated £500,000 this year to £1,650,000 in three years time.'

Finally, Precision Valves Ltd has the following summary for its UK plan:

'Although sales of our core product of cast iron ball valves have fallen in recent years, we have seen growth in other products, such as the small type 'S' stainless steel valves for specialised applications. We also sell these valves in packages. With the new investment programmes being announced by the majority of the water companies, we believe that prospects are good to grow these sales further. In addition, the sourcing of castings for our cast iron ball valves from China gives us the opportunity to sell these products at a lower price (competing with imported products), and also to increase our margins.

'The objective of this plan is to increase UK sales by 40 per cent in real terms over the next three years, from an estimate of £2 million this year to £3,140,000 in 20X8.'

EXERCISE

Sketch out below your first attempt at an executive summary for your plan. This should then be checked and, if necessary, amended when your plan is complete:

....

....

....

SITUATION ANALYSIS

In the written plan, the situation analysis should include only the summaries of the external and internal marketing research and the key resulting SWOT analysis. These are included under the headings:

- the assumptions;
- a summary of historical and budgeted sales;
- a review of strategic markets;
- a review of key products;
- a review of key sales areas.

There will be some overlap between the reviews of strategic markets, key products and key sales areas, because it is possible to show the mix in different ways. The important thing is to present the information in a manner that highlights the key points you are trying to convey to those who read the plan. Often the SWOT analyses are put together in the appendix.

Assumptions

These are the key facts and assumptions on which the plan is based. They should be few in number and should relate only to the key issues that would significantly affect the likelihood of the plan's marketing objectives being achieved. Each assumption should be a brief factual statement.

If it is possible for the plan to be implemented regardless of an assumption, then that assumption is not necessary and should be removed from the plan. The only assumptions included in the plan should be the key planning assumptions that would significantly affect the likelihood of the marketing objectives being achieved. They would normally relate to external factors over which the company has no control.

Our sample companies listed their assumptions in Chapter 4.

The example of assumptions for Jane's Beauty & Health in its plan is:

▪ inflation will remain at 3 per cent in 20X6, rising to 4 per cent in 20X7 and 20X8;
▪ interest rates will remain in the range 5 to 6 per cent over the period of the plan;
▪ company wage increases will not exceed inflation over the next three years.

EXERCISE

Check the list of the assumptions that you prepared in Chapter 4 and list below the assumptions that you will include in your marketing plan:

....
....
....
....

Sales

In this section you should include historical sales going back three years together with sales forecasts for the next three years. Unless you state otherwise, it will be assumed that the years shown in your forecast are calendar years. You should use invoiced sales rather than order intake figures as the basis of the plan, because other departments in the company, such as production and finance, can only operate on sales figures. You will, however, need to include order intake figures in your plan as well, because these will be the order budgets that the sales department will work to. More detail would normally be included with regard to the next 12 months' sales forecast since this will become the annual budget for the product or area covered by the plan.

In this section under 'sales' you would normally only include the sales projection for the total area and products. A more detailed breakdown into individual products and sub-areas would be included under key products, key sales areas or in the appendix to the plan. The format for setting out this information follows the guidelines given in Chapter 2.

The sales projection for AH Building is shown in Table 10.1.

Table 10.1 Sales projection for AH Building

AH BUILDING						
SALES FIGURES (Historical and Forecast)						
SALES AREA: ALL				forecast		
YEAR	**20X3**	**20X4**	**20X5**	**20X6**	**20X7**	**20X8**
(all values in £k)						
EXTENSIONS	120	180	220	250	280	300
MODIFICATIONS	250	220	230	230	230	230
DAMP TREATMENT	90	80	100	100	100	100
ROOFING	20	50	100	150	200	250
OTHER	40	60	50	50	50	50
TOTAL	520	590	700	780	860	930

EXERCISE

Prepare a sales projection for your own company for your plan:

....
....
....

Strategic markets

In this section you should include historical information and forecasts for the company's sales in key industry sectors. The information can be presented in two ways: 1) showing the percentage of company sales into each market, or 2) showing the percentage share of individual markets that the company believes that it has.

Only include your key markets – ideally this should be between three and six industries, because if you sell to only one industry you will be very vulnerable to changes or fluctuations within that industry. This type of information can be presented in either tabular or graphical form.

Table 10.2 Presentation of sales by strategic market, Global Fuels

GLOBAL FUELS	SALES – STRATEGIC MARKETS			
YEAR	**20X5** **£k**	**%**	**20X8** **£k**	**%**
HOME HEATING	900	50	960	41
INDUSTRIAL	660	37	850	36
FARMING	120	7	270	11
LEISURE	70	4	220	9
OTHER	50	3	50	2
TOTAL	1800	100	2350	100

Table 10.2 is a representation for Global Fuels in tabular form and Figures 10.2 and 10.3 are representations in graphical form. You should also include some background notes on the key industries.

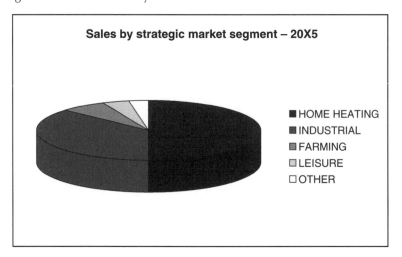

Sales by strategic market segment – 20X5

- ■ HOME HEATING
- ■ INDUSTRIAL
- ■ FARMING
- ▫ LEISURE
- ▫ OTHER

Figure 10.2 Presentation of sales by strategic market in graphical form, Global Fuels: 20X5

Here are Global Fuels' notes on its strategic markets.

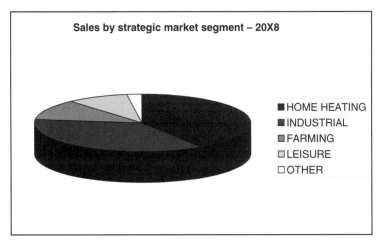

Figure 10.3 Presentation of sales by strategic market in graphical form, Global Fuels, 20X8

Strategic markets

Home heating

'This is a steady sector, making up about half of our sales (four years ago this was 90 per cent of sales). Business is mainly in the winter months, although an increasing number of customers take advantage of our "summer discount" incentives. Margins are low in this competitive market.'

Industrial

'Our main customers in this sector take heavy fuel oils (for industrial burners) and lubricating oils, which are becoming a growing part of our product offering.'

Farming

'Our sales in farming used to be exclusively heating oils, but since we expanded into selling red diesel, this has been an increasing part of our farming sales. We tend to deal with the smaller farmers and smallholders, who appreciate our policy of delivering any quantity. For the really large farms we tend to lose out to the national fuel supply companies, which offer large discounts for bulk deliveries that we cannot compete with.'

Leisure

'This is a relatively new sector for us and sales are mainly red diesel. John knows the leisure market from his days at Atkins plc and he is actively expanding our sales. We are particularly keen to break into the powerboat market based around Weston-super-Mare and Newquay.'

EXERCISE

Prepare information on your strategic markets for inclusion into your marketing plan.

....
....
....

Key products

This section lists your key products and details technological and commercial factors relating to them. This would include the results of the SWOT analysis on your products and your competitors' products. The information could also be included in a product portfolio matrix.

A SWOT analysis for a product and the product portfolio matrix for Prestige Cars are shown in Figures 10.4 and 10.5.

The narrative for the portfolio matrix shown in figure 10.5 reads:

'"Chauffeur-driven cars" are a good cash cow. Prestige Cars is well known for this service, so no advertising is necessary, but margins are fairly good.

'"Chauffeur-driven people carriers" are already a star, and 'chauffeur-driven luxury cars", although still a question mark, are rapidly moving into star territory.

'"Taxis" are fast becoming a dog, but at the moment are too large a part of the turnover to consider dropping.'

This is followed by a summary of the company's key products:

Key products

Taxi hire

'This was our original business, but it is low margin and highly competitive. As we have moved upmarket, we have tried to farm out more of this to contract drivers.'

STRENGTHS	WEAKNESSES
– good range of products: Rolls Royce, Bentley, stretched limos – product enthuses luxury	– each car costs £50k+ – high running costs – need high usage rate to make profit
OPPORTUNITIES	**THREATS**
– add specialist large old US cars (50s/60s type)	– if competitors move into this product, it could start a price war

Figure 10.4   Prestige Cars SWOT for a product – chauffeur-driven luxury cars

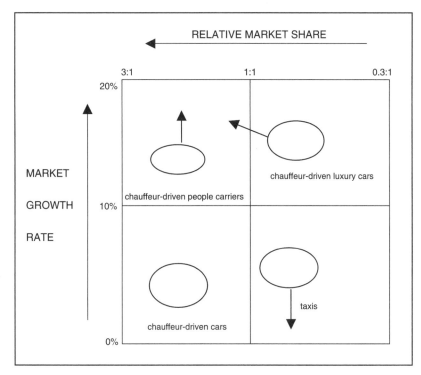

Figure 10.5 Portfolio matrix for Prestige Cars

Chauffeur-driven cars

'The main activity with this product is for business customers. The cars are used extensively for airport runs and customer hotel collections. There is also a growing market for supermarket runs for retired people who no longer want to drive themselves.'

Chauffeur-driven people carriers

'These are used mainly for groups. This can be business customers going to/from restaurants, but also families going out for parties, to restaurants, etc. Birthday party collections is a new activity that we are developing in conjunction with various playgroups in the town.'

Chauffeur-driven luxury cars

'This is a rapidly growing area for us. We have two Rolls Royces, one Bentley and two stretched limos. This is a luxury product and is often sold for birthdays, weddings and other special occasions. We want to expand into children's birthday parties, with one of the Rolls Royces marketed as "Chitty Chitty Bang Bang". We are the only company in the locality offering this type of product, so margins are good even if running costs are high. The high cost of the cars is a barrier to entry to competitors.'

EXERCISE

Prepare key product information for the products included in your plan:

....

....

....

Key sales areas

This information is presented in the same way as the information on strategic markets, but gives the information relating to geographical areas instead of industry sectors. The information can be presented in tabular form as in Table 10.3 or in graphical form as in Figure 10.6. The information shown is included by Precision Valves Ltd in its marketing plan – some in the main text and some in the appendix.

Table 10.3 Representation of key sales areas, Precision Valves Ltd

PRECISION VALVES LTD
KEY SALES AREAS

YEAR	20X5		20X8	
	£k	%	£k	%
SOUTH	800	40	1500	48
MIDLANDS	420	21	590	19
NORTH	640	32	850	27
WALES	60	3	70	2
SCOTLAND/NI	80	4	130	4
TOTAL	2000	100	3140	100

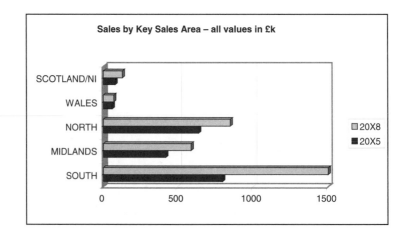

Figure 10.6 Graphical representation of key sales areas, Precision Valves Ltd

The narrative in Precision Valves Ltd plan reads as follows:

Key sales areas

South

'This is a good market for us, accounting for 40 per cent of UK sales. There is a large industrial base, and also many major water and sewage works for towns such as London, Reading, Southampton, etc. The main water-treatment contractors with UK and export business are also based here – Black & Veach, Biwater and Veolia.'

Midlands

'A declining market for us. Only Severn Trent Water remains as a major customer.'

North

'This area accounts for 32 per cent of UK sales. As well as North West and Northumbrian Water, the North is home to the major remaining chemical plants in the UK. This is concentrated in the Manchester/Liverpool and Teesside areas.'

Wales

'Major customers in Wales include Welsh Water and BP.'

Scotland/NI

'We find it difficult to penetrate this market, but now that the Ace Valve Company have sacked their Scottish distributor, we have an opportunity.'

EXERCISE

Now prepare similar information on your own key areas:

....

....

....

In the narrative of your plan you should include relevant information on the size of each key market, growth rates, and your position in each market now and projected for the future. You should also include comments that may relate to your distributor, agent or other methods of distribution in that market.

MARKETING OBJECTIVES

This is a list of the objectives that are to be achieved, quantified in terms of order intake, sales turnover, market share and profit. In the written plan you should list your key objectives only. The key objectives are overall objectives.

The marketing objectives included by The Pure Fruit Jam Company in its UK plan are as follows:

- to increase sales of marmalades by 28 per cent in real terms in three years;
- to increase sales of mini-pots by 44 per cent in real terms in three years;
- to increase by five times our sales of gift packs in three years;
- to increase sales of special products by 41 per cent in real terms in three years.

The objectives for its export marketing plan are:

- to double sales of standard jams in three years;
- to triple sales of marmalades in three years;
- to quadruple sales of mini-pots in three years;
- to increase by five times our sales of gift packs in three years.

EXERCISE

Now list the key objectives for your marketing plan:

....
....
....

MARKETING STRATEGIES

You should indicate whether you are adopting defensive, developing or attacking strategies – or a mixture of different types. The individual strategies should then be listed under the headings of the four main elements of the marketing mix:

- strategies relating to *products;*
- strategies relating to *pricing;*
- strategies relating to *advertising/promotion;*
- strategies relating to *distribution.*

There may be some overlap between the individual categories, but this does not matter so long as all of the strategies are listed.

In its marketing plan, Global Fuels will be using defensive strategies to protect its existing sales of heating oils and developing strategies to expand its sales of red diesel in the leisure industries. It will be using developing strategies with existing customers (which purchase other products) and attacking strategies (to find new customers) for a range of lubricating oils used in vacuum applications. It has identified the chemical industry around Bristol as a target with the introduction of ATEX regulations for explosive atmospheres. It sees good potential to expand lubricating oil sales into this sector.

Products

expand product range	– increase range of lubricating oils on offer to include special vacuum oils.
Pricing,	– for summer deliveries (heating oil);
discount policy	– for winter deliveries (red diesel for leisure use).
Promotion	
change advertising/	– take part in local exhibitions;
sales promotion;	– mailshots/e-mailshots to local chemical and food; processing companies;
	– mailshots/e-mailshots to boat clubs.
Distribution, telesales	– to chemical and food producers for vacuum oils;
	– to promote red diesel through garden centres;
expand website	– to take orders online.

EXERCISE

Now list the key strategies for your marketing plan.
Products

....
....
....

Price

....
....
....

Promotion

....

....

....

Distribution

....

....

....

SCHEDULE OF WHAT/WHERE/HOW

This is the master schedule showing the programme for the implementation of the action plans. Each action plan would be listed either in the master schedule or in a sub-schedule for the functions of product, pricing, promotion or distribution. These schedules indicate to each department and to each member of staff their responsibilities and the timetable for carrying them out. They should take the form of bar charts. An example from the marketing plan of Precision Valves Ltd is shown in Table 10.4.

The detailed action plans would not be included in the main body of the marketing plan, but could be included in an appendix.

Table 10.4   Master schedule for UK plan for Precision Valves Ltd

MASTER SCHEDULE		
Year: 20X6		

Month	1 2 3 4 5 6 7 8 9 10 11 12	**Responsibility**	
Action Plan		**Dept**	**Person**
Mailshot	⟶	Marketing	AJK
Press advertising	⟶	Marketing	AJK
Exhibition	⟶	Marketing	AJK
Pricing	⟶	Sales	EGM
Distribution	⟶	Marketing	AJK
Expand website	⟶	IT	JAF

EXERCISE

Prepare a master schedule for your own plan:

....

....

....

SALES PROMOTION

Under this heading you should detail your advertising and promotions plan. This includes your personnel requirements as well as advertising and sales promotion.

You should define the mix of distribution channels that you will be using and the structure of your sales organisation, including any changes that you intend to make as part of your plan. You should include a list of existing and additional sales personnel as well as an organisation chart for the sales department. The charts can be included as an appendix to the main plan. Examples of the sales organisation charts and the presentation of existing and additional personnel used by our sample companies were given in Chapter 7 in Figures 7.4 to 7.15.

You should include the details and costs of your advertising and sales promotion campaigns. A detailed advertising and promotions schedule for the next 12 months should also be included where appropriate.

BUDGETS AND THE PROFIT AND LOSS ACCOUNT

The minimum information that should be included is the total cost of implementing the plan. This needs to confirm that the return in increased contribution and profit justifies the expenditure in the action plans and the advertising and promotion plan. The budgeted extra costs will have an effect on the company profit and loss account. The additional sales projected by the plan and the extra costs involved must be presented in the written plan in a way that shows the extra contribution that the plan will make to company profits. They can also be presented as a complete profit and loss account for the area and products of the plan. Examples of this were given in Chapter 9.

The operating expenses budget for the sales department of Global Fuels for the first year of its plan is shown in Table 10.5.

A partial profit and loss account for Precision Valves Ltd for its UK plan is shown in Table 10.6.

Table 10.5 Operating expenses budget for sales department, Global Fuels

GLOBAL FUELS

OPERATING EXPENSES BUDGET FOR 20X6

Department: Sales

Item	20X5 expenses £k	Inflation %	Inflation £k	Growth £k	Other £k	20X6 expenses £k
Salaries	55	3	1.65			56.65
Recruitment	8	3	0.24			8.24
Travel/entertaining	14	3	0.42	5		19.42
Car costs	11	3	0.33	3		14.33
Advertising	19	3	0.57		5	24.57
Exhibitions	9	3	0.27	2		11.27
Literature	20	3	0.6			20.6
Sundry items	12	3	0.36		10	22.36
		3	0			0
Total	148	3	4.44	10	15	177.44

Table 10.6 Partial P&L account for the additional sales included in Precision Valves Ltd UK plan

PRECISION VALVES LTD

EFFECT ON PROFIT & LOSS ACCOUNT OF EXTRA SALES

(all values in £k)

	20X6	20X7	20X8
Invoiced sales	400	770	1140
less Cost of sales	240	462	684
Gross profit	160	308	456
Sales & Marketing costs			
Salaries	26	2	3
Recruitment	9	3	0
Travel/entertaining	7	5	5
Car costs	8	5	7
Advertising	12	7	9
Exhibitions	28	5	8
Literature	8	3	5
Sundry items	5	5	5
Total sales costs	104	35	42
Administration costs	10	20	30
IT costs	15	15	15
Distribution costs	20	38	57
Total operating expenses	149	108	144
Operating profit	11	200	312

Our final example is the full profit and loss account for The Pure Fruit Jam Company (Table 10.7).

Table 10.7 Total P&L account for The Pure Fruit Jam Company for the period of its plans

THE PURE FRUIT JAM COMPANY

PROFIT & LOSS ACCOUNT

(all values in £k)	20X6	20X7	20X8
Invoiced sales	3090	3690	4390
less Cost of sales	1528	1868	2260
Gross profit	1562	1822	2130
Sales & Marketing costs			
Salaries	134	134	136
Recruitment	12	15	22
Travel/entertaining	70	46	48
Car costs	28	26	30
Advertising	85	76	83
Exhibitions	129	50	58
Literature	71	48	53
Sundry items	55	34	34
Total sales costs	584	429	464
Administration costs	235	230	232
Data processing costs	75	75	75
Distribution costs	110	110	110
Total operating expenses	1004	844	881
Operating profit	558	978	1249

EXERCISE

Prepare a profit and loss account for your plan:

....
....
....

CONTROLS AND UPDATE PROCEDURES

It is important to have a suitable monitoring and control system to measure performance in achieving the objectives of the marketing plan and to recommend corrective action where necessary. The control process involves:

- Establishing standards – these would relate to the budgeted sales and costs and the timescales for the implementation of the action plans.
- Measuring performance – this would compare actual performance against the standards.
- Proposing measures to correct deviations from the standard – by detailing corrective procedures to be implemented if the variation from the standard exceeds certain limits. These limits should be defined in the written plan.

The control system will operate on the people who are responsible for implementing the plan rather than on the schedules and costs themselves. It should be easy to operate and should allow reasonable variations from the standards before it comes into action.

For a complex plan for a medium-sized company, the controls should be detailed in the written plan. Precision Valves Ltd has included the following controls in its plan: 'There will be quarterly marketing plan meetings. A summary of costs against budget and actual progress against the schedules will be prepared for these meetings. A report on the implementation of the action plans will also be presented at these meetings.'

Your marketing plan is not set in stone. As you implement it you will find that economic conditions may change, certain strategies may not be as effective as you thought and there may be delays in the implementation of some action plans. Conversely the plan may prove more successful than you anticipated and order intake levels expected in two years may be achieved in one year.

Because of this, an update procedure should be included in the written plan. This may simply state 'This plan is to be revised every 12 months.' Certainly all marketing plans should be updated on an annual basis.

EXERCISE

State the controls and update procedures for your plan:

....
....
....

PRESENTING THE PLAN, FOLLOW UP AND REVISION

If you have been preparing sections of your plan as you have worked your way through this book, you should now have completed your plan. You can compare it with the final versions of the marketing plans for our sample companies, which are shown in Appendix 1.

Your task is not over when the written plan is complete. It must then be communicated – both to those who must agree to its implementation and to those who will implement it. If a plan is not properly communicated, it will fail. It will fail to be approved and it will fail in its implementation. So it is important to present the plan and to make sure that everyone understands it. If you have consulted properly during the preparation of the plan, it will be 'our plan' rather than 'my plan'. Remember that the contributors to the plan will be better motivated to help implement it if they have been involved in the planning process.

Presenting the plan

The requirements to present the plan will depend on the type and size of company you are and the reasons for the presentation – to your own staff, to your bank, or to your financial advisers. Presentation of the plan needs to be even more clear and concise than the written document itself. You may only have an hour – or even less – to present a plan that has taken many months to prepare.

Nowadays, everyone uses overhead presentations, but some types of presentation package make a greater impact than others. I favour the use of the Microsoft Office software package with the PowerPoint presentation programme. PowerPoint is *extremely powerful* and if used properly it can make a tremendous impression. The slides are prepared on your PC. They can be used as a presentation package on the PC or they can be printed off onto overhead transparencies. The package itself is in colour – *so use it!*

If you prepare the presentation on overhead transparencies they can be printed in colour. However, PowerPoint really comes into its own if you make the presentation from a PC. This can be done in a number of ways:

- You can use a PC with a reasonably large screen.
- You can connect a laptop to a larger PC screen.
- You can connect your PC directly to a projector.

It is important that all present can easily see the presentation and read all the slides. This means that you should use large font sizes on your slides, that you should use a large screen and make sure that the projector is powerful enough for the presentation to be seen clearly without the need to darken the room.

It looks more professional if you prepare a template with your company name and logo (if you have one) on it. A template can be prepared to be used with the whole presentation. In PowerPoint, headings such as the plan's name and your company name and logo can be added to the slide master.

Figures 10.7 and 10.8 show the PowerPoint slide masters that Jane's Beauty & Health and The Pure Fruit Jam Company have prepared for use in their presentations. This is Jane's Beauty & Health's first ever presentation and the slide master is kept simple. The words 'Pure Fruit' and the seal at the bottom of the slide template are The Pure Fruit Jam Company's corporate logo and housemark and are used on all company presentations. The heading 'MARKETING PLAN 20X6' is used just for this presentation.

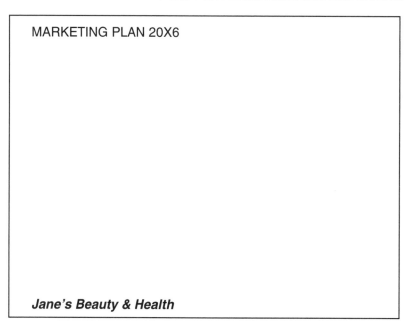

Figure 10.7   PowerPoint slide master for use in marketing plan presentation by Jane's Beauty & Health

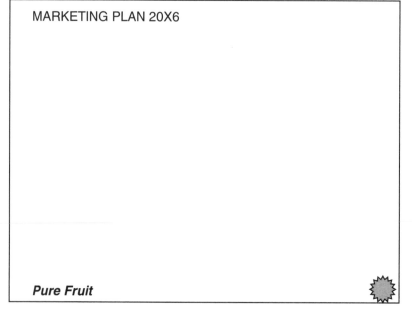

Figure 10.8   PowerPoint slide master for use in marketing plan presentation by The Pure Fruit Jam Company

MARKETING PLAN 20X6

MARKETING PLAN 20X6

Jane's Beauty & Health

Figure 10.9

A background colour could also be applied.

The beauty of using PowerPoint is that you can prepare slides from scratch, or you can import files from Word or Excel. These can be text, tables or graphics. PowerPoint also includes a full range of graphic images called 'Clipart'. These include maps of countries and continents, images of computers, and little cartoon people. You can also import digital photographs. The use of some of these items in the right places will brighten up any presentation. But do not overdo it!

Other techniques that can be used include bringing in bullet points one by one on a slide to avoid your audience trying to read the whole slide instead of listening to your presentation. Sound and video can also be used, but again they should be used in moderation or they will detract from the presentation rather than support it.

I have included some examples of a few of the PowerPoint slides that our sample companies have prepared for the presentation of their marketing plans.

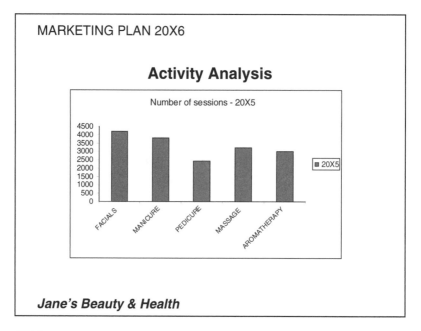

Figure 10.10

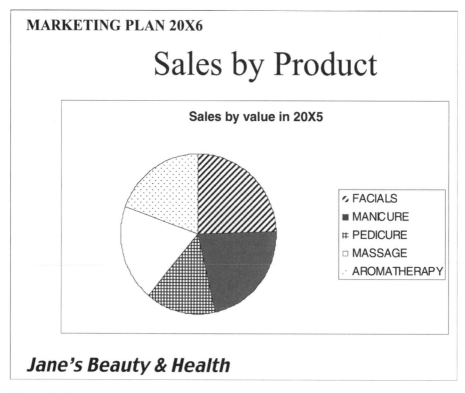

Figure 10.11

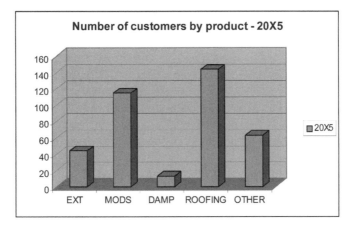

Figure 10.12

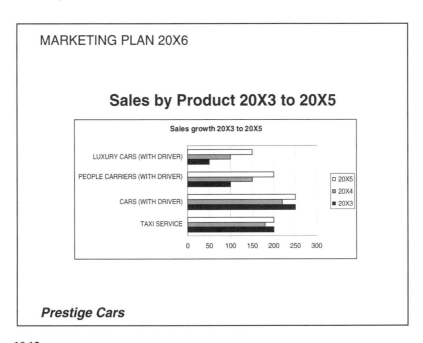

Figure 10.13

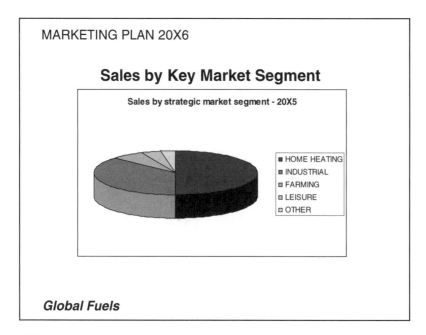

Figure 10.14

Figure 10.15

MARKETING PLAN 20X6

Assumptions

- Inflation will remain at 3% in 20X6, rising to 4% in 20X7 and 20X8
- Interest rates will remain in the range 5–6% over the period of the plan
- Company wage increases will not exceed inflation over the next three years
- UK GDP will grow at 2–3% per year over the next three years
- The £:€ exchange rate will remain in the range of £1:€1.4 to £1:€1.6 over the next three years

Pure Fruit

Figure 10.16

MARKETING PLAN 20X6

Key Objectives

- To increase sales of marmalades by 28% in real terms in three years
- To increase sales of mini-pots by 44% in real terms in three years
- To increase by five times our sales of gift packs in three years
- To increase sales of special products by 41% in real terms in three years

Pure Fruit

Figure 10.17

MARKETING PLAN 20X6

KEY STRATEGIES

Distribution

Add distribution channels

- Expand outlets in major cities in North and Scotland

- Sell mini-pots through Hotel Catering Services Ltd

- Expand website to allow online purchases

Pure Fruit

Figure 10.18

MARKETING PLAN 20X6

OPERATING EXPENSES BUDGET FOR 20X6

Department: UK Sales

Item	20X5 expenses £k	Inflation %	Inflation £k	Growth £k	Other £k	20X6 expenses £k
Salaries	80	3	2.4			82.4
Recruitment	0	3	0			0
Travel/entertaining	14	3	0.42	5		19.42
Car costs	11	3	0.33	3		14.33
Advertising	30	3	0.9		30	60.9
Exhibitions	10	3	0.3	2	54	66.3
Literature	20	3	0.6		10	30.6
Sundry items	12	3	0.36		20	32.36
		3	0			0
Total	177	3	5.31	10	114	306.31

Pure Fruit

Figure 10.19

MARKETING PLAN 20X6

PROFIT & LOSS ACCOUNT			
	20X6	20X7	20X8
(all values in £k)			
Invoiced sales	3090	3690	4390
less cost of sales	1528	1868	2260
Gross profit	1562	1822	2130
Sales & Marketing costs			
Salaries	134	134	136
Recruitment	12	15	22
Travel/entertaining	70	46	48
Car costs	28	26	30
Advertising	85	76	83
Exhibitions	129	50	58
Literature	71	48	53
Sundry items	55	34	34
Total sales costs	584	429	464
Administration costs	235	230	232
Data processing costs	75	75	75
Distribution costs	110	110	110
Total operating expenses	1004	844	881
	0	0	0
Operating profit	558	978	1249

Pure Fruit

Figure 10.20

MARKETING PLAN 20X6

MARKETING PLAN 20X6

UK MARKET

Precision Valves Ltd

Figure 10.21

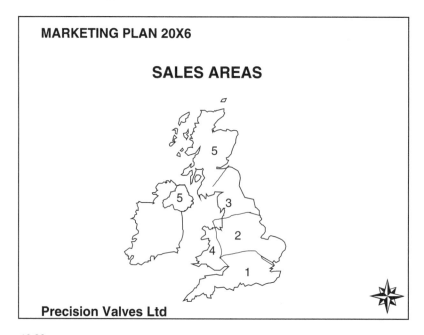

Figure 10.22

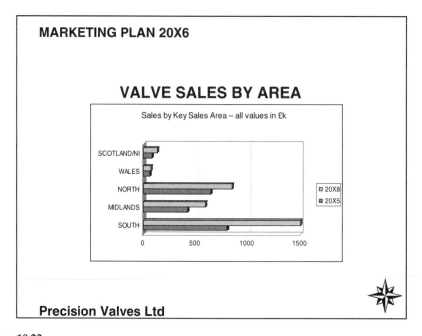

Figure 10.23

MARKETING PLAN 20X6

Key Objectives

- To increase sales by 40% in real terms in three years

- To increase sales of Type 'A' valves by 50% in real terms in three years

- To increase sales of Type 'S' valves by 50% in real terms in three years

- To more than double sales of packages in three years

- To increase margins from 28% to 33% in three years

Precision Valves Ltd

Figure 10.24

MARKETING PLAN 20X6

Key Strategies

Promotion

Change salesforce organisation
- Recruit salesman for the water industry

Change advertising/sales promotion
- Increase advertising
- Use mailshots/e-mailshots
- Increase exhibition coverage
- Expand website to use 'web analytics'
  for e-marketing

Precision Valves Ltd

Figure 10.25

Follow up and revision

Having written and presented your plan, you now have to implement it. The schedules and action plans will be followed and you will start to see the results. You have included controls and update procedures so that you can monitor progress and make changes as necessary.

Most companies use their marketing plans as a basis for the annual budgeting process. As you proceed with your plan, you can list the things that have gone well over the previous year and also the things that have gone badly. You should list your key tasks and give a status report on which have been completed and which have not.

And so the iterative process continues – from marketing plan to budget – from budget to update/revision of marketing plan – and on to the next budget.

This iterative procedure can be simplified if you set up basic formats for both your marketing plans and budgets on your PC. The layout of the marketing plan that I have shown you in this book lends itself to being set up as a blank format in Word, with blank spreadsheets in Excel. If you lay it out with numbered pages, you can enforce a discipline with others in your company so that a common company standard is used for marketing plans, budgets and the presentation of both. This will also make it easier for those with less training or experience in marketing planning than you, to prepare the plans that are necessary for their part of the business.

The biggest advantage of a common format is that any individual plan can easily be incorporated into the overall company marketing plan, and sets of figures can be added together in interlinked spreadsheets.

SUMMARY

The written plan is the document that will transmit the detail of the plan to those who will implement it. It should only contain the key information that needs to be communicated. Excessive and irrelevant detail should be excluded.

The information should be presented in a logical order. It should include an introduction giving the background to the plan, the reasons for its preparation and its purposes and uses. It should also include an executive summary, which should present the key points of the plan in a clear and concise form.

The assumptions on which the plan is based should be clearly stated and information on sales, strategic markets, key products and key sales areas should be presented. The marketing objectives are the aims of the plan and the strategies explain how these objectives will be achieved. The master schedule is the programme for implementation of the action plans.

The advertising and promotions plan includes the personnel requirements as well as advertising and sales promotion. The total cost of implementing the plan and its justification must be shown.

The plan needs to include a suitable control system to measure performance in achieving its objectives and to recommend corrective action where necessary.

Appendix 1

Individual Plans

MARKETING PLAN
FOR
JANE'S BEAUTY& HEALTH

20X6

3 February 20X6

CONTENTS

1. INTRODUCTION

We have grown the business steadily since we started out five years ago. We feel that we have reached the limits that we can with our current set-up at our city centre salon. We therefore decided to analyse our business to decide how we could best carry out our next stage of expansion.

2. EXECUTIVE SUMMARY

Although our sales have grown steadily over the last five years, we have seen a plateau in our standard treatments of facials, manicure and pedicure. Massage and aromatherapy have been our biggest growth areas in recent years. We believe that we can grow this business further, both from our existing premises and also by providing a 'home-visiting' service. We also believe that we can expand our traditional business by means of 'home-visiting', without the need to expand our premises or take on the heavy financial commitment of additional premises.

The objective of this plan is to grow the business by 15 per cent a year in real terms over the next three years. If we are successful, we will consider opening new outlets as the second stage of our expansion plan.

3. SITUATION ANALYSIS

3.1. Assumptions

■ Inflation will remain at 3 per cent in 20X6, rising to 4 per cent in 20X7 and 20X8.
■ Interest rates will remain in the range of 5 to 6 per cent over the period of the plan.
■ Company wage increases will not exceed inflation over the next three years.

3.2. Sales (History/Budget)

JANE'S BEAUTY & HEALTH
SALES FIGURES (Historical and Forecast)

SALES AREA: ALL

YEAR (all values in £k)	20X3	20X4	20X5	20X6	forecast 20X7	20X8
FACIALS	90	100	100	105	110	110
MANICURE	70	80	90	100	110	120
PEDICURE	40	50	60	65	70	75
MASSAGE	20	40	80	120	150	190
AROMATHERAPY	60	70	80	100	120	150
TOTAL	280	340	410	490	560	645

3.3. Strategic markets

Young singles

Young singles tend to concentrate on manicures and pedicures. They mainly come in just prior to the weekend to get ready for Saturday night. There is also a naturalistic trend to using aromatherapy. They have money.

Mature business

Mature customers are big users of facials, massage and aromatherapy. They are also one reason why we are expanding our treatments to include electrolysis. They are usually relatively affluent. Business is more spread throughout the week.

Young mothers

Young mothers come in mainly for stress relief, massage and aromatherapy. They tend to be on a lower budget and are keen on our reduced rate bi-weekly session charges.

Preferring home visits

This category includes mothers with babies and also older less-mobile people. The main categories are massage and reflexology, but older clients would also make use of a visiting service for facials, manicure and pedicure, if it were available.

3.4. Key products

Facials

These treatments are designed to deep cleanse, exfoliate, hydrate and nourish skin. We use only the finest products in conjunction with acupressure and lymphatic drainage massage to produce the ultimate effect on any skin type, thereby restoring the skin with freshness and radiance. We offer a range of facial treatments for different skin types:

- delicate – for sensitive reddening skins to desensitise;
- purifying – for oily acne-prone skin to eliminate impurities;
- nourishing – for dry skin to moisturise/improve skin tone;
- hydrating – for normal/combination skins to re-balance.

Facials are one of the mainstays of our business. There is potential to expand from skin treatments into hair removal and other areas. We also sell a lot of creams to our customers and can expand the range of products available.

Manicure

In our manicures the cuticles are cared for with oils and creams, the nail shape is perfected and finally treatment basecoats and colour are applied for the perfect finish. We also include a hand and arm massage.

Pedicure

With our pedicure, the feet and cuticles are exfoliated, massaged and nourished to keep them attractive and healthy. Toenails and cuticles are cared for and shaped, then colour is applied for the perfect finish.

Massage

Massage for stress relief is our fastest-growing product. We see tremendous potential to grow this product by taking it into people's homes. We offer a traditional invigorating massage that will stimulate blood and lymphatic circulation. It will also improve muscle tone, reduce muscular tension and soothe aches and pains. We offer Indian head massage, upper body massage, as well as full body massage. We also offer additional massage techniques such as deep tissue massage and acupressure. We are now expanding to offer arm and hand massage with manicure and leg and foot massage with pedicure.

Aromatherapy

Aromatherapy applies to any use of essential oils that benefits an individual. These treatments involve relaxing mind, body and soul. The art of aromatherapy is to use 100 per cent pure essential oils derived from plant materials to create a prescriptive blend of massage oil, cream or solution for inhalation to assist the body to return to homeostasis. We obtain our materials from Aromatherapy Products Ltd and sell the products individually as well as using them in our treatments.

Our product portfolio matrix is shown below.

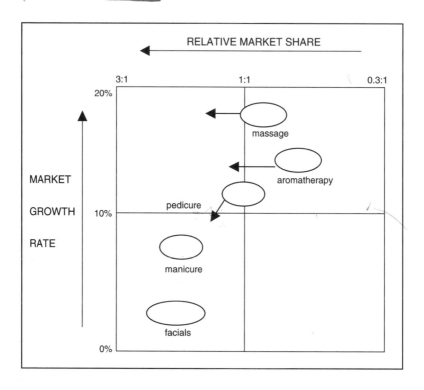

We believe that 'facials' and 'manicures' will continue as cash cows in a stable market. Their turnover will not grow in real terms, but the products will continue to be profitable. A small level of growth is possible as a spin-off of our home-visiting service.

As 'pedicures' have grown to take up a large part of the clientele for 'manicures' the potential for growth in this product is now limited. Over the next three years its growth rate will drop significantly as its relative market share approaches that of 'manicure'.

'Massage' and 'aromatherapy' will become stars, as their market growth rate continues to rise and their relative market share increases. We will need to invest in advertising to help achieve this level of growth

3.5. Key sales areas

City centre

Since we are based in the city centre we get a lot of custom from people living in or near the city centre. There are two main areas. There is the Templemead area on the edge of the centre with upmarket maisonettes and flats. Many of our young single business types and mature older clients live there. There is also the Greenlime area with small Victorian terraces. This is a less affluent area, but does bring in some business from young mothers and young singles.

Suburbs

This area has an affluent customer base and no local competitor sited there. Transport links into town are good and we get a lot of business from mature clients. This is also a target area for us for home visits.

Out of town

This is not a large market for us. We do have some clients who come in and visit us when doing other things in town, but many potential clients find it as easy to travel into London from Winkelsfield station and use the facilities there.

Home

This is a small but growing market for us. There is potential, not only from mothers with young babies, but also from older clients who find it more convenient to use our services at home. The time to do the work is longer, because of time lost in travelling from appointment to appointment, but profits are higher, because we can make the same margins without having to increase the size of our salon to accommodate more workstations.

4. MARKETING OBJECTIVES

- To increase sales by 15 per cent per year in real terms for the next three years.
- To double our massage business in real terms within three years.
- To increase our aromatherapy business by 70 per cent in real terms within three years.
- To increase 'home visiting' sales from £20,000 to £50,000 within three years.
- To increase margins from 51 to 55 per cent over three years.

5. MARKETING STRATEGIES

Products
Package products

      – manicure + pedicure
      – massage + aromatherapy

Develop new products

      – expand range of aromatherapy offerings

Pricing
Discount policy

      – for multiple sessions
      – for students with student card

Promotion
Change advertising/sales promotion

      – leaflet campaign for home visiting
      – bonus scheme for frequent users
      – e-mail aromatherapy offers to massage customers

Increase web coverage

      – expand website
      – add 'web analytics' for e-marketing
      – web links from suppliers' sites

Distribution
Increase sales channels

      – expand home visiting
        use contract workers

6. SCHEDULES

MASTER SCHEDULE

Year:20X6

Month	1 2 3 4 5 6 7 8 9 10 11 12	Responsibility
Action Plan		**Person**
Leaflet campaign	⟶	JNB
Bonus scheme	⟶	JNB
Expand website	⟶	JFS
Supplier links	⟶	JFS
Press advertising	⟶	JNB

7. SALES PROMOTION

Only Jane Bainbridge and Jenny Smith are involved in sales. Jenny is our receptionist. The existing organisation is shown below.

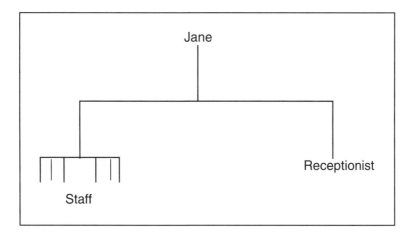

With this structure only Jane Bainbridge and the receptionist are able to take orders. This means that Jane Bainbridge and Jenny Smith can only fit in half a day working on beauty treatments, since they must spend half of the day on reception.

We intend to change this structure. We will train up two of the other members of staff to take phone calls and look after the reception area. There will be a general roster, but if one of the four of them does not have a client, they will take over reception. At the busiest times of the day or week, they will use the answerphone so that all eight employees can be working with clients.

The new structure is shown below.

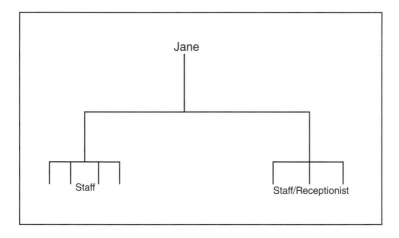

PRESS ADVERTISING
YEAR: 20X6

MEDIA	No	Rate per insertion £	Total cost £	J	F	M	A	M	J	J	A	S	O	N	D
Gazette (Wednesday)	4	50	200	x			x			x			x		
Herald (Friday)	4	50	200	x			x			x			x		
Friday Ad	6	40	240	x		x		x		x		x		x	

Our main advertising expenditure will be used on a leaflet campaign for home visiting and for advertising in the local press. As well as normal advertising, we are looking at the 'Here's my business card' promotion at *The Herald*. We will be expanding our website to take orders online. We will also be adding 'web analytics' software to enable us to analyse hits on our website and to use this information to prepare targeted e-mail campaigns to specific customers with specific offers. We intend to use this particularly to offer aromatherapy to customers who purchase or are interested in massage.

Our advertising schedule for 20X6 is shown above.

8. BUDGETS/PROFIT AND LOSS ACCOUNT

We are recruiting three direct workers, one in each year of the plan. Since these are direct workers, their costs are included in the 'cost of sales'. We will see a significant increase in operating expenses in the first year of the plan and the increase in sales will not be enough to achieve a profit during that first year. However, in subsequent years the plan will produce a significant additional profit.

The effect of the additional sales and the revised profit and loss account for the next three years are shown below.

The revised profit and loss account including additional turnover based on this plan is shown below.

EFFECT ON PROFIT & LOSS ACCOUNT OF EXTRA SALES

(all values in £k)	20X6	20X7	20X8
SALES TURNOVER	80	150	235
less COST OF SALES	30	60	90
GROSS PROFIT	50	90	145
ADMINISTRATION	5	10	15
RENT	5	5	5
RATES	5	5	5
TELEPHONE	7	10	15
ADVERTISING/MARKETING	20	13	16
OVERHEADS	5	10	15
DEPRECIATION	5	10	15
TOTAL OPERATING EXPENSES	52	63	86
OPERATING PROFIT	–2	27	59

PROFIT & LOSS ACCOUNT

(all values in £k)	20X6	20X7	20X8
SALES TURNOVER	490	560	645
less COST OF SALES	230	260	290
GROSS PROFIT	260	300	355
ADMINISTRATION	20	25	30
RENT	55	55	55
RATES	25	25	25
TELEPHONE	17	20	25
ADVERTISING/MARKETING	30	23	26
OVERHEADS	40	45	50
DEPRECIATION	25	30	35
TOTAL OPERATING EXPENSES	212	223	246
OPERATING PROFIT	48	77	109

9. CONTROLS AND UPDATE PROCEDURES

This plan is to be revised every 12 months.

APPENDICES

Copies of company accounts for the last three years together with further analysis work are included as appendices to this report.

MARKETING PLAN
FOR
AH BUILDING

20X6

3 February 20X6

CONTENTS

Section

1. INTRODUCTION

After the stagnation of two to three years ago, we have made significant sales growth in the last year – principally with our home extensions. We have now decided to analyse our business to decide how we can grow it further in a profitable way.

2. EXECUTIVE SUMMARY

The company is now solid and has started to grow since we took on the Monarch range of home extensions and conservatories. We see further potential to grow this side of the business and also to expand our roofing business, which we only started two years ago.

The objective of this plan is to grow the business by about 10 per cent a year in real terms over the next three years.

3. SITUATION ANALYSIS

3.1. Assumptions

- Inflation will remain at 3 per cent in 20X6, rising to 4 per cent in 20X7 and 20X8.
- Interest rates will remain in the range 5 to 6 per cent over the period of the plan.
- Company wage increases will not exceed inflation over the next three years.

3.2. Sales (History/Budget)

AH BUILDING
SALES FIGURES (Historical and Forecast)

SALES AREA: ALL

YEAR (all values in £k)	20X3	20X4	20X5	20X6	forecast 20X7	20X8
EXTENSIONS	120	180	220	250	280	300
MODIFICATIONS	250	220	230	230	230	230
DAMP TREATMENT	90	80	100	100	100	100
ROOFING	20	50	100	150	200	250
OTHER	40	60	50	50	50	50
TOTAL	520	590	700	780	860	930

3.3. Strategic markets

Renovators

This category covers people buying a property in need of renovation to live in themselves. Competition is always fierce, because they are often short of money and will often do what work they can themselves. We have devised standard renovation packages that we can quickly cost up and allow us to carry out the work in a speedy manner.

Expanding families

This work normally involves making more space. This can involve knocking down or moving walls, strengthening support beams and putting in loft extensions. It can also involve boarding over lofts and fitting additional window units.

Affluent retired

This type of customer is normally getting the property how they want it. There is therefore often a considerable amount of work over a one- or two-year period and then none after that. Finance is not usually a problem. There is a limit to the number of projects, so we have continually to find new customers.

Do up/resell

This category consists mainly of property investors who do up and resell property. They may be a couple doing one property at a time or a property company. Competition is always fierce and often the professional renovator does what work he can himself. As with renovations, we have devised standard packages that we can quickly cost up and that allow us to carry out the work in a speedy manor.

3.4. Key products

Extensions

This product is based around the Monarch range of home extensions, which includes wood and glass add-ons and conservatories. We also have the ability to combine this with brickwork to give us greater flexibility and to offer a wider range to our customers. It is a high-quality product.

Modifications

This has been the mainstay of our business and covers everything from knocking down walls and making good, to building garages and crazy paving paths. It is not easy to expand the level of this basic business, because the product we are offering is straightforward and one-man companies can offer the same at a lower price.

Damp treatment

We offer the Sleepsafe product, which is injected into holes drilled through the cavity of the wall. We are not the only company offering this product and margins are therefore low. For this reason, we are not considering trying to grow this part of the business.

Roofing

We only started roofing work two years ago and have found it to be lucrative, since a more limited number of local companies will take it on. Personnel insurance is higher for this product, but margins are also higher, which more than compensates.

Other

This covers work that does not fall into any of the other categories. In many cases it is a 'one-off' of a specialist type of job. We are not actively looking for this type of work.

Our product portfolio matrix is shown in the figure below.

'Modifications' are a cash cow and even if we cannot grow the business, we make good margins on them and will continue to sell them.

'Extensions' are stars – we are still having to advertise to make the product known. It has been growing rapidly but we now expect the growth to slow.

'Roofing' is moving from being a question mark to becoming a star.

The dog of the pack is 'damp treatment' and we will soon have to decide whether to drop this product completely.

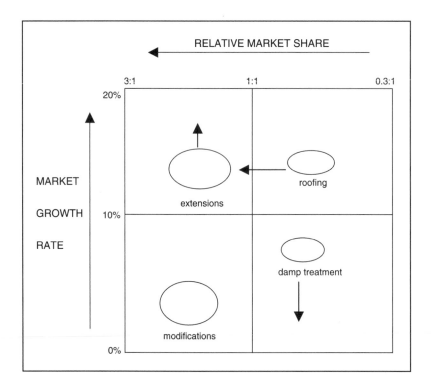

3.5. Key sales areas

Town centre

This consists mainly of older properties, many of which have already been converted into flats. We get a lot of work here doing conversions and also renovating and modernising existing flats.

Old Town

This area consists mainly of larger houses, and customers tend to be affluent working or affluent retired. There is a lot of roofing work available on the larger houses and council grants are often available to modernise more run-down properties. There is a good level of extension work, but it is mainly conservatories.

Seaside

This area consists mainly of smaller terraced properties – 'two up, two downs'. Work is mainly renovation, modernisation and also some roofing and reroofing requirements.

Suburbs

The housing stock here is similar to that found in Old Town, but is generally more modern. The main business for us here is in extensions and conservatories, also building new pathways and front garden walls.

4. MARKETING OBJECTIVES

- To increase sales by 10 per cent per year for the next three years.
- To increase our extensions business by a third within three years.
- To double our roofing business within two years.
- To increase margins from 43 to 46 per cent over three years.

5. MARKETING STRATEGIES

Products
Develop new product
– expand Monarch home extensions to include brickwork
– extend roofing range to include seagull removal

Pricing
Discount policy
– for repeat orders within nine months

Promotion
Change advertising/
sales promotion
– advertise in Yellow Pages
– increase advertising in local paper/free newspapers
– set up a website
– take part in local 'Ideal Homes' show

Distribution

Increase sales channels

– get supplier of 'seagull spikes' to forward leads in return for using their materials

– train key workers to give budget pricing

6. SCHEDULES

MASTER SCHEDULE

Year:20X6

Month	1 2 3 4 5 6 7 8 9 10 11 12	Responsibility
Action Plan		**Person**
Press advertising	————————————————→	JAJ
Expand website	———→	SJS
Ideal Homes Show	————→	JAJ

7. SALES PROMOTION

In our company only John James (managing director) does the selling. So there is no real sales structure – just a company structure, as shown below.

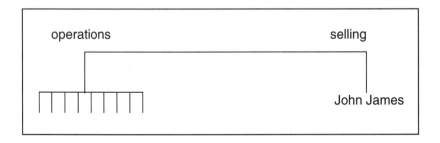

operations   selling

                                              John James

We intend to train up our two senior foremen so that they can give budget quotations. They will also feed these to Susan in the office, who will prepare and send out the written quotations. The new organisation is shown below.

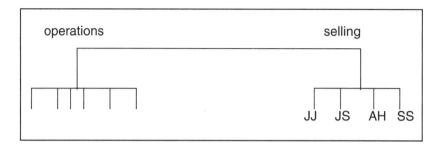

Our main advertising expenditure in 20X6 will be for advertising in Yellow Pages, the local press (£250) and taking part in the 'Ideal Homes' show in town. Details of the exhibition costs are given below.

We also intend to set up a website for which we are budgeting £5,000.

EXHIBITION COSTS

Name of exhibition: Ideal Homes
Location: Downtown Sports Arena
Date: 8–10 June 20X6

Stand size: 6 m² (2 m x 3 m)

COSTS	£
Stand space rental	120
Artwork, photographic panels	500
Rental of table/chairs	200
TOTAL	**880**

8. BUDGETS AND PROFIT AND LOSS ACCOUNT

Jim Smith will be retiring in the first year of the plan, but we intend to take on two apprentice bricklayers. The costs of the two new apprentices will be the same as the current costs of Jim Smith, so there are no additional labour costs in the plan overleaf.

The effect of the additional sales and the additional costs is shown below.

The revised profit and loss account, including total turnover based on this plan is shown overleaf.

EFFECT ON PROFIT & LOSS ACCOUNT OF EXTRA SALES

(all values in £k)	20X6	20X7	20X8
SALES TURNOVER	80	160	230
less COST OF SALES	45	90	102
GROSS PROFIT	35	70	128
ADMINISTRATION	5	10	15
RENT	5	5	5
RATES	2	3	5
TELEPHONE	5	8	12
ADVERTISING/MARKETING	10	5	5
OVERHEADS	5	10	15
DEPRECIATION	0	0	0
TOTAL OPERATING EXPENSES	32	41	57
OPERATING PROFIT	3	29	71

PROFIT & LOSS ACCOUNT

(all values in £k)	20X6	20X7	20X8
SALES TURNOVER	780	860	930
less COST OF SALES	445	490	502
GROSS PROFIT	335	370	428
ADMINISTRATION	45	50	55
RENT	70	70	70
RATES	32	33	35
TELEPHONE	20	23	27
ADVERTISING/MARKETING	20	15	15
OVERHEADS	65	70	75
DEPRECIATION	30	30	30
TOTAL OPERATING EXPENSES	282	291	307
OPERATING PROFIT	53	79	121

9. CONTROLS AND UPDATE PROCEDURES

This plan is to be revised every 12 months.

APPENDICES

As appendices, please find attached our latest set of audited accounts. We also include brochures for the Monarch range of home extensions.

MARKETING PLAN
FOR
PRESTIGE CARS

20X6

3 February 20X6

CONTENTS

Section

1. INTRODUCTION

Prestige Cars started off as a taxi company. With the transfer of the business to new owners three years ago, we have moved the business rapidly into a chauffeur hire company. This plan analyses our business and recommends ways to expand from our present customer base.

2. EXECUTIVE SUMMARY

Four years ago, the company was a small taxi firm competing with many other taxi companies in the locality. Over the last three years we have not tried to expand this part of the business. Instead we have expanded our chauffeur hire business. Recently we have put significant additional effort into two new areas – people carriers and luxury cars.

Our business with people carriers is growing steadily, but our chauffeur-drive luxury car hire has expanded rapidly. We see scope to develop both of these parts of our business further – particularly the luxury car hire.

The objective of this plan is to grow the business by 9 per cent a year in real terms over the next three years.

3. SITUATION ANALYSIS

3.1. Assumptions

▦ Inflation will remain at 3 per cent in 20X6, rising to 4 per cent in 20X7 and 20X8.
▦ Interest rates will remain in the range of 5 to 6 per cent over the period of the plan.
▦ Company wage increases will not exceed inflation over the next three years.

3.2. Sales (History/Budget)

PRESTIGE CARS
SALES FIGURES (Historical and Forecast)

SALES AREA: ALL

YEAR (all values in £k)	20X3	20X4	20X5	20X6	forecast 20X7	20X8
TAXI SERVICE	200	180	200	200	200	200
CARS (WITH DRIVER)	250	220	250	250	250	250
PEOPLE CARRIERS (WITH DRIVER)	100	150	200	250	300	350
LUXURY CARS (WITH DRIVER)	50	100	150	200	250	300
TOTAL	600	650	800	900	1000	1100

3.3. Strategic markets

Business

Our business travel work has been expanded in the last few years and we now cater for more than a dozen local firms. This work includes collecting the companies' clients and distributors from the airport or taking them from local hotels to the company offices and back. We also supply chauffeur-driven people carriers on occasions of company sales meetings, budget meetings, distributor meetings, etc.

Leisure

This relates mainly to taking people to/from theatres and cinemas, and to/from parties. This type of work is more heavily biased to the winter months and in particular around the Christmas and New Year period.

Travel

This involves mainly the airport run to Heathrow, Gatwick or Stansted. Because holidays are pre-booked, we can get bookings ahead of time. We offer a standard rate for each journey, which clients like. It does, however, mean that in some cases we have to absorb and pay for wasted time when flights are delayed. It is competitive low-margin business, but is a regular source of baseline business.

3.4. Key products

Taxi hire

This was our original business, but it is low margin and highly competitive. As we have moved upmarket, we have tried to farm out more of this to contract drivers.

Chauffeur-driven cars

The main activity with this product is for business customers. The cars are used extensively for airport runs and customer hotel collections. There is also a growing market for supermarket runs for retired people who no longer want to drive themselves.

Chauffeur-driven people carriers

These are used mainly for groups. This can be business customers going to/from restaurants, but also families going out for parties, to restaurants, etc. Birthday party collections is a new activity that we are developing in conjunction with various playgroups in the town.

Chauffeur-driven luxury cars

This is a rapidly growing area for us. We have two Rolls Royces, one Bentley and two stretched limos. This is a luxury product and is often sold for birthdays, weddings and other special occasions. We want to expand into children's birthday parties, with one of the Rolls Royces marketed as 'Chitty Chitty Bang Bang'. We are the only company in the locality offering this type of product, so margins are good even if running costs are high. The high cost of the cars is a barrier to entry to competitors.

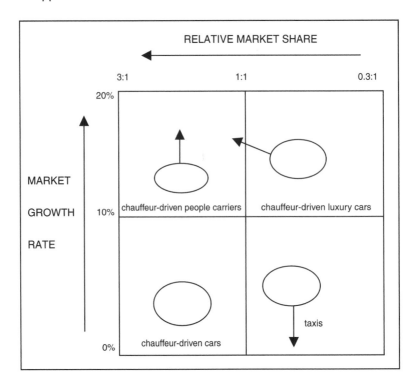

'Chauffeur-driven cars' are a good cash cow. We are well known for this service, so no advertising is necessary, but margins are fairly good.

'Chauffeur-driven people carriers' are already a star, and 'chauffeur-driven luxury cars', although still a question mark, are rapidly moving into star territory.

'Taxis' are fast becoming a dog, but at the moment are too large a part of our turnover to consider dropping.

3.5. Key sales areas

Town centre

This is not our best area. In the town centre, we have to compete with a large number of small taxi firms based near the railway station.

Suburbs

This is our best area. On the southern and eastern side of town, the suburbs comprise larger size houses and an affluent type of customer. On the north side of town, we have the Belsize Business Park, which is where most of our business customers are based.

Out of town

Although some of our customers here are farmers, the bulk are business people working either locally or in London. Most houses are large and the customer base is affluent. Business is mainly airport runs and party/entertainment related. Business levels would be higher if London-based customers did not spend evenings out in London rather than locally.

4. MARKETING OBJECTIVES

- To increase sales by 9 per cent per year in real terms for the next three years.
- To increase sales value from people carriers by 60 per cent within three years.
- To increase sales value from luxury car hire by 80 per cent within three years.
- To maintain margins at 38 per cent over three years.

5. MARKETING STRATEGIES

Products
Modify products — modify offering to expand people carriers and luxury cars into the children's party and playgroup markets

Pricing
Discount policy — offer discounts for 'supermarket runs' out of peak hours

Promotion
Change advertising/ — increase coverage in Yellow Pages
sales promotion — mailshots/e-mailshots to playgroups and businesses
— add 'web analytics' for e-marketing
— give new leaflets/cards to each customer with their bill

Distribution
Expand website — to allow online bookings

6. SCHEDULES

MASTER SCHEDULE

Year: 20X6

Month	1 2 3 4 5 6 7 8 9 10 11 12	Responsibility
Action Plan		**Person**
Mailshot playgroups	⟶	ILH
Mailshot businesses	⟶	ILH
Expand website	⟶	ALT
New leaflet	⟶	NBF
Press advertising	⟶	ALT

7. SALES PROMOTION

We have a full-time receptionist, who is in effect *the* salesperson. The structure of the company is shown below.

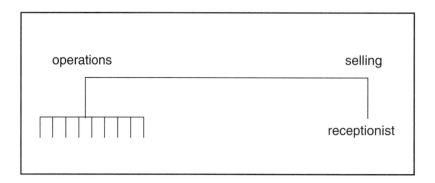

Alan Taylor will get involved in selling himself and we will give responsibility to the senior drivers in luxury cars, people carriers and chauffeur cars for promoting and selling their products.

The proposed structure is shown.

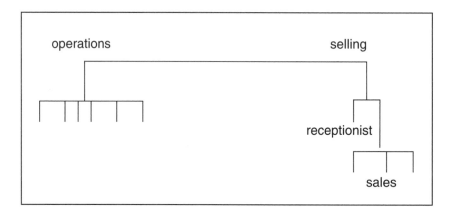

In 20X6 we will be advertising in the local press and will be increasing our coverage in Yellow Pages with a block advert. Our main promotions will be by means of various mailshots/e-mailshots that we are planning to local playgroups and local businesses. We also intend to expand our website to allow online booking of car hire and will add software for 'web analytics'.

The action plan for our mailshot to local businesses is shown above.

ACTION PLAN – e-mailshot to local businesses
DEPARTMENT: SALES

Aim	Current position	Action	By	Start	Finish	Cost
Carry out e-mailshot	Need 'opt in' e-mail list of local companies	Purchase list	ALT	10.1.X6	10.1.X6	£200
	Need link to website	Prepare text create link on e-mail	JDT JDT	10.1.X6 20.1.X5	20.1.X6 20.1.X6	£25 £10
		Send out	ILH	1.2.X6	1.2.X6	£100

8. BUDGETS AND PROFIT AND LOSS ACCOUNT

During the course of our plan, we are not intending to purchase any additional cars, although some will be replaced when they get to their replacement age. We will also be continuing to move towards contract workers for our taxi business.

We have carried out a full appraisal of the idea of introducing electric cars as a special project, but have decided against it for now.

The effect of the additional sales and the additional costs for the next three years are shown below.

EFFECT ON PROFIT & LOSS ACCOUNT OF EXTRA SALES

(all values in £k)	20X6	20X7	20X8
SALES TURNOVER	100	200	300
less COST OF SALES	62	125	187
GROSS PROFIT	38	75	113
ADMINISTRATION	10	15	20
RENT	5	5	5
RATES	2	3	5
TELEPHONE	5	8	12
ADVERTISING/MARKETING	10	10	10
OVERHEADS	5	10	15
DEPRECIATION	10	20	20
TOTAL OPERATING EXPENSES	47	71	87
OPERATING PROFIT	–9	4	26

The revised profit and loss account including total turnover based on this plan is shown below.

PROFIT & LOSS ACCOUNT

(all values in £k)	20X6	20X7	20X8
SALES TURNOVER	900	1000	1100
less COST OF SALES	562	625	687
GROSS PROFIT	338	375	413
ADMINISTRATION	40	45	50
RENT	55	55	55
RATES	22	23	25
TELEPHONE	15	18	22
ADVERTISING/MARKETING	15	15	15
OVERHEADS	45	50	55
DEPRECIATION	105	115	115
TOTAL OPERATING EXPENSES	297	321	337
OPERATING PROFIT	41	54	76

9. CONTROLS AND UPDATE PROCEDURES

This plan is to be revised every 12 months.

APPENDICES

Our latest set of accounts is included in the appendix together with further analysis of our sales areas and key applications.

MARKETING PLAN
FOR
GLOBAL FUELS

20X6

3 February 20X6

CONTENTS

Section

1. INTRODUCTION

Global Fuels is a supplier of bulk oil products in the South West of England. We have a mix of customers, ranging from individual homes and farms, to large industrial companies. We started in home heating oils, but have expanded into diesel and lubricating oils.

2. EXECUTIVE SUMMARY

Our business was stagnating until we decided to move into related products. We are now making a good return with red diesel and lubricating oils and see great possibilities to grow our business with these products.

The objective of this plan is to grow the business by 25 per cent over the next three years.

3. SITUATION ANALYSIS

3.1. Assumptions

▪ Tax increases on our products will be in line with inflation at 3 per cent in 20X6, rising to 4 per cent in 20X7 and 20X8.
▪ The oil price will remain in the range of $25 to $40 per barrel over the next three years.
▪ The £:$ exchange rate will remain in the range of £1:$1.65 to £1:$1.85 over the next three years.
▪ There will be no governmental changes relating to the sale of red diesel.

3.2. Sales (History/Budget)

GLOBAL FUELS
SALES FIGURES (Historical and Forecast)

SALES AREA: ALL

Net sales after deducting tax & duty

YEAR (all values in £k)	20X3	20X4	20X5	20X6	20X7 forecast	20X8
FUEL OILS	850	920	900	900	915	930
HEAVY FUEL OILS	300	280	300	300	310	320
DIESEL	270	310	300	300	275	350
RED DIESEL	50	100	200	300	400	500
LUBRICATING OILS	60	80	100	150	200	250
TOTAL	1530	1690	1800	1950	2100	2350

3.3. Strategic markets

Home heating

This is a steady sector, making up about half of our sales. (Four years ago this was 90 per cent of sales.) Business is mainly in the winter months, although an increasing number of customers take advantage of our 'summer discount' incentives. Margins are low in this competitive market.

Industrial

Our main customers in this sector take heavy fuel oils (for industrial burners) and lubricating oils, which are becoming a growing part of our product offering.

Farming

Our sales in farming used to be exclusively heating oils, but since we expanded into selling red diesel, this has been an increasing part of our farming sales. We tend to deal with the smaller farmers and smallholders, who appreciate our policy of delivering any quantity. For the really large farms we tend to lose out to the national fuel supply companies, which offer large discounts for bulk deliveries that we cannot compete with.

Leisure

This is a relatively new sector for us and sales are mainly red diesel. John knows the leisure market from his days at Atkins plc and he is actively expanding our sales. We are particularly keen to break into the powerboat market based around Weston-super-Mare and Newquay.

3.4. Key products

Fuel oils

This was our original product. Its main application is in home heating, which is a competitive market. Although our level of sales has remained relatively static, they are down from 90 per cent of sales four years ago to about 50 per cent now as we expand sales of our other products.

Heavy fuel oils

Mainly sold to business customers, the heavy fuel oils need industrial burners, rather than home oil-heating boilers. This is a steady business, but we see no possibility of expanding sales.

Diesel

We sell this product to farmers for on-road use and also for heavy garden machinery. Sales have always been steady, but will not grow. Red diesel is replacing these sales for off-road use. We cannot compete with garages for sales to private motorists.

Red diesel

This is a simple product with a range of markets, including farmers, gardeners and the leisure industry. Since John joined us from Atkins plc, we have moved into this market with a considerable degree of success.

Lubricating oils

We only started selling lubricating oils three years ago and have really seen this product take off. Not many companies stock the range that we do and this has brought us a number of loyal business accounts. With the recent introduction of ATEX regulations for explosive areas, we see potential to grow sales by offering special vacuum oils, particularly synthetic oils for use in oxygen-rich atmospheres. We see this as our main growth product for the future.

Our product portfolio matrix is show below.

'Fuel oils', 'heavy fuel oils' and 'diesel' are cash cows and bring in the bulk of the company's profits. We expect 'fuel oils' to be steady and may see a small level of growth. Heavy fuel oils will not change. We have a fixed number of customers and their requirements do not change. We expect sales and market share for 'diesel' to start to decline over the next three years, moving this product into the dogs category.

'Red diesel' is already a star and we expect further growth from this product.

'Lubricating oils' have been a question mark, but are now moving into the star sector. We expect dramatic growth in sales of this product.

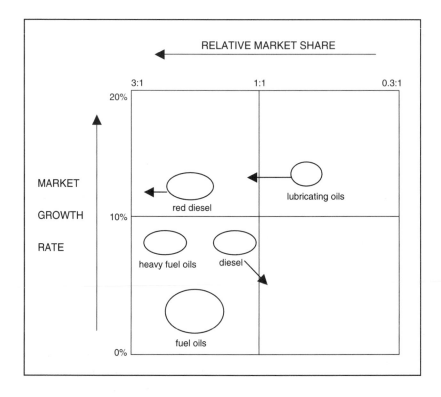

3.5. Key sales areas

Devon/Cornwall

Apart from our home-heating application, sales in this area are mainly into farming and leisure. There are few industrial bases apart from St Austell and Exeter, and business customers are few. Distances from our base in the Bristol area also increase the cost of small deliveries.

Somerset/Wiltshire

Our biggest customers here are in farming, although we also have some good industrial customers in Taunton, Bridgewater and Devises. We also do good business in home-heating oils, because of the rural nature of the area. We are optimistic about expanding our leisure sales in and around Weston-super-Mare.

Bristol/Avon

This is by far our biggest area, which is why we separate it from the rest of Somerset. It is near to our home base and contains major centres of industry in Bristol and Avonmouth as well as major centres of population in Bristol and Bath. Our main sales in this area are to industrial users and over 80 per cent of our industrial sales are sited here. But there are also a significant number of population areas without access to natural gas, which make up a significant proportion of our home-heating oil customers.

4. MARKETING OBJECTIVES

- To increase sales by 30 per cent over the next three years.
- To increase sales of red diesel by 250 per cent in volume terms in three years.
- To increase sales of lubricating oils by 250 per cent in three years.
- To increase margins from 33 to 36 per cent over three years.

5. MARKETING STRATEGIES

Products	
Expand product range	– increase range of lubricating oils on offer to include special vacuum oils
Pricing	– for summer deliveries (heating oil)
Discount policy	– for winter deliveries (red diesel for leisure use)
Promotion	
Change advertising/ sales promotion	– take part in local exhibitions
	–mailshots/e-mailshots to local chemical and food-processing companies
	– mailshots/e-mailshots to boat clubs
	– add 'web analytics' for e-marketing

Distribution Telesales

Expand website

– to chemical and food producers for vacuum oils
– to promote red diesel through garden centres
– to take orders online

6. SCHEDULES

MASTER SCHEDULE

Year: 20X6

Month	1 2 3 4 5 6 7 8 9 10 11 12	Responsibility	
Action Plan		Dept	Person
Mailshot – boats	───────────▶	Sales	JBS
Mailshot – chemicals	──▶	Sales	JBS
Mailshot – food	─────▶	Sales	JBS
Bristol Chemshow	─────────▶	Mgmt	AJF
Agricultural show	──────▶	Mgmt	AJF
Expand website	──────▶	Accounts/IT	GGH

7. SALES PROMOTION

At present the managing director manages the major distributors and our sales manager manages direct sales and minor distributors.

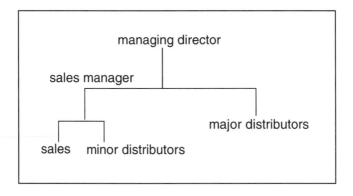

We have decided that the sales manager will concentrate on the leisure market, which he knows well. He will take over managing distributors for the leisure industry and the managing director will manage the others. The managing director will also manage the telesales, for which we will use Gillian, the accounts clerk, two hours a day. The new structure is shown below.

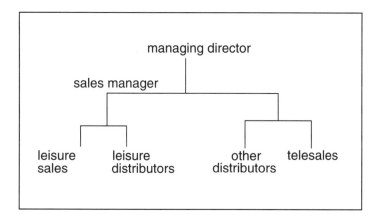

During 20X6 we intend to take part in two local exhibitions – the Bristol Chemshow and the West of England Agricultural Show. We will also be carrying out separate mailshots/e-mailshots for the boating, chemical and food industries. We will be revamping our website and adding in the facility to take orders online and 'web analytics' for e-marketing. We will be spending about £10,000 each on the exhibitions and our website project.

The schedule for our exhibition expenditure is given below.

EXHIBITION COSTS

Name of exhibition:	Bristol Chemshow
Location:	Avon Exhibition Centre
Date:	4–6 October 20X6
Stand size:	9 m² (3 m × 3 m)
Stand and artwork:	Riverside Design

COSTS

	£
Stand space rental	800
Shell scheme rental	2,000
Artwork, photographic panels	2,000
Rental of carpets, furniture, lights	800
TOTAL	**5,600**

EXHIBITION COSTS

Name of exhibition: Agricultural Show
Location: West of England Showground
Date: 18–22 June 20X6

Stand size: 6 m² (2 m × 3 m)

COSTS

	£
Stand space rental	600
Artwork, photographic panels	2,000
Rental of furniture, lights	400
TOTAL	**3,000**

8. BUDGETS AND PROFIT AND LOSS ACCOUNT

Operating expenses will increase to fund the additional sales costs of the plan. The detailed operating expenses budget for the sales department for the first year of the plan is shown below.

OPERATING EXPENSES BUDGET FOR 20X6

Department: Sales

Item	20X5 expenses £k	Inflation %	Inflation £k	Growth	Other £k	20X6 expenses £k
Salaries	55	3	1.65			56.55
Recruitment	8	3	0.24			8.24
Travel/entertaining	14	3	0.42	5		19.42
Car costs	11	3	0.33	3	5	14.33
Advertising	19	3	0.57			24.57
Exhibitions	9	3	0.27	2		11.27
Literature	20	3	0.6			20.6
Sundry items	12	3	0.36		10	22.36
		3	0			0
Total	148	3	4.44	10	15	177.44

Under 'sundry items, other', we have included £10,000 to expand our website. An additional £5,000 to support mailshots is shown under 'advertising'.

Our plan will do little more than break even during its first year. Profits will grow much more quickly as volume growth accelerates in the second and third years.

The revised profit and loss account for our operations during the course of the plan is shown below.

PROFIT & LOSS ACCOUNT

(all values in £k)	20X6	20X7	20X8
Invoiced sales	1950	2100	2350
less cost of sales	1300	1400	1504
Gross profit	650	700	846
Sales & Marketing costs			
Salaries	57	57	58
Recruitment	8	11	8
Travel/entertaining	19	19	19
Car costs	14	16	18
Advertising	25	26	28
Exhibitions	11	14	17
Literature	21	23	25
Sundry items	22	17	17
Total sales costs	177	183	190
Administration costs	160	160	161
Data processing costs	49	49	50
Distribution costs	103	104	105
Total operating expenses	489	496	506
Operating profit	161	204	340

9. CONTROLS AND UPDATE PROCEDURES

This plan is to be revised every 12 months.

APPENDICES

In the appendices we include a further breakdown of current sales, by product, by area and by application. We also include our customer list and a list of target customers in the chemical and vacuum industries.

MARKETING PLAN
FOR
THE UK MARKET
20X6

THE PURE FRUIT JAM COMPANY LTD

3 February 20X6

CONTENTS

Section

1. INTRODUCTION

The Pure Fruit Jam Company is a manufacturer of specialist jams and conserves. The company uses only fresh fruit and ingredients and we have had considerable success with the trend towards organic and 'non-synthetic' products. We intend to build on our success.

2. EXECUTIVE SUMMARY

Sales growth in the UK has been sporadic, with stagnation in the sales of standard jams and marmalades. However, our mini-pots have been well received by hotel chains and airlines.

We have also seen growth in our special products, particularly the whisky and brandy 'Scottish' and 'French' breakfast marmalades.

With added sales from our website and the relaunch of our gift packs, we are confident of a rapid rise in sales over the next three years.

The objective of this plan is to increase UK sales by 23 per cent over the next three years, from an estimate of £2 million this year to £2,740,000 in 20X8.

3. SITUATION ANALYSIS

3.1. Assumptions

- Inflation will remain at 3 per cent in 20X6, rising to 4 per cent in 20X7 and 20X8.
- Interest rates will remain in the range of 5 to 6 per cent over the period of the plan.
- Company wage increases will not exceed inflation over the next three years.
- UK GDP will grow at 2 to 3 per cent per year over the next three years.
- The £:€ exchange rate will remain in the range of £1:€1.4 to £1:€1.6 over the next three years.

3.2. Sales (History/Budget)

THE PURE FRUIT JAM COMPANY
SALES FIGURES (Historical and Forecast)

SALES AREA: UK

YEAR (all values in £k)	20X3	20X4	20X5	20X6	forecast 20X7	20X8
STANDARD JAMS (340 gm)	1000	1000	1000	1030	1030	1050
MARMALADES (340 gm)	350	350	420	470	520	600
MINI-POTS	100	180	250	320	350	400
GIFT PACKS	90	70	50	100	180	250
SPECIAL PRODUCTS	150	200	280	340	380	440
TOTAL	1690	1800	2000	2260	2460	2740

3.3 Strategic markets

Supermarkets

We have contracts with Waitrose. Tesco sells our black cherry and blueberry flavours, but nothing else. This is a very competitive market and we lose out to our bigger continental rivals – La Belle Confiture and Rein Konfitüre.

Quality shops

We have contracts with Marks & Spencer and with House of Fraser food halls. Apart from that, this sector consists of a wide range of individual shops and delicatessens. There are a limited number of such shops, but also the sales effort is high in contacting a large number of individual buyers to gain sales.

Hotels

Most of our business with hotels is with our mini-pots. We have secured contracts in recent years with Jarvis Hotels and also with the MacDonalds chain. The northern hotels are particularly keen on our range of 'Scottish' and 'French' breakfast marmalades, with whisky and brandy flavours.

Airlines

Again with airlines, the emphasis is on mini-pots. British Airways serves our alpine straw-berry range with clotted cream teas on its transatlantic and Japanese flights. This resulted in our largest ever contract for mini-pots. The UK airlines seem more interested in jams than their continental rivals.

3.4. Key products

Standard jams

Even our standard jams use natural ingredients. But it is difficult to compete for standard flavours like strawberry and raspberry with fresh fruit jams from bulk manufacturers. That is why we have moved steadily into more exotic flavours, such as alpine strawberry, fig, mango and blueberry. Sales of standard jams have stagnated in recent years and we are fighting just to stand still.

Marmalades

We have seen an improvement in marmalade sales since we moved away from traditional Seville breakfast marmalades to flavoured marmalades. Our 'Scottish' and 'French' mar-malades with whisky and brandy are now becoming big sellers and we will be adding a rum and a Cointreau flavour next year. We expect specialist flavours to boost sales signifi-cantly at the expense of our traditional flavours.

Mini-pots

Sales of mini-pots have grown dramatically with the contracts with British Airways, Jarvis and MacDonalds. Sales are always by contract and so we either have a significant jump in sales or no growth at all. It is not worthwhile to sell mini-pots individually.

Gift packs

Gift packs consist of either two specialist standard size jars of jam or marmalade or six mini-pots of different flavours. This business is growing and has really started to take off since the opening of our website sales unit. We hope that sales of gift packs will increase further, but that also once customers have tasted particular flavours they will start to pur-chase the standard size jars of the flavours they like most.

Special products

These are own-label products for prestige stores such as Harrods, Fortnum & Mason, etc. They can be based on the top end of our standard jams and marmalades or progressively on our gift packs.

Our portfolio matrix is shown above.

'Standard jams' are cash cows and we do not expect significant growth.

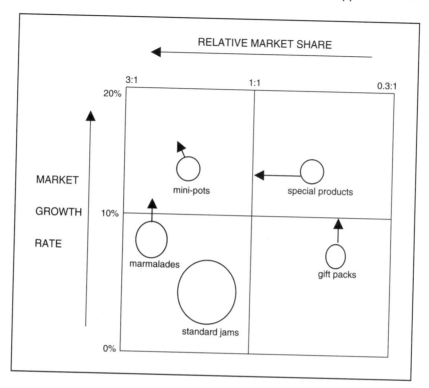

'Marmalades' are also cash cows, but with the advent of our new flavoured marmalades they are moving back towards the star quadrant and we expect this to continue over the next three years.

'Mini-pots' and our 'special products' are both stars and we expect considerable growth over the next three years.

'Gift packs' have been a dog, largely because so much of the sales of this product have been as own-label special products. But this has sparked interest from our ordinary customers, which has generated demand for this product under our own name.

We expect 'special products' to move from being a question mark to become a star.

3.5. Key sales areas

South

This is our largest sales area, because it includes the purchasing offices of a number of key customers such as British Airways, Marks & Spencer and some of the major London specialist stores.

North

Customers here include some of the smaller supermarkets and a number of delicatessen chains in the Birmingham, Manchester and Leeds areas.

Wales

After the euphoria of signing a deal with the Welsh Tourist Agency for Welsh World Cup marmalade, we have been disappointed with sales, which have hardly grown from 20X3 levels.

Scotland/NI

Our biggest customers in Scotland are Jarvis and MacDonalds, both of whom purchase product through their Scottish purchasing offices for all of their hotels. We also do good business with specialist shops in Edinburgh and Aberdeen. Our 'Scottish' breakfast marmalade has gone down well north of the border.

4. MARKETING OBJECTIVES

- To increase sales of marmalades by 28 per cent in real terms in three years.
- To increase sales of mini-pots by 44 per cent in real terms in three years.
- To increase by five times our sales of gift packs in three years.
- To increase sales of special products by 41 per cent in real terms in three years.

5. MARKETING STRATEGIES

Products
Add/modify products

- launch new-look gift packs
- launch rum and Cointreau flavoured marmalades
- drop 'bulk' jams – strawberry, raspberry

Pricing
Discount policies

- offer retrospective discount to major outlets based on level of annual purchases

Promotion
Change advertising/
sales promotion

- carry out high-key product launch for rum and Cointreau flavoured marmalades
- increase advertising in Scotland
- add 'web analytics' for e-marketing

Distribution

Add distribution channels – expand outlets in major cities in North and Scotland

– sell mini pots through Hotel Catering Services Ltd

Expand website – to allow online purchases

6. SCHEDULES

MASTER SCHEDULE

Year: 20X6

Month	1 2 3 4 5 6 7 8 9 10 11 12	Responsibility	
Action Plan		**Dept**	**Person**
Product launch (Marmalades)	———————→	Marketing	FNB
Product launch (Gift packs)	———————→	Marketing	FNB
Press advertising (General)	——————————————→	Marketing	BKS
Press advertising (Scotland)	——————————→	Marketing	BKS
Foodex Exhibition	——→	Marketing	LFR
Expand website	——————→	IT	OJT

7. SALES PROMOTION

In The Pure Fruit Jam Company we have a sales director, a new sales manager, and a marketing assistant who handles advertising, publicity and exhibitions.

Our existing sales structure is shown below.

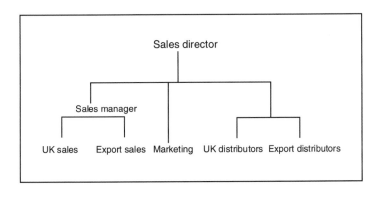

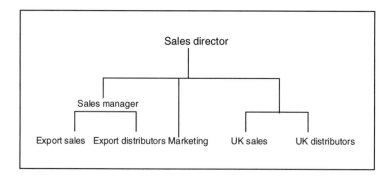

The new sales manager has a lot of experience in export sales, so our intention is to give him full responsibility for export sales. The sales director will concentrate mainly on UK sales and overall marketing.

During 20X6 we will be carrying out a high-profile product launch for our new range of breakfast marmalades, with a press launch on 26 June and a trade launch on 27 June. We will also be relaunching our gift packs at the Foodex exhibition in March. We will be adding distribution channels in Scotland and the North of England and will be carrying out a press advertising campaign to support that.

Details of our product launch and exhibition expenditure are given below.

PRODUCT LAUNCH COSTS

Name of product:	New marmalade range
Location:	Cumberland Hotel
Date:	26–27 June 20X6
Agency:	Top Notch Advertising

COSTS	£
Hire of hotel room and facilities	3,000
Design, supply and build launch stand	8,000
Artwork, photographic panels	5,000
Launch video	10,000
Sample packs	3,000
Launch dinner	3,000
Hotel bills/expenditure for launch staff	2,000
TOTAL	**34,000**

EXHIBITION COSTS

Name of exhibition:	Foodex
Location:	NEC Birmingham
Date:	6–8 March 20X6
Stand size:	32 m² (4 m x 8 m)
Stand contractor	Top Notch Advertising

COSTS	£
Stand space rental	4,000
Design, supply and build	8,000
Artwork, photographic panels	4,000
Rental of carpets, furniture, lights, phone, etc	2,000
Hotel bills/expenditure for stand staff	2,000
TOTAL	**20,000**

Separate schedules for our press advertising campaigns for Scotland and England are included in an appendix to this plan, together with individual action plans.

We will also be adding 'web analytics' software to our website for e-marketing.

8. BUDGETS AND PROFIT AND LOSS ACCOUNTS

Operating expenses will increase significantly to fund the additional sales costs of the plan. The operating expenses budget for the UK sales department for the first year of the plan is shown below.

OPERATING EXPENSES BUDGET FOR 20X6

Department: UK Sales

Item	20X5 expenses £k	Inflation %	Inflation £k	Growth £k	Other £k	20X6 expenses £k
Salaries	80	3	2.4			82.4
Recruitment	0	3	0			0
Travel/entertaining	14	3	0.42	5		19.42
Car costs	11	3	0.33	3		14.33
Advertising	30	3	0.9		30	60.9
Exhibitions	10	3	0.3	2	54	66.3
Literature	20	3	0.6		10	30.6
Sundry items	12	3	0.36		20	32.36
		3	0			0
Total	177	3	5.31	10	114	306.31

Advertising for 20X6 includes the cost of increased advertising in Scotland. Exhibition costs are to cover the Foodex Exhibition and also the cost of the product launch for the new marmalade range. The costs of expanding our website are also being charged to the UK sales department budget under 'sundry items'.

A partial profit and loss account for the additional sales included in this plan is shown below.

EFFECT ON PROFIT & LOSS ACCOUNT OF EXTRA UK SALES

(all values in £k)	20X6	20X7	20X8
Invoiced sales	260	460	740
less cost of sales	130	230	370
Gross profit	130	230	370
Sales & Marketing costs			
Salaries	2	2	3
Recruitment	0	0	10
Travel/entertaining	5	7	9
Car costs	3	5	7
Advertising	31	20	25
Exhibitions	56	25	30
Literature	11	15	18
Sundry items	20	5	5
Total sales costs	129	79	107
Administration costs	10	5	6
IT costs	5	5	5
Distribution costs	5	5	5
Total operating expenses	149	94	123
Operating profit	−19	136	247

9. CONTROLS AND UPDATE PROCEDURES

This plan is to be revised every 12 months.

APPENDICES

In the appendices we include details of sales by product, key market and key sales area, with forecasts for these for the next three years.

MARKETING PLAN
FOR
EXPORT MARKETS

20X6

THE PURE FRUIT JAM COMPANY LTD

3 February 20X6

CONTENTS

Section

1. INTRODUCTION

The Pure Fruit Jam Company is a manufacturer of specialist jams and conserves. The company uses only fresh fruit and ingredients and we have had considerable success with the trend towards organic and 'non-synthetic' products. We intend to build on our success.

2. EXECUTIVE SUMMARY

We only started in the export market five years ago and have made considerable progress, so that export sales now represent 20 per cent of our total sales.

Our marmalades are selling well in North America and Europe and our mini - pots are well received by hotel chains and airlines. Our website is also progressing well and with the introduction of our online purchasing service we expect to increase sales of our gift packs and special products.

Our new sales manager has experience of export markets and will help us in our growth.

The objective of this plan is to triple our export sales from an estimated £500,000 this year to £1,650,000 in three years' time.

3. SITUATION ANALYSIS

3.1. Assumptions

∎   Inflation will remain at 3 per cent in 20X6, rising to 4 per cent in 20X7 and 20X8.
∎   Company wage increases will not exceed inflation over the next three years.
∎   The £:$ exchange rate will remain in the range of £1:$1.65 to £1: $1.85 over the next three years.
∎   The £:€ exchange rate will remain in the range of £1:€1.4 to £1:€1.6 over the next three years.

3.3. Strategic markets

Supermarkets

Although this is a major market for us in the UK, we have not made progress in this market overseas, with the exception of Japan where the Seikokku chain has started taking our gift packs and mini gift packs. We are targeting up-market supermarket chains in North America and Australasia.

3.2. Sales (History/Budget)

THE PURE FRUIT JAM COMPANY
SALES FIGURES (Historical and Forecast)

SALES AREA: EXPORT

YEAR (all values in £k)	20X3	20X4	20X5	20X6	20X7	20X8
				forecast		
STANDARD JAMS (340 gm)	100	200	300	400	500	600
MARMALADES (340 gm)	50	80	100	150	200	300
MINI-POTS	0	20	50	80	150	200
GIFT PACKS	0	30	50	100	180	250
SPECIAL PRODUCTS				100	200	300
TOTAL	150	330	500	830	1230	1650

Quality shops

We have had some success with a quality delicatessen chain in Canada – particularly with our 'Scottish' breakfast marmalade. Our new sales manager James McGuire has some contacts in New York and Boston, which we will be following up.

Hotels

The Four Seasons chain in North America and the Golden Apricot chain in Japan have signed contracts to purchase our mini-pots.

Airlines

Air Canada and Qantas have followed the lead of British Airways and are purchasing mini-pots for 'afternoon tea' in business class.

3.4. Key products

Standard jams

Our standard jams use natural ingredients. But it is difficult to compete for standard flavours like strawberry and raspberry with fresh fruit jams from bulk manufacturers. That is why we have moved steadily into more exotic flavours, such as alpine strawberry, fig, mango and blueberry. We are not pushing this product line as a priority overseas.

Marmalades

Our marmalades are selling well in North America and Europe. Our 'Scottish' and 'French' marmalades with whisky and brandy are now becoming big sellers and we will be adding a rum and a Cointreau flavour next year. We expect specialist flavours to boost sales significantly at the expense of our traditional flavours.

Mini-pots

Contracts have only recently been signed with a number of major airlines and hotel chains. So we expect to see sales of this product grow dramatically over the next three years

Gift packs

Gift packs consist of either two specialist standard size jars of jam or marmalade or a gift pack of six mini-pots of different flavours. This business has really taken off in Japan with Seikokku and we hope to secure other major contracts shortly.

Special products

We are considering special products for individual export markets including maple syrup flavoured marmalade for the North American market and mandarin orange marmalade for the Japanese market. These products will be packaged with local style packaging and may be sold as own-label products through prestige stores.

Our portfolio matrix for export markets only is shown below.

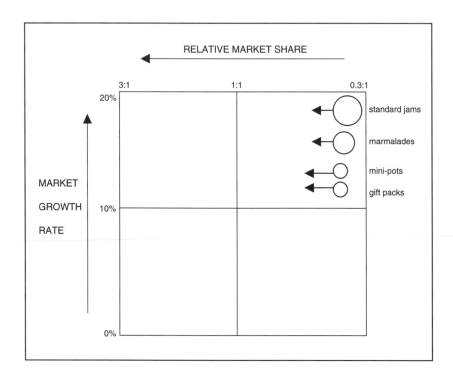

At present all of our products are so new in export markets that they remain question marks. We hope that during the course of the next three years some, if not all of them, will move towards the star area.

3.5. Key sales areas

North America

Our sales in North America are mainly to Four Seasons Hotels, Air Canada and the Brady's delicatessen chain in Canada. We are only scraping the surface of this huge market and are optimistic of our chances of expanding further.

Europe

The European market is difficult for us, because of the presence of our major competitors La Belle Confiture and Rein Konfitüre. We are not making this a priority market.

Japan

Our contracts with Golden Apricot and Seikokku have given us good experience of how business is carried out in Japan. Given the 'prestige' of British quality products, we are confident of major expansion here.

Australia

We have had good success with the Quality Deli chain in Australia and New Zealand. They have stores in major cities including Sydney, Melbourne, Perth, Adelaide, Brisbane and Auckland. They have taken our specialist marmalades and gift packs.

4. MARKETING OBJECTIVES

- To double sales of standard jams in three years.
- To triple sales of marmalades in three years.
- To quadruple sales of mini - pots in three years.
- To increase by five times our sales of gift packs in three years.

5. MARKETING STRATEGIES

Products
Change product   – make different versions of the product with different names for different markets

Pricing
Change pricing   – introduce new discount structure for distributors
Premium pricing   – for alcohol - based marmalades

Promotion

Restructure sales management	– new sales manager will take over responsibility for export sales
Increase exhibition coverage	– use government assistance for exhibitions – add 'web analytics' for e-marketing

Distribution

Change channels	– appoint new distributors for North America – appoint new distributor for west of Japan
Expand website	– to allow online purchases

6. SCHEDULES

MASTER SCHEDULE

Year: 20X6

Month	1 2 3 4 5 6 7 8 9 10 11 12	Responsibility	
Action Plan		**Dept**	**Person**
Japan	————————————————→	Sales/Mkting	JNM
North America	————————————————→	Sales/Mkting	JNM
Exhibition	————————————→	Marketing	LFR
Press advertising	————————————————→	Marketing	BKS
Expand website	——————————→	IT	OJT

7. SALES PROMOTION

In The Pure Fruit Jam Company we have a sales director, a new sales manager, and a marketing assistant who handles advertising, publicity and exhibitions.

Our existing sales structure is shown overleaf.

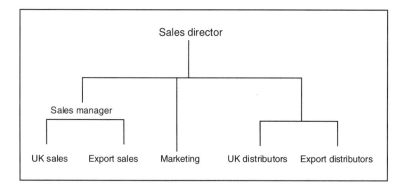

The new sales manager has a lot of experience in export sales, so our intention is to give him full responsibility for export sales. The sales director will concentrate mainly on UK sales and overall marketing.

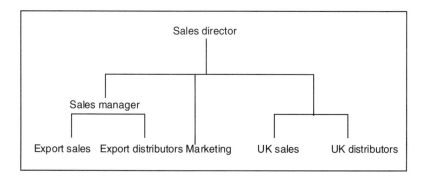

In 20X6 we will be concentrating particularly on North America and Japan and will be introducing 'local' products and 'local' packaging in a number of key markets.

For the Japanese market, we will be repackaging gift packs and adding a sake flavoured marmalade range. We are using government grants to produce Japanese sales literature and also to support taking part in the Nippon Food Show in Osaka as part of the British Pavilion.

For the North American market we will take part in Hotel Suppliers 20X6 in Chicago and will support local distributors with targeted advertising

Details of advertising expenditure are given in the next section and our action plans are included in an appendix to this plan.

Details of exhibition expenditure are shown overleaf.

EXHIBITION COSTS

Name of exhibition:	Nippon Food Show
Location:	International Exhibition Centre, Osaka
Date:	12–14 May 20X6
Stand size:	32 m^2 (4 m x 8 m)
Stand contractor:	Brit-Ex Contracting

COSTS	£
Stand space rental	6,000
Design, supply and build	10,000
Artwork, photographic panels	6,000
Rental of carpets, furniture, lights, phone, etc	3,000
Hotel bills/expenditure for stand staff	3,000
Air fares	3,000
TOTAL	31,000
less government grants of £3,000 **TOTAL COST**	**28,000**

EXHIBITION COSTS

Name of exhibition:	Hotel Suppliers 20X6
Location:	Carnegie Center, Chicago
Date:	11–15 September 20X6
Stand size:	20 m^2 (4 m x 8 m)
Stand contractor:	Brit-Ex Contracting

COSTS	£
Stand space rental	5,000
Design, supply and build	8,000
Artwork, photographic panels	5,000
Rental of carpets, furniture, lights, phone, etc	2,000
Hotel bills/expenditure for stand staff	2,000
Air fares	3,000
TOTAL	25,000
less government grants of £3,000 **TOTAL COST**	**22,000**

8. BUDGETS AND PROFIT AND LOSS ACCOUNT

Operating expenses will increase significantly to fund the additional sales costs of the plan. The operating expenses budget for the export sales department for the first year of the plan is shown below.

OPERATING EXPENSES BUDGET FOR 20X6

Department: Export Sales

Item	20X5 expenses £k	Inflation %	Inflation £k	Growth £k	Other £k	20X6 expenses £k
Salaries	50	3	1.5			51.5
Recruitment	12	3				
Travel/entertaining	20	3	0.6	20	10	50.6
Car costs	5	3	0.15	3	6	14.15
Advertising	19	3	0.57		5	24.57
Exhibitions	10	3	0.3	2	50	62.3
Literature	10	3	0.3		30	40.3
Sundry items	12	3	0.36		10	22.36
		3	0			0
Total	138	3	3.78	25	111	265.78

Increased travelling costs are shown under 'growth' for the sales manager's costs and under 'other' for travel costs for the sales director to support major overseas exhibitions. Exhibition costs are for the Nippon Food Show in Osaka, Japan and Hotel Suppliers 20X6 in Chicago, USA. Literature costs include the provision of Japanese literature and also the cost of specific materials for the USA exhibition.

A partial profit and loss account for the additional sales included in this plan is shown.

9. CONTROLS AND UPDATE PROCEDURES

This plan is to be revised every 12 months.

EFFECT ON PROFIT & LOSS ACCOUNT OF EXTRA EXPORT SALES

(all values in £k)	20X6	20X7	20X8
Invoiced sales	330	730	1150
less cost of sales	198	438	690
Gross profit	132	292	460
Sales & Marketing costs			
Salaries	2	2	3
Recruitment	0	3	0
Travel/entertaining	31	5	5
Car costs	9	5	7
Advertising	6	7	9
Exhibitions	52	5	8
Literature	30	3	5
Sundry items	10	5	5
Total sales costs	140	35	42
Administration costs	5	5	6
IT costs	5	5	5
Distribution costs	5	5	5
Total operating expenses	155	50	58
Operating profit	−23	242	402

APPENDICES

In the appendices we include details of sales by product, key market and key sales area (split by region and country), with forecasts for these for the next three years.

MARKETING PLAN
FOR
THE UK MARKET
20X6

PRECISION VALVES LTD

3 February 20X6

CONTENTS

Section

1. INTRODUCTON

UK sales have stagnated in recent years. The water industry has always been our main industry. After privatisation of the Water Authorities the company did well, but the private water companies have cut back on investment in recent years. With the enforcement of EU directives for water treatment and sewage disposal, the industry is now again carrying out a major capital improvement programme. It was therefore felt by the sales and marketing director that we needed to analyse our position in the market and prepare for growth to take advantage of the increased level of spending by the industry.

2. EXECUTIVE SUMMARY

Although sales of our core product of cast iron ball valves have fallen in recent years, we have seen growth in other products, such as the small type 'S' stainless steel valves for specialised applications. We also sell these valves in packages.

With the new investment programmes being announced by the majority of the water companies, we believe that prospects are good to grow these sales further. In addition, the sourcing of castings for our cast iron ball valves from China gives us the opportunity to sell these products at a lower price (competing with imported products), and also to increase our margins.

The objective of this plan is to increase UK sales by 40 per cent in real terms over the next three years, from an estimate of £2 million this year to £3,140,000 in 20X8.

3. SITUATION ANALYSIS

3.1. Assumptions

- Inflation will remain at 3 per cent in 20X6, rising to 4 per cent in 20X7 and 20X8.
- Company wage increases will not exceed inflation over the next three years.
- UK GDP will grow at 2 to 3 per cent per year over the next three years.
- Interest rates will remain in the range of 5 to 6 per cent over the period of the plan.
- The £:$ exchange rate will remain in the range £1:$1.65 to £1:$1.85 over the next three years.
- The £:€ exchange rate will remain in the range of £1:€1.4 to £1:€1.6 over the next three years.
- There will be no delay in the timescale for the UK water industry to implement the EU directives on drinking water and effluent.

3.2. Sales (History/Budget)

PRECISION VALVES LTD						
SALES FIGURES (Historical and Forecast)						

SALES AREA: UK

					forecast	
YEAR (all values in £k)	20X3	20X4	20X5	20X6	20X7	20X8
TYPE 'A' VALVES	450	450	400	500	600	700
TYPE 'B' VALVES	1000	900	800	900	950	1000
TYPE 'S' VALVES	100	200	400	500	600	700
PACKAGES	50	100	200	300	400	500
SPARE PARTS	180	180	200	200	220	240
TOTAL	1780	1830	2000	2400	2770	3140

3.3. Strategic markets

Water treatment

This is our main industry, accounting for 34 per cent of UK sales. The industry is carrying out a major capital investment programme to comply with EU directives for water treatment. We expect to be able to take advantage of the increased level of spending in the industry.

Waste water

After water treatment, this is our second market, accounting of 24 per cent of UK sales. Again, as a result of EU directives on sewage treatment discharge quality, we expect major investment in this sector. We expect to be able to take advantage of this.

Chemicals

The chemical industry has been growing for us and now accounts for 18 per cent of UK sales. Our sales here are of specialist packages and our type 'S' stainless steel valves. It is a difficult market as capacity moves to lower - cost manufacturing countries. Our main business is in speciality chemicals and pharmaceuticals.

Other

We sell a reasonable amount into the sugar and paper industries, but are not specifically targeting these for our growth plan.

3.4. Key products

Type 'A' valves

Sales of our actuated type 'A' valve have been declining in recent years, but with the launch of the new activator unit within the next few months, we are confident of significant growth.

Type 'B' valves

Our standard cast iron ball valve has become much more competitive with the sourcing of components from China. This will help us to hold and even grow our market share of this product.

Type 'S' valves

The launch of our type 'S' stainless steel valve, three years ago, finally gave us the corrosion-resistant product that we needed for the chemical industry. Growth here has been rapid. It also gives us an advantage in dosing systems for water and sewage applications and also on alum dosing on water - treatment plants.

Packages

Our packages are based around our type 'S' valves and are aimed at providing a complete solution for the control of chemical and polymer dosing. We expect major growth with this product to the UK water companies.

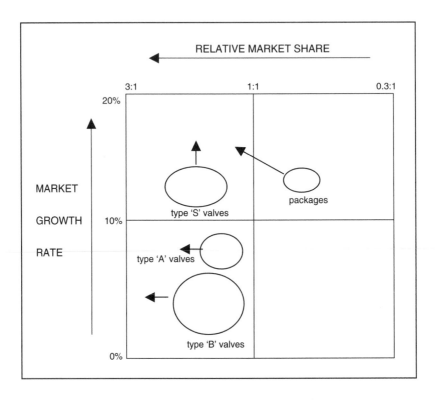

Both our type 'A' and type 'B' valves are cash cows. They have been moving towards being dogs, but we hope that with the sales of our new actuators on type 'A' valves and with targeted price reductions on our type 'B' valves (benefiting from reduced costs), we will start to move these products back firmly into the centre of the cash cow quadrant.

Type 'S' valves are stars and we expect this growth to continue as investment in updating water - treatment facilities increases over the next three years.

Our packages are based around the type 'S' valve and are moving from being question marks to stars. We expect this product to constitute a significant part of our UK turnover in three years time.

3.5. Key sales areas

South

This is a good market for us, accounting for 40 per cent of UK sales. There is a large industrial base, and also many major water and sewage works for towns such as London, Reading, Southampton, etc. The main water - treatment contractors with UK and export business are also based here – Black & Veach, Biwater and Veolia.

Midlands

A declining market for us. Only Severn Trent Water remains as a major customer.

North

This area accounts for 32 per cent of UK sales. As well as North West and Northumbrian Water, the North is home to the major remaining chemical plants in the UK. This is concentrated in the Manchester/Liverpool and Teesside areas.

Wales

Major customers in Wales include Welsh Water and BP.

Scotland/NI

We find it difficult to penetrate this market, but now that the Ace Valve Company has sacked its Scottish distributor, we have an opportunity.

4. MARKETING OBJECTIVES

- To increase sales by 40 per cent in real terms in three years.
- To increase sales of type 'A' valves by 50 per cent in real terms in three years.
- To increase sales of type 'S' valves 50 per cent in real terms in three years.
- To more than double sales of packages in three years.
- To increase margins from 38 to 40 per cent in three years.

5. MARKETING STRATEGIES

Products
Develop new products
- new activator for type 'A' valve
- expand range of packages
- add control package to type 'S' valve

Pricing
Penetration policy
- offer lower pricing for type 'B' valves to achieve framework agreements (favoured supplier) with water companies

Discount policy
- offer discount to new distributors for initial stock orders

Promotion
Change sales force organisation
- recruit salesman for the water industry

Change advertising/ sales promotion
- increase advertising
- use mailshots/e-mailshots
- Increase exhibition coverage
- Add 'web analytics' for e-marketing

Distribution
Change distribution
- appoint new distributor in Scotland

Increase sales coverage
- recruit salesman for the water industry

6. SCHEDULES

MASTER SCHEDULE

Year: 20X6

Month	1 2 3 4 5 6 7 8 9 10 11 12	Responsibility	
Action Plan		**Dept**	**Person**
Mailshot	⟶	Marketing	AJK
Press advertising	⟶	Marketing	AJK
Exhibition	⟶	Marketing	AJK
Pricing	⟶	Sales	EGM
Distribution	⟶	Marketing	AJK
Expand website	⟶	IT	JAF

7. SALES PROMOTION

Our existing UK sales organisation is shown in the figure below.

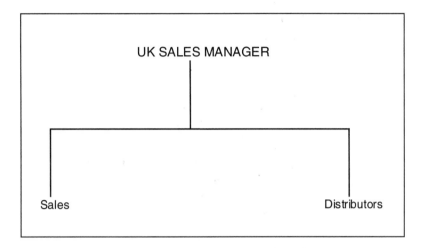

At present we have only one person doing the selling in the UK. (The sales and marketing director is handling the export business and marketing.) We intend to recruit a sales engineer to handle the water and waste - water industries. We will then change the sales structure to that shown below.

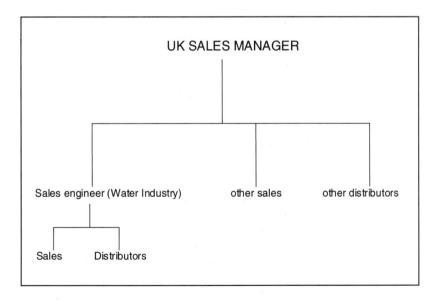

This structure adds one person to our overall sales organisation. This change is shown in the figure above and is included in our budget.

For 20X6 we are targeting the water industry. The next two tables on the following page show the press advertising schedule and exhibition cost schedule that we have prepared.

Position	Existing Personnel	New Personnel	Total
Sales Director	1		1
Water Industry Manager	1		1
Sales Engineer		1	1
Total	2	1	3

PRESS ADVERTISING

APPLICATION: WATER INDUSTRY   **YEAR: 20X6**

Media	No	Rate per insertion £	Total cost £	J	F	M	A	M	J	J	A	S	O	N	D
Water & Waste Treatment	2	1800	3600					x				x			
Water Services	2	1500	3000						x				x		
Water Bulletin	3	800	2400				x			x			x		
Water Yearbook	1	2000	2000	x											
TOTAL COST			11000												

EXHIBITION COSTS

Name of exhibition: Iwex
Location: NEC Birmingham
Date: 6–8 November 20X6

Stand size: 64 m² (8 m x 8 m)
Stand contractor: Exhibition Contractors Ltd

COSTS	£
Stand space rental	8,000
Design, supply and build	10,000
Artwork, photographic panels	5,000
Rental of carpets, furniture, lights, phone, etc	3,000
Hotel bills/expenditure for stand staff	2,000
TOTAL	**28,000**

We will also be carrying out some targeted mailshots/e-mailshots and expanding our website to include 'web analytics' for e-marketing.

8. BUDGETS AND PROFIT AND LOSS ACCOUNT

Operating expenses will increase significantly to fund the additional sales costs of the plan. The operating expenses budget for the UK sales department for the first year of the plan is shown below.

Salary costs shown for this year include the sales manager's salary and related costs. In 20X6 a new sales engineer will be recruited for water industry sales. Under 'other' we have included his salary and related costs and also the costs for his company car and for travel and entertaining. Under 'advertising' we have included the cost of our advertising campaign and mailshots/e-mailshots for the water industry and under 'exhibitions' we include the costs of the Iwex exhibition in Birmingham.

OPERATING EXPENSES BUDGET FOR 20X6						
Department: Sales						
Item	**20X5 expenses**	**Inflation**	**Inflation**	**Growth**	**Other**	**20X6 expenses**
	£k	%	£k	£k	£k	£k
Salaries	45	3	1.35		25	71.35
Recruitment	2	3	0.06		9	11.06
Travel/entertaining	9	3	0.27		7	16.27
Car costs	11	3	0.33		8	19.33
Advertising	19	3	0.57		11	30.57
Exhibitions	9	3	0.27		28	37.27
Literature	20	3	0.6		7	27.6
Sundry items	6	3	0.18		5	11.18
		3	0			0
Total	121	3	3.63	0	100	224.63

The revised profit and loss account for our UK operations during the course of the plan is shown overleaf.

PROFIT & LOSS ACCOUNT (UK operations only)

(all values in £k)	20X6	20X7	20X8
Invoiced sales	2400	2770	3140
less cost of sales	1440	1662	1884
Gross profit	960	1108	1256
Sales & Marketing costs			
Salaries	71	47	48
Recruitment	11	5	2
Travel/entertaining	16	14	14
Car costs	19	16	18
Advertising	31	26	28
Exhibitions	37	14	17
Literature	28	23	25
Sundry items	11	11	11
Total sales costs	225	156	163
Administration costs	158	168	178
Data processing costs	62	62	62
Distribution costs	120	138	157
Total operating expenses	565	524	560
Operating profit	395	584	696

9. CONTROLS AND UPDATE PROCEDURES

There will be quarterly marketing plan meetings. A summary of costs against budget and actual progress against the schedules will be prepared for these meetings. A report on the implementation of the action plans will also be presented at these meetings.

This plan is to be revised every 12 months.

APPENDICES

In the appendices we include sales history and budgets by product, by key applications and by key sales areas. There is also a list of customers by invoiced sales value for each of the last three years. We include a competitor analysis, SWOT analyses and individual action plans.

Appendix 2

Useful websites

GOVERNMENT STATISTICS

www.dti.gov.uk – Department of Trade and Industry

www.statistics.gov.uk – government statistics including economy, regional trends, consumer trends and Product Sales Reports (PRODCOM) information

www.thestationeryoffice.com – government bookshop, both online and with various branches around the country

GOVERNMENT SUPPORT FOR EXPORTERS

www.britishchambers.org.uk/exportzone – British Chambers of Commerce export information

www.businesslink.gov.uk – local support for business, including export services

www.export.org.uk – The Institute of Export – The UK Centre of Exporting Excellence

www.iccwbo.org – International Chambers of Commerce

www.uktradeinvest.gov.uk – government organisation providing support for exporters, including market reports, country reports and support for exhibitions, trade missions, etc

E-MARKETING

www.emailfactory.co.uk – The Email Factory UK

www.emailvision.com – Emailvision UK Ltd

EXHIBITION INFORMATION

www.aeo.org.uk – Association of Exhibition Organisers

www.expoguide.com – information on international exhibitions

DIRECTORIES

www.euromonitor.com
www.mintel.co.uk – Mintel International Group

FINANCIAL DATA

www.companieshouse.gov.uk – company accounts for UK companies
www.dnb.com/uk – Dunn & Bradstreet – financial information on companies

BUSINESS RATIO REPORTS

www.theprospectshop.co.uk

MARKET REPORTS

www.eiu.com – Economist Intelligence Unit – country reports
www.euromonitor.com
www.frost.com – Frost & Sullivan
www.keynote.co.uk
www.trade.uktradeinvest.gov.uk

MARKET RESEARCH ORGANISATIONS

www.bmra.org.uk – British Market Research Association
www.caci.com
www.marketresearch.org.uk – Market Research Society

TRADE ASSOCIATIONS

www.taforum.org – Trade Association Forum – find trade associations in your industry

OTHER GENERAL SOURCES

www.eiu.com – Economist Intelligence Unit
www.kompass.com – 'the business to business search engine'

www.oecd.org – Organization for Economic Cooperation and Development – GDP data and a wide range of statistics for OECD members
www.tremnet.com – Thomas Register of European Manufacturers
www.worldatlas.com – worldwide country information

OTHER USEFUL WEBSITES

www.cim.co.uk – Chartered Institute of Marketing
www.ft.com – Financial Times
www.iod.com – Institute of Directors
www.ismm.co.uk – Institute of Sales and Marketing Management
www.marketing-society.org.uk – Marketing Society
www.patent.gov.uk – The Patent Office
www.uspto.gov – US Patent Office
www.theidm.co.uk – The Institute of Direct Marketing

Index

Index of advertisers

ALSO AVAILABLE FROM KOGAN PAGE IN *THE SUNDAY TIMES* BUSINESS ENTERPRISE SERIES:

The Business Enterprise Handbook by Colin Barrow, Robert Brown and Liz Clarke (0 7494 4100 3)

The Business Plan Workbook, 5th edition by Colin Barrow, Paul Barrow and Robert Brown (07494 4346 4)

The Company Secretary's Handbook: A Guide to Duties and Responsibilities, 3rd edition by Helen Ashton (07494 4119 4)

Complete Guide to Selling Your Business, 2nd edition by Paul S Sperry, Beatrice H Mitchell (07494 4161 5)

The Customer Service Workbook by Neville Lake & Kristen Hickey (07494 3789 8)

E-Business for the Small Business: Making Profit from the Internet by John G Fisher (0 7494 3479 1)

Financial Management for the Small Business, 5th edition by Colin Barrow (0 7494 3500 3)

Forming a Limited Company, 8th edition by Patricia Clayton (0 7494 4150 X)

How to Prepare a Business Plan, revised 4th edition by Edward Blackwell (0 7494 4191 7)

Law for the Small Business, 11th edition by Patricia Clayton (0 7494 4149 6)

Managing People in a Small Business by John Stredwick (0 7494 3662 0)

Practical Marketing and PR for the Small Business, 2nd edition by Moi Ali (0 7494 3823 1)

Raising Finance: A Practical Guide for Business Start Up & Expansion by Paul Barrow (07494 4260 3)

Selling by Telephone: How to Turn Business Cold Calling into Hot Profit, 4th edition by Chris De Winter (0 7494 3682 4)

Starting a Successful Business, 5th edition by Michael J Morris (0 7494 4413 4)

Successful Marketing for the Small Business: A Practical Guide, 5th edition by Dave Patten (0 7494 3524 0)